Edited by
GREG WILKINSON
HUGH FREEMAN

The Provision of Mental Health Services in Britain: The Way Ahead

GASKELL

ISBN 0 902241 15 X

Gaskell is an imprint of the Royal College of
Psychiatrists, 17 Belgrave Square, London SW1

Distributed in North America
by American Psychiatric Press, Inc.

ISBN 0-88048-234-6

Typeset by Dobbie Typesetting Service, Plymouth, Devon
Printed in Britain at the Alden Press, Oxford

Contents

Implementation: Services for the mentally handicapped

Problems in community care

List of Contributors

Tom Arie, Professor of Health Care of the Elderly, University of Nottingham

John Chant, Director, Social Services, Somerset

D. S. Coleman, Director of Nursing Services (Psychiatry), Bexley Health Authority

Chris Cullen, Secretary, Division of Clinical Psychology, British Psychological Society

Ken Day, Consultant Psychiatrist, Northgate Hospital, Morpeth

Ben Essex, General Practitioner, Royal College of General Practitioners

Stuart Etherington, Director, Good Practices in Mental Health Project, British Association of Social Workers

Hugh Freeman, Consultant Psychiatrist, Hope Hospital, Salford, Manchester; Editor *British Journal of Psychiatry*

Lord Glenarthur, Joint Parliamentary Under-Secretary of State, DHSS

Howard Glennerster, Professor of Social Administration, London School of Economics and Political Science

David Goldberg, Professor of Psychiatry, University of Manchester

Tessa Jowell, Assistant Director, Training and Education, MIND

Nancy Korman, Research Officer, Department of Social Science and Administration, London School of Economics and Political Science

Julian Leff, Consultant Psychiatrist, MRC Social Psychiatry Unit, Friern Hospital, London N11

Peter Mellor, Nurse Adviser, Society of Psychiatric Nursing, Royal College of Nursing

Kenneth Rawnsley, Professor, Department of Psychological Medicine, University of Wales College of Medicine

James Ross, Director of Welfare, Legal and Counselling Department, MENCAP

Frank Seymour, Regional Medical Officer, North-West Thames Regional Health Authority

G. B. Simon, Professor of Mental Handicap, Department of Psychiatry, University of Birmingham

Greg Wilkinson, Honorary Lecturer and Honorary Senior Registrar, General Practice Research Unit, Institute of Psychiatry, London SE5

John Wing, Professor of Psychiatry, MRC Social Psychiatry Unit, Institute of Psychiatry, London SE5

Lorna Wing, Member of Scientific Staff, MRC Social Psychiatry Unit, Institute of Psychiatry, London SE5

Introduction

GREG WILKINSON and
HUGH FREEMAN

This book consists of the proceedings of a conference on planning mental health services, organised jointly by the Royal College of Psychiatrists and the Department of Health and Social Security, which was held in London on 7 and 8 March 1985.

The conference concentrated on the difficulties associated with the implementation of government policies for these services in England and Wales. The main themes were the development of alternative resources during the process of closing some mental and mental handicap hospitals, and the overall implications of these changes for patients, their families, and the community. Emphasis was placed on the problems of transition from a hospital-based to a community-based mental health service, and on the special needs of the chronically mentally ill, the elderly, and the mentally handicapped which will most likely result from these changes. Concern about the long-term care of these vulnerable groups was expressed by many of the participants, who felt that the problems of chronic disability were tending to be set aside, because they were not easily accommodated into the new pattern of services.

The last such conference was held in October 1972, and its theme was the planning of comprehensive district psychiatric services. At that time, the largely informal and piecemeal process of experimentation, which had begun in the late 1950s, was becoming embodied in official policy documents both on mental health and on the organisation of health services in general. The prediction that 'the policies are virtually on a 20-year scale' was certainly not an overestimate (McLachlan, 1973), though this forecast had been made in an optimistic climate of new resources, which has now totally disappeared. The hope was expressed that there would be further meetings of this kind — and now there has been one.

In the book that emerged then, *Policy for Action*, Cawley (1973) came to the still pertinent conclusion that there was:

. . . a need for much clarification of theories, assumptions, and logistics concerned with practice. Interdisciplinary consultation may be expected to improve the quality of care, as well as throwing light on particular problems of different regions or localities. There is a serious lack of reliable information about geographical variations in availability of services and in the patterns of services considered desirable by those engaged in practice. This information can be provided only by interdisciplinary collaboration and systematic inquiry. The professions engaged in psychiatry share with local authorities and the DHSS the responsibility for providing information and interpreting it in such a way as to facilitate the best possible psychiatric service in every area. The quality of the consultation process between the management, in central and local government, and the professions, will play a large part in determining the quality of the psychiatric services in the future. As far as this process is concerned, the initiative shown by the DHSS has brought us successfully to the end of the beginning.

The present publication indicates both the scope of subsequent developments in mental health service provision and the major obstacles to future progress. Whilst the contribution made by psychiatrists is crucial to this process, and is again well documented here, much attention is also rightly given to the views and perspectives of the other necessary participants: regional and district health authorities, local authorities, the professions that make up both psychiatric and primary care multidisciplinary teams, families, and voluntary and other non-statutory care-giving agencies, including the private sector.

Since 1973, interprofessional inequalities of status have much diminished, so that clinical psychology, for instance, is now a wholly independent discipline. Medical authority counts for less, in view of the more hierarchical managerial structure of the NHS, and psychiatric practice has been put under greater legal constraint since the 1983 Mental Health Act. The voice of the consumer is also being expressed more strongly through organisations such as the National Schizophrenia Fellowship, MIND, and MENCAP.

A synopsis of the policy of the Department of Health and Social Security in this field is outlined in the documents constituting the Appendix. With this material, the principles and practices of planning British mental health services can be examined in the context both of general health care and of the responsibilities of social services.

The long-term aim of this policy is to create a comprehensive range of psychiatric services within each district, but it has to be done in relation to a regional plan, which takes account both of districts' needs and resources and of nationally determined priorities and policy. That means taking account — in each district — of the contribution of social, educational, housing, and employment resources, as well as of the voluntary, statutory, and independent services which are directly related to mental health.

In 1973, Cawley pointed out that psychiatric practice had advanced through an understanding of the social processes which influence the identification, aetiology, content, and treatment of mental disorders, as well as through progress in medicine, psychopharmacology, and psychology. He suggested that because 'mental illness' was too definite and circumscribed a term, services would be better described as 'psychiatric', at the same time making it clear that their practice is multidisciplinary. However, such a change has not yet been made in official terminology.

Cawley also drew attention to several assumptions which were embedded, explicitly or implicitly, in national plans for mental health services. The first of these was that 'it is always better to be out of hospital than in'; yet this seemed inappropriate to many severely disabled people, mostly schizophrenic or brain-damaged. Therefore, some suitably modernised mental hospitals ought to remain, because 'nobody who has seen the best of such places can fail to be impressed by what they have to offer in terms of care, shelter, occupation, and comparative freedom of movement to some very handicapped people'. Twelve years later, though, it is by no means clear that some 'asylum' care of this kind will be allowed to continue in the long-term, either for the mentally ill or mentally handicapped, and this has become a major source of concern.

The second assumption was that 'the local authorities will provide'; yet, 'it is likely that for many years to come there will be striking contrasts between different local authorities in the adequacy of provision . . . for the psychiatrically disabled. And it is hard to see how the DHSS can do much to influence this situation . . .' In 1985 these contrasts remain as widely apart as ever, while the financial climate provides little hope that 'a wide range of highly important, and as yet substantially undefined, material facilities and skilled manpower' will be provided at an acceptable level by all local authorities. Mental health services are seen officially as a partnership between the NHS, local authorities, and voluntary organisations; but what is to be done if at least one partner is failing to provide his share of the resources? This question remains unanswered, as does the concern of psychiatrists that the Seebohm 'integration' of social work resulted in the disintegration of mental health services, where these had become established on a local basis (Jones, 1979).

The next assumption identified by Cawley was that 'neurotic patients need no special provision'. Yet more and more people could be expected to consult psychiatrists 'because they experience recurrent neurotic symptoms associated with problems of social adjustment or interpersonal difficulties . . . The only realistic treatment may be some kind of formal psychotherapy, behavioural modification . . ., or intensive social casework, or a combination of these . . . But the available manpower . . . is gravely deficient.' The issues raised by this problem appeared then to have been side-stepped in DHSS policy documents, yet they raised fundamental questions about the quality of psychiatric service which the country could afford, and about the distribution of existing resources. By 1985 skilled manpower had significantly increased — particularly clinical psychologists — and more was being done for neurotic patients in some places at the primary care level, but it could not be said that the policy issues involved had been either confronted or resolved. Psychotherapy resources remain overwhelmingly concentrated in Greater London, and there is very little sign that this will change.

Finally, Cawley discussed the assumptions that 'all medical staff should be trainees or consultants' and that 'general practitioner trainees can ease the manpower situation'. His conclusion that 'there may be strong arguments for reviewing the medical staffing structure' was also reached by the House of Commons Social Services Committee (1985), which recommended a much higher proportion of consultants among hospital medical staff; experimental all-consultant psychiatric services are at present being set up in several places. At the same time, the associate specialist grade (rejected by most other specialties) helps to provide the stability and continuity of medical care which may be lacking when trainees are either absent or constantly changing. So far as GP trainees in psychiatry are concerned, Cawley pointed out that they need teaching and supervision by consultants — as they continue to do — and this demands a reasonable investment of time. Medical manpower, though, is one aspect of the mental health service which has seen substantial improvement since 1973, largely as a result of the increased numbers of graduates being produced by British medical schools; trainee posts in 1985 are, on average, now held by doctors of a much higher standard.

A number of critical issues still remain to be clarified and resolved. These concern: firstly, the identification of appropriate health and social services in each district, and the balance of their components; secondly, the co-ordination of these services and the identification of gaps between them; and finally, the evaluation of the provision, and assessment of the financial consequences of changes in it, in a context of static or even diminishing resources. These interrelated topics represent the main agenda for consideration, practice, and innovation over the next decade.

It is clear from these conference proceedings that the outcome of the planning, research, and development which is now taking place in the mental health services will depend greatly on both the clinical and administrative skills of the various professions concerned. Those who have a part to play in the process, or who wish to study the evolution of British social policy in an important area of public intervention, now have an unusual opportunity here of comparing two major assessments of it, twelve years apart. The conclusion to be drawn from this comparison could be mainly optimistic or pessimistic, depending on which aspects of the scene seem most important. One could be impressed, for instance, by the continuity of themes over the last two hundred years, or alternatively by the risks and uncertainties associated with the widespread closure of large mental hospitals — and it would be possible to take either a positive or a negative view of each of these, according to experience or ideology. It is claimed that huge resources can be released by running down the hospital sector of care, and that these could then be used to provide a better pattern of services on a mainly non-institutional basis. In our view, though, it has still to be shown that this can be done for *all* the mentally ill and mentally handicapped (including the most disabled), and that it can be done in a way which maintains high standards over long periods. We would agree with Mrs Renée Short, MP, Chairman of the House of Commons Social Services Committee, that 'any fool can close a mental hospital'. In itself, this does no more than provide an opportunity for creating something better.

Shortly after this conference, the death occurred of one of the shrewdest observers of the mental health scene in Britain — Professor F. M. Martin. In his last book on the subject (Martin, 1984), he ended with the warning:

We do not have a comprehensive national mental health service, nor in the fullest sense is there hope of achieving one. The task is rather one of creating systems which while acknowledging existing divisions provide a framework for joint planning and joint action . . . But without a firm governmental commitment to the principle of active community-based mental health services and a corresponding recognition of the practical implications of the principle, the national scene will not have significantly improved by the end of the century; such advances as are achieved through small-scale local initiatives will be counter-balanced by the growing . . . problems of . . . the elderly mentally infirm.

This comment, from one who had studied the medical and social services involved for over thirty years, should be taken most seriously, as we look both back to the discussions of 1972 and forward to the next chapter of the story.

References

CAWLEY, R. H. (1973) Postscript. In *Policy for Action* (eds. R. H. Cawley and G. McLachlan). London: Oxford University Press.
JONES, K. (1979) Integration or disintegration of the mental health service: Some reflections and developments in Britain since the 1950s. In *New Methods of Mental Health Care* (ed. M. Meacher). Oxford: Pergamon Press.
MARTIN, F. M. (1984) *Between the Acts.* London: Nuffield Provincial Hospitals Trust.
McLACHLAN, G. (1973) Foreword. In *Policy for Action* (eds. R. H. Cawley and G. McLachlan). London: Oxford University Press.
PARLIAMENTARY SOCIAL SERVICES COMMITTEE, HOUSE OF COMMONS (1985) *Community Care with Special Reference to Adult Mentally Ill and Mentally Handicapped People: Second Report from the Social Services Committee.* (HC 13 I, II, III). London: HMSO.

1 Introduction and current developments

LORD GLENARTHUR

The timing of this conference is particularly opportune because the Parliamentary Social Services Select Committee (1985) has just published its report on community care, with special reference to adult mentally ill and mentally handicapped people.

I very much welcome the Committee's support for the policy of community care; they have made the important points that it takes time, thought, and consultation, and that it is not to be done on the cheap. I am most interested in the role of the DHSS in carrying community care policies forward through the planning system, financial initiatives, and the promulgation of policy guidance.

The very fact that this conference is being held points to: first of all, the priority which is being given to the development of better services for mentally disordered people, both by central government and the field services; and secondly, the highly complex task facing service planners.

Key policy objectives

Two of the conference papers summarise our policies for the development of services for mentally ill and mentally handicapped people (see Appendix). The key features which services must display are that they must be: (i) local — so that they help people where the people are; (ii) flexible — so that they meet people's real needs; (iii) comprehensive — so that they leave no gaps through which people may fall; (iv) integrated — so that they do not leave the client to pull together the loose ends; (v) relevant — dictated by need not organisation; (vi) multidisciplinary — pulling together, not apart; (vii) sensitive — responsive to changing needs; and (viii) accessible — so that the consumer can get to them.

Community care policies are designed to provide a better quality of life for the consumers. The Government is not looking to save money through

1

these policies, but to use money more efficiently to achieve that aim; in commercial jargon, the customer comes first. Community care means building up alternatives to care in the long-stay hospital, providing care for people already in the community, and preventing unnecessary admission to hospital. It is the creation of alternatives which will make hospital closures possible. We shall still need psychiatrists, nurses, social workers, psychologists, and other professionals, but their ways of working are already changing, and will need to develop further to meet the new pattern of service. The Government is convinced that these objectives are achievable, though it does not underestimate the difficulties of making progress.

We have made great progress already. Firstly, firm plans are being jointly devised by the NHS and local authorities, which are realistic in the light of resources. Some parts of the country are certainly moving faster than others, but overall, the priority which is being given to the planning of mental health services is very encouraging. Secondly, the mental illness and mental handicap fact sheet (see Appendix III) shows that progress is being made in reducing the number of patients in the long-stay hospitals, that community provision is increasing, and that staffing levels are improving. There has also been real progress in the development of the regional secure unit programme; patients are now being admitted to 12 permanent units, two more have been completed, and six more are being developed.

There is a broad measure of agreement within the professions that the policy we are embarked on is the right one — though there is still lively debate and sometimes disagreement about the detail. There is evidence that the field authorities want to make progress, and both the National Development Team for Mentally Handicapped People and the Health Advisory Service will continue to be available to advise authorities on their present and planned services. But the size, complexity, and sensitivity of the task should not be underestimated. A number of challenges must be faced.

Resources and their management

The Government has already demonstrated its commitment to the health service in terms of resources. In the period 1979–85, the cost to the taxpayer of the National Health Service increased by 20% in real terms. This increase was sufficient to allow the hospital and community health services to grow more quickly than the demographic pressures on them, and to finance the expansion of the family practitioner services. Capital expenditure in 1984/85 was also higher — by some 23% in real terms than in 1978/79.

The Government remains committed to the health service. In the 1985 White Paper on Public Expenditure, its commitment was underlined by providing for an increase of 1% a year above inflation for each of the three years from 1984/85 to 1987/88. This is at a time when public expenditure as a whole is being held broadly static in real terms.

Local authorities decide their own priorities for spending, but the Government does take account, in the annual rate support grant settlements, of demographic and other pressures (such as tapering off of joint finance) on personal social services. The challenge service planners now face is how to manage the resources available in the most effective way. There are two aspects to this: (i) managing the finance; and (ii) managing the staffing implications.

Practising good housekeeping and using the savings to achieve progress must make sense. Regional health authorities have to realise the savings from running down the large hospitals and transfer those savings to the new services being developed. There will be periods when the old service and the new overlap, and many regions are, in fact, already using funding mechanisms to deal with this transitional 'hump'.

The DHSS can act as a 'broker' to help regions which face such a capital expenditure hump. Arrangements have been operating for some years by which regions can borrow funds from others which have surplus capital in any particular year, and pay the money back later in the planning period. The Select Committee recommended a central bridging fund, additional to other revenue and capital expenditure, and that recommendation will be examined carefully.

Administrative obstacles to shifting patients from hospital care to care in the community have already been removed through the *Care in the Community* initiative (see Appendix IV).

It is recognised that social security funding is an important part of community care; new decisions on board and lodging will respond to the enormous volume of reactions to the consultation process on social security.

Manpower is the other vital resource, which must be supported and skilfully managed during the transition period. Every effort needs to be made to ensure that where hospitals run down, their trained staff do not drift away for lack of certainty about their future role; we will continue to need their skills. To achieve this, health authorities and social services departments must jointly work out the manpower implications of their plans. They must decide what staff numbers they will need, and what skills they should possess.

Training programmes also need to be initiated, so that hospital staff can build on their existing skills for the new community setting. Following the reports of the Joint Working Group, set up by the Central Council for Education and Training in Social Work (CCETSW) and the nursing bodies, some progress is being made in joint training of nurses and social workers, especially post-basic. CCETSW and the English National Board are being encouraged to pursue this.

Training for all staff (including local authority employees) should reflect the new objectives for mental illness and mental handicap services. A new look at training is needed, including that for management; this is a matter for the relevant professional bodies.

New collaboration

Good collaboration between health authorities, local authorities, and voluntary organisations is essential, yet complaints still occur that sometimes this does not happen as well as it should. Consultation structures are important; but they are not enough — they need to be used.

Health authorities and social services departments need to get together at the earliest stage in the planning process; they need also to involve the housing and education departments, the Manpower Services Commission, and voluntary organisations. All of them need to contribute to a comprehensive range of services, and it has now been ensured that voluntary organisations are statutorily represented on joint consultative committees.

Collaboration is a two-way process. Health authorities should resist the temptation to go it alone on untested assumptions about what local authorities will or will not do. Some local authorities have, in the past, been reluctant to get closely involved in planning for mental health services in the community because they fear the resource implications. The 'care in the community' initiative was designed to help overcome this difficulty.

Health and local authorities need to agree at the outset the general shape of the new services and their respective responsibilities. As work proceeds, they need to keep in step, so that everybody knows who will be providing what, with what objectives, to what timetable, and with what financial and manpower implications.

A local authority associations', National Association of Health Authorities', and DHSS working group is looking at the present arrangements for joint planning, including those for transferring resources. It is hoped that their efforts will point the way to closer collaboration and to a better use of resources for the benefit of patients and clients.

Collaboration is also needed at the level of service delivery. There should be joint, multidisciplinary assessments to determine what form of care is appropriate for each patient. For mentally handicapped people, community mental handicap teams provide a firm starting point, and many authorities are making progress towards the National Development Team targets of one team per 60,000–80,000 general population. For mental illness, there are some community mental health teams, crisis intervention teams, and also approved social workers, who it is hoped will help to ensure an improved service. By fulfilling the wide role that Parliament had in mind for them when passing the 1983 Mental Health Act, they can harness together all the available resources for the benefit of their clients. Mentally disordered people also have the same general health care needs as the rest of us: they fall ill, have accidents, and get old like the rest of us.

Attitudes

So far as attitudes are concerned, we cannot expect people to exercise choice without information about the options available and without awareness of their own needs. To take advantage of new possibilities, patients may well need careful and sensitive preparation. Secondly, relatives are bound to question community care if they can see the advantages of the existing service and are not taken into the confidence of those who are planning the new one. Attitudes of the general public also matter: good local schemes can be shipwrecked by local opposition. The Parliamentary Social Services Committee suggested a national education campaign, but the answer might lie in local education.

Thirdly, planners themselves should consider the human implications of the transfer to community care. Hospital has become home to some patients, and they have made their own friendships there; they cannot simply be shifted without their interests being consulted.

Patients with special needs

The Government does recognise that some mentally ill people are very much in need of a hospital service, while others need long-term care in a domestic setting with professional support. Similarly, some mentally handicapped people have special needs, and a service network which does not recognise those needs is incomplete, while the special service needs of children, adolescents and elderly people must not be neglected.

Achieving the standards and range of services that we all want requires both imagination and hard work. The Parliamentary Social Services Committee made the point that there are many good things happening, but that these are not widely enough known or practised. Perhaps I could end with one sentence from the DHSS evidence to the Select Committee: 'The only reason for developing care in the community and reducing the dependence on institutional care for so many patients is the *welfare of the patient*.'

Reference

PARLIAMENTARY SOCIAL SERVICES COMMITTEE, HOUSE OF COMMONS (1985) *Community Care with Special Reference to Adult Mentally Ill and Mentally Handicapped People: Second Report from the Social Services Committee.* (HC 13 I,II,III). London: HMSO.

2 Regional perspectives on planning mental health services

FRANK SEYMOUR

I was appointed Regional Medical Officer in North-West Thames Region in 1982. What has surprised me most since then is the complexity of the planning task, with its requirement to establish a rational basis for providing a comprehensive health service within the region. There is the need to improve access to the health service for widely differing and changing populations and to evaluate their differing health care needs, whilst at the same time developing centres for medical education, tertiary referral and research. Demands for resources arise continuously from many diverse sources; for example, from the increasing incidence of AIDS and drug misuse, and from the need to improve services for patients with end-stage renal failure, to develop the clinical genetics service, and to respond to the increasing number of very elderly people in the population, particularly the elderly mentally ill. All of this within the constraints of being a losing region under RAWP (Resource Allocation Working Party).

There is the added dimension that the NHS does not stand alone but is part of a complex network of services, of which the psychiatric services, with their links with social services, education, housing, the prison and probation services, social security, the employment service and the voluntary agencies, to name but a few, are an outstanding example. What then are the essential prerequisites for planning and the implementation of change to be successful?

Shared sense of priority

There needs to be a clear and shared sense of priority at every level within the NHS, complemented by a harmonisation of policies and priorities between the different agencies involved in effecting change.

I described above some of the many priorities which exist within the health service at present. Because of the sheer number of developments which are being awarded the status of a 'priority' I believe that there is a very real

6

danger that the meaning of the word will become debased. If an optimum impact is to be made, it is essential that there be a limited number of priorities that are common to all the major agencies involved, be they at government, regional or district/local authority level.

One needs no imagination to envisage the tensions created by the competing priorities of the individual spending departments of government and between these departments and the Treasury. These are, of course, replicated within and between local authorities and health authorities. Nevertheless, choices have to be made by authorities albeit that they have very different responsibilities.

There is no formal mechanism for joint planning with other agencies at regional level, although this is a requirement at district level and, hopefully, takes place between government departments. With regard to the latter, be it justified or not, the perceived wisdom at officer level within the statutory services is that insufficient attention is paid to this within government. In North-West Thames we have sought to overcome this problem at regional level through a network of informal consultation with directors of social service, the Prison Medical Service and a number of voluntary bodies.

Nevertheless, it remains a fact that however well intentioned joint planning is, the priorities of different agencies will not always coincide. I would argue strongly that every effort should be made at government level to ensure that the policies and priorities of government departments are mutually compatible and resources equal to the development required. This is a dimension of management which I hope the NHS Management Board will confront.

Continuity of management

The sheer complexity of the task of closing a large hospital is well illustrated by Leavesden, a hospital for mentally handicapped patients within the North-West Thames Region. It has 1,050 patients from 64 local authorities and their associated district health authorities. The hospital has been afflicted by numerous changes of senior staff over the last decade, and by two NHS reorganisations. The staff are now speculating on the implications of the fundamental change in management philosophy arising from Griffiths. At the time of writing, no appointment has been made of the district general manager, so the appointment of the unit general manager will also not be made for some time.

I happen to support the ideas behind the 1982 reorganisation and the development of a 'general management' approach. Nevertheless, in the real world, one has to recognise that the benefits accruing from such fundamental and frequent changes in management will have to be very substantial to overcome the setbacks to the development and implementation of policy which inevitably arise during a period of change and uncertainty. In my judgement the NHS requires, above all else, a period of managerial stability following the implementation of the Griffiths proposals. Stability is not synonymous with stagnation and can in itself promote development and evolution.

Resources

It is essential to have the resources to bring about change both in terms of money and manpower. I would admit that all too often in the past the staff of the NHS have looked too readily to the injection of fresh resources to achieve change. Indeed, I count it as a major achievement of this Government, painful though it has been, that a sense of reality has been brought to the management of the NHS, particularly in the area of resource use. It is necessary for all who have responsibility for using resources to question if they are being used to the greatest advantage of the overall community. The days are past when clinicians can seek to divorce themselves from this aspect of the service.

Those responsible for the services for the mentally ill and mentally handicapped are not immune to this discipline, which has an added urgency in my own region, which has to free-up revenue to pass to less well endowed regions whilst at the same time finding the revenue and manpower from within its own resources to develop and change existing services.

I would question the extent to which most departments of psychiatry have developed, or are developing, measures of efficiency and effectiveness. To what extent are joint studies being undertaken with general practitioners to measure the differential use made of the consultant-based psychiatric services? Do general practitioners refer patients at the most appropriate stage for effective treatment? Are services being directed to those most in need, even if they are the patients who may well cause the greatest disruption within the psychiatric unit, or do they too closely reflect the clinical interest of consultants? Are staff used in the most efficient and effective manner possible?

Fundamental to these questions is the development of a sound information base, and essential to this is greater agreement on the definition of clinical conditions. I must admit to a sense of frustration on receiving psychiatric reports on the same patient which reach different conclusions on diagnosis and treatment. I realise that it is inherent in the nature of the specialty that this will happen, but I would question whether peer review and audit play as significant a role as they should.

I acknowledge the difficulties inherent in this approach, which, although it is becoming more common is, I suspect, still revolutionary to many. I do not apologise for my questions, however, as it is essential that the specialty accepts that the public require of us that the money and resources entrusted to the NHS are spent to maximum effect, and in a way which gives the maximum benefit to the community as a whole and to those in greatest need.

Policies

Clear policies are needed, which are supported by the majority of clinical staff and based on sound epidemiological research. I believe that the DHSS, the Royal Colleges, COHSE, various national advisory committees and the national voluntary agencies, to mention but some, have made immensely valuable contributions to the clarification of policy. However, there remain a number of areas where there is need for further clarification. For example:

(i) What sort of provision should be made for those long-stay patients who cannot be rehabilitated to the extent that they can be transferred to a life fully integrated within the local community? Is it true that there is a continuing need for a form of 'asylum', and what is the nature and extent of the provision to be made?

(ii) What is the future role of psychotherapy within the NHS and what is the extent of the provision to be made? What are the future training requirements?

(iii) What is the long-term specialist role of medical and nursing staff in relation to the care of the mentally handicapped?

(iv) What is the role of the NHS, and the psychiatric services in particular, in relation to the treatment and care of persons who behave in a socially unacceptable manner, but who are not necessarily mentally ill? I would argue that society is not over-interested in the subtleties of whether the person is mentally ill or not, but rather in ensuring that the staff with the most appropriate skills should provide care and treatment. In expressing this view I am not implying any changes to the terms of the Mental Health Act.

(v) What role have the NHS, and, in particular, the psychiatric services in the treatment of persons with severe behaviour disorders?

(vi) What is the potential case load that it would be appropriate to transfer to the NHS from the courts and prison service? What would be the resource implications of such a policy?

Psychiatry lies, at times uncomfortably, at the interface between conflicts inherent within society regarding the treatment of the mentally ill, the mentally handicapped and the socially unacceptable. Society does not want such persons to be institutionalised, but, as individuals, members of society find great difficulty in accepting the consequences of such policies. In my view, there is much to be gained by a greater investment of time on the part of all those involved in these services to stimulate more open local debate on these conflicts and a more active role on the part of the voluntary agencies.

An essential prerequisite to the clarification of policy is an increase in the amount of epidemiological and other research undertaken in the psychiatric field. Obviously much research is already undertaken. In addition, the NHS can fund such activities, be it through the locally organised research schemes, or through university or other departments. My own region, for example, has offered to fund a Chair in the Mental Illness of Old Age. Whilst the RHA was very supportive of this policy, its very necessity leads one to question whether the universities, medical schools and postgraduate institutions have necessarily got their own priorities right. Are the emerging problems of drug misuse, the elderly mentally ill, the behaviour disordered, and mentally handicapped really being given an appropriate allocation of university resources? I realise this is a particularly inopportune time to raise such questions, but it must be recognised that a time of economic stringency could well make the relative deprivation of these areas of clinical activity even greater and longer lived.

Commitment to management

Key staff need to be committed to the management of the health service, and there needs to be a wider understanding of the management process by individual clinicians. It is perhaps worth spending a short time exploring one possible reason why the so-called 'Cinderella services' are just that. A recurring source of amazement to me, travelling around the region, is the presence in even the least well endowed district general hospital of a passable intensive therapy unit with reasonable staffing levels, associated with a plethora of high technology equipment. Go to the matching psychiatric unit, which might in some districts still be substantially based in a large psychiatric hospital, and there is likely to be no equivalent intensive care service. A different expression of this difference of impact on the public is shown in the vast sums of money raised by voluntary effort to purchase high-technology equipment such as CT scanners. However, it must be said that such appeals are normally only successful when the clinicians involved adopt a high profile and put an immense amount of personal effort into projecting their schemes to the public. This attitude is reflected by the active involvement of clinicians who work in the acute sector, in the management process, and the way they use every (I was going to say legitimate, but that description at times is hardly appropriate) means to ensure that their priorities for development are brought directly to the attention of those at every level of the service who influence policy and make decisions.

I realise that psychiatrists are relatively few in number, but I would suggest that many psychiatrists, albeit with some outstanding exceptions, could well pause to reflect if their contribution to the management of the health service is as pro-active as it could be. It is an absolutely essential prerequisite to the development of the services for there to be active involvement of psychiatrists in the management process, not least to sustain and keep on course those managers exposed to many other pressures.

Commitment to implementation of policies

Members and general managers need to be committed to the implementation of policy. Banstead Hospital is a large psychiatric hospital in the North-West Thames Region which is on course for closure. This could not be achieved without the continued and wholehearted support of the Chairman, members, chief officers, and now the general manager, of the managing authority. This has been absolutely critical to the success so far achieved.

In the future there will be an added dimension to the commitment of management to the achievement of objectives, which serves to highlight the potential, 'post Griffiths', for the sharpening of managerial accountability. The successful achievement, for example, of an authority's plans for the progression of the closure of a large psychiatric hospital or the development of local psychiatric services could quite appropriately be written into the district general manager's objectives. The nature and extent of the progress made could then be used as a measure of success when the general manager's contract was considered for renewal. It is not unreasonable to anticipate that the vibrations of this accountability will be felt throughout the service. We live in exciting times!

Notwithstanding the emergence of 'general management' as a new force, I think it important to emphasise the key role of the chairmen and members of authorities in determining policy and priorities. Thought should be given by the specialty to the process by which these judgements are formed and the ways, if appropriate, they can be influenced.

Building on success

For me, one of the most important successes has been the emergence of the 'medium secure psychiatric service' which gives every indication of filling a major gap in the psychiatric services. Already, valuable links are being forged with the Prison Medical Service and an out-patient service has been developed. Concurrently, there is an increasing willingness on the part of psychiatrists and nursing staff to accept what are still described as 'difficult to place patients'.

Psychiatrists and nursing staff are increasingly accepting that a comprehensive local service has to be provided. The needs of all patients, even if they suffer from conditions lying outside the immediate interest of local psychiatrists, have to be met until such time as a colleague with a special interest is appointed, or specialist units established.

Strong leadership

The RHA must provide clear planning guidelines and resources, and not baulk at playing a strong leadership role. It should do its job properly, but what are the essential elements of this job? I would suggest the following:

(i) To establish, in collaboration with district health authorities, a clear strategic plan defining objectives; and through the issue of planning guidelines, giving a time-framework for change. An essential part of this plan is the development of comprehensive local psychiatric services, coupled with the identification and development of specialist services where necessary, and the provision of alternative and more appropriate facilities for patients at present residing in the large psychiatric institutions;

(ii) To ensure that individual district plans are compatible with the region's overall strategy;

(iii) To ensure that the revenue, capital, and manpower resources necessary are available and sufficient to achieve the changes required;

(iv) To ensure that the necessary training and personnel services are available for the re-training and support of staff affected by change;

(v) To ensure that interdependent developments involving a number of districts are kept on schedule;

(vi) To monitor the results of the changes in service to ensure that the essential needs of patients are met.

For those who think I am over critical in this paper may I plead that I am very conscious that regional health authorities and their officers bear a major share of the responsibility for the fact that a conference such as this is necessary. My criticism is, I hope, constructive and is motivated by a strong personal commitment to the improvement of the quality of services available for mentally ill, mentally handicapped and socially inadequate persons and their families.

3 The issues as seen from the perspective of a Director of Nursing

D. S. COLEMAN

Nurses at all levels are fully involved in the debate and action to develop improved services for the mentally ill. Indeed, without the commitment and involvement of nurses it is doubtful that worthwhile changes can be made, as they represent by far the largest single group of staff involved in the care of people with psychiatric problems.

It is often interesting to identify why ideas and plans are made, or how significant decisions are reached. I doubt that historians will find the source of current developments in our services as simple to identify as in the case of the decision to build the asylums in the 19th century. The first identifiable step then was a letter from Sir George Onesiphorus Paul of Gloucester, who wrote to the Secretary of State for the Home Department in 1806, proposing the establishment of 'asylums for the insane' at public expense. By the end of the century we had, in all parts of the country, a network of large remote institutions. No doubt, at the time, these were considered the model for the world to follow. With hindsight, it appears that these did in fact work remarkably well, with few reported problems and a relatively humane approach in comparison to the situation found in previous centuries.

Recent developments in the care of the mentally ill lend themselves more to evolution than revolution. Although significant steps can be identified, like the development of phenothiazines in the 1950s and the 1959 Mental Health Act, most of the progress was gradual and depended upon personal vision and leadership by medical superintendents, and others.

We now know that the old arrangements, where the care of the mentally ill was largely in remote mental hospitals, cannot be maintained. A change of huge proportions is required to overcome the mental hospitals' problems of geographical isolation, public scandals, management difficulties, and deteriorating old fashioned buildings, no longer suitable for the patients they house. There has been increasing support for the view that it is no longer appropriate to care for the mentally ill in Victorian institutions, and all the large hospitals have reduced beds over the last 20 years.

The position has now been reached where the majority of health authorities are planning with local authorities for the development of local community-based mental illness services, and the consequent run-down or closure of the mental hospital. However, there are still many people who are doubtful about the wisdom of this move, and it is far from easy to get agreement about the requirements of this new service, or about the timing of such a move. The process is very complex and some of the problems experienced are worth examining.

What should be done in a particular district sometimes becomes an issue as to who should decide. There may be differing views between different disciplines, or between individuals from the same discipline. The health authority may find itself with substantial agreement, but be confronted by a local authority with different plans. I believe that it is important to spend time on discussing options and ideas with all parties before concentrating on precise plans for the closure or run-down of mental hospitals. Too often the alternative or replacement facilities are an after-thought, whereas there needs to be a clear understanding about the type of service required and how to move to this, before identifying the effects on the mental hospital. Various interests must be considered in forming the plan, including those of existing patients, the public (through community health councils and representative organisations), the various staff involved, as well as the planning groups from health authorities and local authorities.

Even when plans have been reached after adequate debate, there are other problems. The most pressing is often the lack of adequate finance, either for capital development or revenue funding. This is not an excuse, and if the Government and health authorities want changes and improvements in their mental health services, they must provide adequate resources. No doubt the position varies from one part of the country to another, but in many districts the evidence is of less money being spent now on mental health than 10 or 15 years ago, despite the priority status applied by governments in successive reports or circulars. Even if you take the view that enough money is now available, the probability is that some bridging money will be necessary, as inevitably, one will find both the old and new services running in tandem for some while.

There is also the loss of 'economy of scale' when new smaller services replace the large hospital. It is likely too that improved standards of care will be expected in the new setting, and these may well require more staff. A most dangerous assumption to make is that local services or community care will cost less than care in the mental hospital. Only time will tell exactly how much a comprehensive local psychiatric service will cost, but the objective should not be to save money. Clearly there is a duty to avoid waste and provide cost-effective care, but one will need a longer time-scale to substantiate economic claims in respect of different mental illness services than for some other specialties.

Another important issue is the ability of smaller local units to cope with some of the more difficult or long-stay patients. Already we know that district general hospital psychiatric units find particular problems with either aggressive patients or those unfit for discharge after one year. These patients, although few in number, can have a very damaging effect upon their work, and the problems are sometimes not containable within the unit and can affect the whole of the district general hospital with both immediate and long-term consequences.

An additional problem is the long-stay patient who has become institutionalised in the mental hospital, but who leaves for a group home, or hostel. Very often he is unprepared for the changes he finds and readmission is necessary. Of course, the failure rate is reduced by effective pre-discharge preparation and support after discharge, but sometimes the intolerance of the community or loss of immediate support provided by hospitals can be overwhelming. What will happen to such people in the future? One important step in planning the closure of the mental hospital is to have accurate information about the needs of patients who reside there. Many 'half-baked' schemes have been shown to be inadequate after a detailed survey of patients and their dependencies. It really is important to ensure that the new services are at least as good as those they replace.

As a nurse manager, and a member of a unit management team of a service which includes a large mental hospital, I am closely involved in the practical problems of developing new services, in co-ordinating the transfer of existing services to new locations, and in the effect all this has on the mental hospital itself. It is difficult to balance the tasks of planning a new service and continuing to maintain the old one. Those districts which have little or no psychiatric services have an advantage in starting from scratch. The districts with the mental hospitals have a much more difficult job.

I have already referred to the need for adequate resources, but I would wish to add to that by giving an example of the dilemma faced by my own health authority. A recent survey has shown there to be a need to spend in excess of £7.3 million to bring the buildings of the mental hospital up to an acceptable standard, with a life span of 20 years. Even assuming that the two other health authorities we serve take all their patients and provide their own services, we would still need to spend £5 million on the buildings required for our own patients. Provisional estimates indicate, however, that new buildings, whether on existing or new sites, would cost more. The likelihood is that such large sums of money will not be available, and the alternatives are to continue in a sub-standard setting or to develop a new type of service which is less dependent upon residential or in-patient care. Unlike some mental hospital sites, the value of land appears modest and disposal would not generate much capital. Some of the most important decisions will be in identifying which groups of patients will need hospital beds, and which can be as effectively helped without these.

Community psychiatric nurses were first employed over 30 years ago, but it is particularly over the last decade that this service has developed. It is now very difficult to imagine how we could manage without them, and the clear need is to extend and develop this service as part of the move towards community care. Progressively, as the number of community psychiatric nurses increases, their role is changing from after care to primary care, and there has been a move towards specialisation into the care of the elderly mentally infirm or into specialties such as alcoholism, drug dependency, or behavioural treatment. There has been enthusiasm among psychiatric nurses for their new work, and many hospital-based staff are also finding satisfaction in a wider role beyond the walls of the hospital.

The major problem has been in balancing the needs of in-patient care against those in the community. Unlike district general nurses or health visitors, who have been additionally funded, the development of community psychiatric nursing services in those districts with a mental hospital has been by withdrawing nurses from the wards. Another difficulty has been in preparing or training nurses for this new role. In the past, a psychiatric nurse's training was almost entirely hospital based, but the revised 1982 registered mental nurse training now includes a minimum of 12 weeks in the community. Those staff who trained under the old syllabus do need additional preparation, and there are various courses available. The training issue is one of the keys to a successful transition to a new style of care, and more work needs to be done in clearly identifying the requirements of the various disciplines, whether for new staff or for those who need refresher courses.

I have been impressed by the interest and enthusiasm of the majority of psychiatric nurses for the development of a new service. For example, over 50% of the trained nurses in my own hospital are interested in new posts that are required for the development of local psychiatric services in adjoining districts. This may, of course, be partly a concern about future job security, but it does show an awareness of the changes afoot. As the process accelerates, and the mental hospitals run down, there will be a number of dangers. One is the effect upon the morale of patients and staff who remain. For this reason it is vital that the new services take a balance of patients, and not just those that are more interesting or manageable. Acute patients are easier to relocate, but it is also relatively easy to transfer psychogeriatric patients who benefit from the easier access of relatives and closer links with the community that stem from being locally based. The most difficult groups, in some ways, are the old long-stay whose home is the mental hospital, and those in the sub-regional specialties that are not required in any single district. Perhaps, therefore, the role of those mental hospitals that will be retained over the next 10 years will be in the care of the old long-stay, and in accommodating a number of specialties, including medium security units.

There needs to be a careful check to ensure that standards are protected in the mental hospital, and monitoring of the work will need to be developed. At the least we should ensure the allocation of resources reflects work-load, that the requirements of the Mental Health Act are met, and that sensitive issues such as seclusion and locking of wards are closely controlled. The recruitment and retention of staff will be a problem for many hospitals, and this will largely depend upon the way the process of change is handled. Staff organisations must be consulted where significant changes are planned, and care needs to be taken to avoid the situation that happened with a large mental handicap hospital that was scheduled for closure by 1983 — it lost most of its staff, failed to recruit replacements, but remains open with poor standards of care. The best laid plans can fail, but there must be some flexibility, particularly in respect of time-scales.

In conclusion, I would wish to draw attention to a few other issues that seem to be particularly important and may prove major stumbling blocks to development. The first of these is the important part to be played by the local authorities in providing services for the mentally ill. As the money from joint finance tapers off and the local authority picks up the cost of these schemes, we may well find greater resistance to further schemes being agreed. The record of many boroughs and councils has been poor, and we know that the needs of the mentally ill receive a low priority in comparison to those groups for which there are statutory obligations. For some urban boroughs the threat of rate capping may produce new budgetary constraints. The added burden from the 'rising tide' of elderly people seems certain to take up all of the growth money available. Secondly, I remain concerned about the reaction of some communities to the placement of the mentally ill in their midst. The view is often that 'community care is a good idea so long as it is not in my street'. Thirdly, psychiatry is a highly labour-intensive specialty, and although there may be new breakthroughs in treatment around the corner, there will probably be a need for more staff in the future. Can we recruit suitable staff, and will developments be thwarted by manpower targets or other such devices? There is evidence to show that although more nurses do not necessarily improve standards of care, too few most certainly have an immediately damaging effect. One of the foremost needs in the future will be for nurses to identify how many staff, and of what grades, will be necessary to provide safe nursing care for the new services. Quite clearly this will be a more complex task in community-based services, and I predict some mistakes and learning from trial and error!

The challenges ahead are enormous, but with adequate consultation, resources, flexibility, team work, and leadership, I see the achievement of an effective and exciting mental health service which will provide the basis for care into the twenty-first century.

4 Making ends meet—
A continuum of care

JOHN CHANT

This paper explores the social services aspects of mental health service planning. It identifies issues which range from the complexities of implementing a national policy, through the problems of planning between complex organisations, to the practical considerations of delivering services which are relevant to people's needs. I argue for clearer definition, integration and articulation of policies for the development of community care at a national level; for the establishment of a financial mechanism which will allow the transfer of resources to promote the development of community-based services; and for the need to develop manpower policies to facilitate and support staff in the transitional arrangement to community-based care.

Setting — the burden of national politics

Personal social services departments have a wide range of responsibilities, many of which are specifically prescribed by statute. The services are administered by local authorities. The relationships of these services to central government through the Secretary of State for Health and Social Services is an indirect one. This is in contrast to the health service or the income maintenance services which are provided by the Department of Health and Social Security, and which are managed directly for the Secretary of State (Table I).

Currently, relationships between local government and central government are poor. This has implications for the development of community-based services. Whilst difficulties are most acute where political differences are at their greatest, poor relationships between the two levels of government exist across the spectrum of political views. Relationships are deteriorating as the struggle over resource allocation grows. This deterioration in relationships between central and local government has a particular

TABLE I

The structure and organisation of health and social services (adapted from the Nodder Report*)

Item	Health service	Social service
Accountability	To DHSS	Largely controlled locally
Membership	Appointed	Elected
Finance	From Exchequer	Nearly two-thirds raised locally
Control/public accountability	Health authorities and CHCs are separate	Elected members perform both roles
Geographical boundaries	Hospital catchments	An amalgamation of traditional communities
Internal structures	RHAs and AHAs are corporate	SSDs are part of local authorities with wider functions
	Confined to health interests	Other duties, for example juvenile delinquency
Dominating skills	Medical/nursing	Social work
	Long history of training	Many staff untrained
Responsibility	Individual clinical responsibility	Most responsibilities are to the local authority, leading to more member involvement
	Dispersed	Managerial control more specific

*DHSS (1981) *Organisational and Management Problems of Mental Illness Hospitals: Report of a Working Group.* London: DHSS.

significance for the personal social services and will have an impact on the way in which these services can be delivered in the field.

The effects of long-term unemployment combine with the demographic growth in the numbers of people who are both very old and frail to press forward the development of community care for the mentally handicapped and mentally ill in a way which, inevitably, determines that more resources are needed. This pressure for service growth directly conflicts with the strategy to seek an overall reduction in local government spending. The political consensus which has tended to surround the provision of personal social services is weakening and the consequent polarisation of political view is likely to impede and distort the pattern of services provided. It is not just collaboration at operational level which is required for the successful development of services.

Unlike other services, in the local authority setting the personal social services must mesh into a broad interface with both the health service and the income maintenance services directly managed by the Department of Health and Social Security. The need for integrated planning between the three arms of these services, in relation to the development of community care, is self-evident. Significant development of services cannot take place unless more resources are made available and those additional resources are protected from the general reduction in local authority expenditure. Neither of these things can happen unless at a political level the Government gives leadership and clear direction to local authorities and secures their co-operation in carrying through agreed programmes.

Faced with these complex issues, which block any real movement of policy, target dates for the closure of long-stay hospitals are being set as the only way forward. Simply deciding a date for implementation will not solve the political and financial problems which have been identified.

To be effective, the personal social services departments of local authorities must collaborate fully in planning community services with the health service and housing authorities. The commitment of all three is vital to progress being made. The extent to which firm commitments can be entered into at local level will reflect the perception each service has of its forward financial position. At a national level, collaboration within the DHSS in relation to the management of the health service, the administration of supplementary benefits and the policy division of the personal social services is essential. The strategy of the DHSS must be more closely co-ordinated with the housing sector of the Department of the Environment, as well as being seen to be reflected in the manpower policies adopted by local government and the strategic targets adopted by the Treasury. The public commitment to a strategy for change needs to be more clearly articulated. The community care strategy is barely mentioned in the White Paper on Public Expenditure for each of the last three years, yet it is said to be a central strategic policy. The present arrangement of one department of government telling local authorities to build up service provision, whilst another department of government seeks to constrain spending and reduce the manpower employed, effectively inhibits movement for change, particularly since the political will to cut spending appears so much stronger than the commitment to promote the development of services in the local government setting.

The new managerialism — performing to targets

Recent initiatives by ministers imply that a new impetus is being given to policies designed to secure the closure of long-stay hospitals for the mentally ill and the mentally handicapped by setting closure dates for such institutions. In the South-West Region, target dates have been agreed between the regional health authority and the responsible minister to close 11 long-stay hospitals. The publicly announced aim is to halve the population of these hospitals within five years and to close them in ten years.

This announcement was made without any prior consultation with local authorities within the region, and without any indication to the local authority associations at national level that firm targets and objectives were going to be set in this way. The theory is, apparently, that targets, like hanging, concentrate the mind. Ironically, the announcement was made just two months after the Somerset Social Services Committee and the Somerset Health Authority had given approval to a jointly agreed plan to move to a further stage in the development of services for mentally handicapped people. These plans will enable the discharge of a minimum of a further

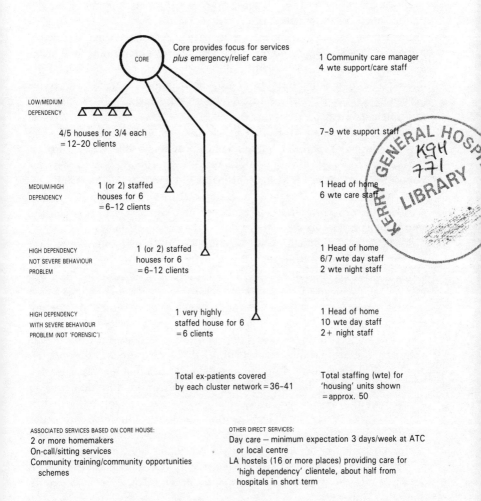

Fig. 1—Somerset: proposed extended core and cluster model. There would be approximately 10 local networks, as shown.

120 (and possibly 160) patients over five years. The projects were approved on the basis of a judgement of what could be realistically achieved within the existing climate of resource constraints. For years practitioners and service managers have been exhorted to establish joint planning mechanisms which will enable collaboration and co-ordination of service delivery. Recent experience suggests that there is little evidence of any joint planning or collaboration between services at regional or national level. Locally, we are proceeding to implement our agreed plan.

In addition, we have embarked on the process of drawing up plans which would allow the closure of the long-stay hospitals for the mentally handicapped in Somerset within eight years (Fig. 1). The cost of implementing such an arrangement, on early provisional estimates, is likely to be of the order of £5 million at current prices. The present total spent on personal social services is £16 million, which indicates the scale of the development that is required. The ratio of development costs to base service provision also gives a useful impression of the effort which will be required to implement such proposals.

Whilst deciding on a target date for closure of long-stay hospitals has the effect of concentrating people's thinking, the benefits must be weighed against the damage that is dealt to staff morale and commitment. There are major implications from planning blight for the maintenance of buildings and staff recruitment. Setting dates that are not realistically achievable may be evidence of conviction and determination, but is unlikely to result in the sound and purposeful management of such a complex task.

The process of regional review, together with the appointment of general managers on short contracts, is clearly designed to make the performance of the health service more responsive to direction. Service objectives will increasingly be targeted and one of the performance measures against which general managers are likely to be judged, will be their success in meeting those targets.

The setting of dates to close long-stay hospitals takes on a particular significance in such arrangements. Setting a date for closure begs the question of whether the goal is to close the hospital or to develop a comprehensive range of community-based services which result in the hospital being no longer required. Social services departments and many staff employed in the health service are concerned to emphasise that community care is not simply about discharging people from hospital: it is about helping people not to be patients, or dependent residents, and about helping them to re-establish themselves as participating members of the community. The objective must be to avoid institutionalisation and dependency, wherever that is possible.

Community care is a term that should be defined in a positive sense. It must say something about the nature of the care that should be provided in the community. It must not be allowed to become a low-cost strategy for the abandonment of people in need, by decanting them from long-stay hospitals into cheap lodgings and the isolated life of a wayfarer. The term 'community care' should be used to describe a commitment to provide services to support families and informal carers wherever possible, to use substitute family care where the family is unable or unwilling to make provision, and to use admission to hospital and residential care only when absolutely necessary. Those who are admitted to hospital as patients need regular assessment, rehabilitation and, where appropriate, access to training to enable their discharge. The prime purpose must be to prevent people being admitted to hospital inappropriately because of a breakdown in their network of family and social care.

Programmes must respect and value the needs of individuals, give opportunity for choice and independence, and assume that the least restrictive alternative in relation to the needs of an individual will guide the placement that is used and the service which is provided. The existence of a network of care services in the community, capable of responding appropriately to a wide variety of individual needs, will provide the best possible framework to support those discharged from hospital who are handicapped by the institutionalising effect of a long stay in hospital or in residential care.

Choosing priorities — support and abandonment

Accepting the reality that service provision must inevitably be constrained by availability of resources, difficult choices must be made. Such choices may involve deciding to focus resources on the needs of one group of people to the exclusion of the needs of another. The alternative of spreading resources thinly to everybody may result in services which are ineffective.

Most authorities will define the first priority as the need to develop services to prevent the unnecessary admission of people to hospital. Already in the community there are large numbers of mentally handicapped people being cared for by elderly parents. To illustrate this point, in Somerset the service will need to find alternative care arrangements for some 200 mentally handicapped people over the next five years. There are currently some 430 people in long-stay hospitals. This latent need for more service development for people already in the community is insufficiently recognised. Similar concerns can be identified in relation to services for the mentally ill.

The level, range and distribution of day care resources and programmes are a key element to the build-up of community-based programmes of care. In particular, it is important that those families caring for the most severely handicapped are provided with day care, which, given the degree of handicap, is likely to be in special care units. There is scope for day care programmes to become more community based. Greater efforts should be made to help people who need such facilities to become involved and participate in ordinary every-day experiences in the community. More and more, they will need to experience the opportunity not solely to receive care, but also to give and contribute. The provision of community-based residential care units for children, together with resources to provide short-term and crisis care facilities, can effectively reduce the level of new cases entering hospital-based care systems.

Thus far the strategies are relatively easy to define and implement. However, without additional resources there comes a point where a clear choice has to be made between developing services to support people in the communities in which they are already living, or using those same resources to develop policies to allow large-scale closure of hospitals. Obviously there is some measure of overlap and a great deal of ingenuity has been used to enable significant numbers of people to leave hospital. However, the core of the problem cannot be tackled without additional resources.

To release the resources locked up in large hospitals, a double-banking of expenditure must occur in the initial years to provide the facilities which are needed to allow closure to take place. The first 30 or 40 people to leave hospital make little impact on reducing the cost of services provided by the health services, but require significant expenditure by the local authorities (both in capital and revenue terms).

Recently, imaginative attempts have been made to break the deadlock of resource transfer by using the provision of the 1983 *Care in the Community* circular to transfer an annual sum reflecting average cost per patient place from health service expenditure to social service expenditure. Increasingly this method is viewed as a possible solution to the growing problems which face local authorities in taking up joint financing and to the objections which local authority associations have to accepting ear-marked funds from Central Government.

The idea is attractively simple: you transfer the patient, together with a sum equal to the cost of his care, from hospital to the community. As and when the consequent services are well established, in three to five years a central book-keeping transfer of funds from the National Health Service budget to the rate-support grant is effected in confirmation of the transfer which has already taken place at operational level.

The solution may be too simple. The implications need to be clearly understood. Transferring resources based on average care costs assumes that responsibility for the total range of care is being transferred. Our own work in drawing up plans to facilitate the discharge of all patients from long-stay hospital provision would suggest that if social services were to assume responsibility for all the low dependency patients currently resident in the hospital, this would transfer responsibility for 33 % of the patient population, but would only release some 10% of the revenue spent on staff. If, in addition, social services accepted responsibility for providing care in the community for medium-dependency patients, they would have 70% of the present patient population, but would only free approximately 40% of the expenditure spent on staff. Average costs can be misleading, and even substantial progress toward placement in the community may not unlock the resources locked into institutional care.

It is, therefore, important that there should be a clear understanding between health and social services about what their long-term objectives are. There needs to be clear understanding about the care arrangements for those who have maximum dependency. There must be agreement about who is to take the primary responsibility for development, and a recognition of the fact that the economics of the process are likely to determine that there will be a point in the process when it has to be accelerated to contain escalating unit costs of care.

Planning and development

Building services between large organisations to meet the needs of individuals in a way which fits in with local cultural patterns is a complex task. Making things happen in terms of service delivery and influencing patterns of professional practice is difficult and not to be confused with the easier task of agreeing plans between managers who are not directly involved in patient care.

The recent reorganisation of the health service has both interrupted and added to the complexities of planning between the health service and the personal social services. As a result of reorganisation there are in many areas greater problems in relation to the lack of geographical co-terminosity between the authorities responsible for the provision of the personal social services, the housing authorities and health districts. It has taken many health authorities longer than anticipated to complete changes of personnel, and in a number of areas this has created a hiatus in joint planning arrangements.

The more recent implementation of proposals to appoint general managers has added to the climate of uncertainty. The planning arrangements for the development of community care strategies need clarification. In some parts of the country strategic planning initiatives are being pursued by regional health authorities, without the full involvement of the local authorities who will be directly affected by the plans produced. This is particularly so, either where a hospital facility has a catchment area involving many local authorities, or there are complex problems of geographical co-terminosity.

In some areas, health authorities are pursuing detailed plans to establish community-based systems of care for people who are disabled by mental handicap or chronic mental illness, without any significant development of community-based services with the involvement of the local authority. It is not known whether this reflects an inability or unwillingness to plan and develop services together or whether it reflects the anxieties and concerns of staff currently employed in long-stay hospitals about their future. The fact that such plans appear to be implemented with the approval of regional health authorities highlights the need for structured, collaborative and integrated planning and decision-making arrangements.

There is a danger of services being developed in a competitive rather than a collaborative way — this could result in a mis-match between needs and resources, a lack of clarity about prime areas of responsibility and unnecessary duplication and wasteful use of resources. Any change involving a reduction of the role of a long-standing institution requires clear aims, strong commitment, careful consultation and determination. Without these there will always be enough ambiguity, prejudice and vested interest to maintain the status quo. The closure of institutions with long history and tradition needs to be done with due regard and recognition of the service commitment which the institution and its staff have given over the years. In the same way that it is necessary to establish a team to commission a new hospital, closing a hospital in a constructive way is an even more complex task. The idea of de-commissioning teams would be worth careful exploration.

Whilst the general objectives to be achieved in service development and the strategic resource parameters are appropriately set within the national and regional forum, we would argue that the detailed plans of service development must be drawn up jointly at a level common to the authorities most directly involved. It is important to ensure that strategic decisions are taken jointly, as it is only in this way that there can be an effective and equal commitment to the outcome. To this end, members of regional health authorities need opportunities to meet and agree policies with the elected members of local authorities.

The complexities of joint planning are frequently underestimated: not only are the nature and structures of local authorities and health authorities very dissimilar (Table I), but the systems of funding and the time-scales of their planning arrangements suffer from a high degree of mis-match. There is more than one experienced director of social services who would sympathise with the view that 'if you wanted to create a structure for health and social services that inhibited co-operation and led to misunderstandings and inertia, you could not do better than re-invent the present structure'.

Implications for staff

The common experience of both the health service and the personal social services is that high standards of care can only be provided if the right calibre of staff are recruited, trained, appreciated and rewarded. We are in danger of overlooking the needs of staff in transition.

In adopting strategies for the development of community services to provide alternative patterns of care for people who have been cared for in hospital on a long-stay basis, it is properly the plans for patients which have predominated people's thinking. It is now clear to a number of authorities that plans for patients from long-stay hospitals cannot be made in isolation from a proper concern for the interests of staff. Failure to acknowledge this issue and deal with it openly may result in service planning for patients being disturbed by the vested interests of staff.

There is plenty of evidence to suggest that the shape and form of service provision is as much influenced by attitudes and prejudice as it is by notions of needs and rights. Attempts at joint training are proceeding all too slowly. More thought needs to be given to mechanisms which will facilitate the movement of staff between various settings. The special pension arrangements of staff who work as mental health officers in long-stay hospitals, and the recruitment processes of local government that require staff not previously employed in this service to complete a probationary year, are two particular examples of the problems which can face experienced members of staff in moving from working in a hospital-based setting into community-based services.

Plans to close hospitals will require manpower policies, setting clear options for staff and ensuring their interests are protected in transition. It is important to acknowledge that there are resources of skill and experience which must also be devolved from the institutional setting. Greater efforts should be made to provide joint training for staff from both the health and personal social services.

Similarly, a greater investment in staff training needs to be made by social services departments if they are to develop the breadth of service and skill that is necessary. The extent to which social services departments are able to provide a satisfactory standard of care for people with high levels of dependency will depend on their ability to recruit people of the right calibre and train them, as well as on the support they can get from health service experts.

A successful model of community care requires close collaboration in practice as well as in planning. In many areas of service provision the joint participation of staff from both health and social service settings, as well as from differing professional backgrounds, will be essential if needs are to be effectively met. To this end, joint in-service training initiatives need to be more widely encouraged. Team-building amongst practitioners from differing disciplines, as well as differing settings, will call for careful review of the existing mechanisms for allocating services. Lines of accountability will need reappraisal.

Central to these issues is the need to establish some clear measure of agreement between service organisations as to where primary responsibilities will lie. The broad consensus within social services would lead to the view that the problems which beset mentally handicapped people are primarily social and educational rather than medical, and for this reason we would take the view that the social services infrastructure should be the base upon which services for mentally handicapped people should be developed. The successful treatment and rehabilitation of those who suffer from mental illness, however, will require a primary involvement of medically-based psychiatric services, and the social services provision must be built up in support of the strategies adopted by the psychiatric services. Clarifying the roles to be played by the staff of the differing agencies involved is important if the service is to be coherent to those who use it as well as those who work within it.

Conclusions

Most of the problems touched on in this paper are on a macro-level. They are the barriers to making large-scale fundamental change. They are the problems related to: political will and confidence, adequate resourcing, inter-agency planning at member and officer level, allocation of task and responsibility, and consideration of the needs of staff in parallel to the needs of patients.

At the practice level, it is important to emphasise that there is a great deal of important development built around the needs of individual clients. In a number of areas, small residential homes no longer required for children have been switched to use for the mentally handicapped. Housing authorities and housing associations have responded positively to the development of care systems based on group homes. The exodus of staff from local authority homes to become non-resident has freed a great deal of accommodation that is often ideally situated to support vulnerable people in the community. There has been a significant development in the private and voluntary sector through the funds which have been made available through housing benefit and supplementary benefit.

This networking of services can proceed in a positive way, but there comes a point in the evolution of such arrangements when the services and support have to be effectively managed and co-ordinated to ensure that people's needs do not get lost or overlooked. At that point, the issues outlined in this paper will need to be confronted by members of all authorities, by service directors, field managers and practitioners. The individual commitment of consultants, nurses and social workers is unlikely to surmount these problems. Failure to seek solutions to these issues in a constructive way will frustrate the vocation of the staff who actually provide the care for people in need. It is likely to lead to a costly and ill-defined service which lacks leadership and direction. Failure to identify solutions is likely to result in long-stay hospitals remaining open for many more years than is currently envisaged, facing even greater problems than they do now in maintaining satisfactory standards of care. Planning is also a doing activity; we must work at these issues if they are not to block progress and distort the provision of services.

5 Planning and organisation

Discussion

Joint planning

A major problem was identified by many of the psychiatrists present; namely, that many local authorities had not given the same priority as health authorities to the need for developments in community care. It was suggested that unless some form of compulsion was provided to local authorities, the facilities needed (for example, day centres, group homes, and sheltered workshops) would not be forthcoming. This outcome was thought to be more likely to be the case if, as Lord Glenarthur pointed out, local authorities were left to set their own priorities. Joint planning between local authorities and health authorities was required, but, so far, such developments were found only in patches around the country. It was thought that there was a need for the Department of the Environment to try to influence local authorities in this regard.

Funding

The impact on the provisions for community care of problems arising from rate capping, and the financial penalties associated with local authorities' overspending ('even for promoting normal services') were also mentioned. These problems, it was pointed out, had to be considered against the background of the totality of public expenditure. On the positive side, it was pointed out that health authorities were not directly affected by rate capping. It was proposed that local authorities had to come to terms with living within their means.

In relation to the general financial issue, a distinction was drawn between bridging finance and bridging loans. The latter appeared not to be working as had been envisaged. The sums of money that were likely to be involved in the future greatly exceeded current expectations. For this reason, speakers welcomed the fact that the further provision of bridging finance was under consideration by the Department of Health and Social Security. At the same time, it was recognised that there were still many unsolved problems regarding joint funding by health authorities and local authorities, and the basis for this was thought to be mutual suspicion and hostility between these authorities.

Housing

It was stated that however good the plans for community care were, new resources would be needed: and the example of housing was highlighted. If the situation which developed in the United States of America and Italy following the closure of large mental hospitals was not to be repeated in this country, local authorities needed to be brought into the discussions early, so that adequate housing was available for patients to reside in the community. This was especially the case for the more independent and less disabled patients. If the local authority was not brought into plans, it was difficult to see how housing provision could be made available at a time when local authority housing budgets were already decreasing.

Long-stay patients

In a number of regions there were plans to combine together long-stay patients from several mental hospitals, in order that the plans for closure of individual hospitals might proceed. This appeared to some to perpetuate the notion of large institutions. The patients' views on such transfers had to be sought: they, and many others, might think it preferable, in the long term, for accommodation to be provided in small units or within a residential portion of a larger hospital — provided this was in an area with which those involved had natural ties or were familiar.

It was recalled that one region had suggested that such an amalgamation might lead to the concentration of 900 patients in one asylum. This was thought to be too large a number, and was said to be 'sacrificing' a generation of patients for reasons of policy, when it was not at all clear that the long-standing and continuing decline in mental hospital in-patient numbers was the result of any particular policy or action. In fact, the reasons for this decline remained obscure.

It was suggested that the DHSS had a role in influencing regional planners with such intentions. Others responded that it might still be in the long-term interests of patient care to release capital and 'free-up overheads' by closing large hospitals, even if the temporary solution was to transfer and amalgamate patients in another mental hospital. However, some speakers stressed that although future patient care might benefit, the group of patients directly concerned in this transfer might be adversely affected.

Transfer of resources

On the issue of the transfer of resources from institutional care to community care, most speakers emphasised that long-stay patients in mental hospitals individually absorbed a small amount of resources at present, and that greater resources would be needed in order to support them with community care services in the future. This was thought likely to be to the detriment of the development of acute psychiatric services. Furthermore, it seemed unlikely that revenue saved or capital acquired by the closure of mental hospitals would, in all cases, be enough to support either new community services or services for the acutely psychiatrically ill. One speaker stated that until accurate financial information became available, there was a need to be cautious in talking of the true costs of community care.

A large number of psychiatric patients and mentally handicapped patients were currently looked after by their parents, attended special schools, or had alternative residential provision. When informal carers were no longer able to provide care for these patients, it was unavoidable that 'new money' would be needed to provide for them. In this case there would be no resources to transfer, as the resources available were for patients who were currently in hospital.

Manpower

Psychiatrists, social workers and nurses, among others, were needed to provide the proposed new mental health services, but it was not at all clear that the manpower consequences had been fully analysed or appreciated. In particular, in view of the restraints on medical manpower, the number and nature of psychiatrists that would be required was uncertain.

Problems often seemed to arise from the nature of the care givers' professional status and background. While supporting the need for flexibility between different organisational structures, such as local authorities and health authorities, there was seen to be a need to recognise, in addition, that there were also great intraorganisational problems, e.g., which was more appropriate, to talk of psychiatric services for the elderly mentally ill or of services for the elderly? It was stressed that clients and patients spanned current organisational structures.

New developments

Across the country, many interesting developments were taking place, but mostly at the instigation of enthusiastic individuals. It was noted that such networks of care required planning and management as they were built up, and that there was a need to manage community resources.

Planning blight

A speaker drew attention to the consequences of 'planning blight' if the mental hospitals continued in operation for the next 10–20 years. It seemed unlikely that Victorian asylums would be maintained properly. It was still possible to agree with the then Minister of Health, 20 years ago, when he said that these Victorian monuments must depart; but, in the meantime, it was necessary to maintain their fabric.

Determining policies and priorities

One speaker claimed that it was insufficiently recognised that senior managers in the National Health Service were not challenged enough — there was a failure generally to understand how policies and priorities are determined. There were immense possibilities of influencing management and opinion and these extended from NHS staff outwith the NHS to patients and voluntary bodies. Not many people were convinced that every penny spent on health services was spent wisely. There was always a need to make it clear that resources were used to their best advantage.

6 The cycle of planning and evaluation

JOHN WING

The programme for this conference states that its particular emphasis is to be 'on the problems of transition from a hospital-based to a community-based mental health service'. The terms of this formulation imply that hospitals do not provide, and even that they cannot provide, a community-based service. Probably the organisers were far from intending the implication but adopted a piece of fashionable jargon without examining it very closely. Nevertheless, it incorporates assumptions about the National Health Service and local government, the nature of mental illness and mental retardation,[1] the functions of 'institutions' and the meaning of 'community' that can vary so widely as to be in total contradiction to each other.

This is not the place to examine this range of assumptions in any detail. Richard Titmuss (1963)[2] called 'community care' (another term that can easily degenerate into a slogan) an 'everlasting cottage-garden trailer'. That was in 1961. He agreed that it conjured up 'a sense of warmth and human kindness', but, after much effort, had tried and failed to discover its social origins. Fortunately, the introduction to our programme goes on to state, in parentheses, what the organisers have in mind, which is to consider the problems created by a continuing decline in the population of the large psychiatric hospitals and by the inadequate development of alternative resources.

[1] The term 'mental handicap', when used to describe only the intellectually and developmentally retarded, excluding those who by default may be called the 'chronic mentally ill', is not only parochial (no other country uses it) but betrays confusion about the concepts of illness and handicap. The term adopted by the WHO and DSM-III is 'mental retardation' which does not imply that the ill cannot be handicapped nor the handicapped ill. In this paper, 'mental disablement' is used to refer to a state of disability due to the combined effect of mental illness and/or retardation, social disadvantages and adverse personal reaction. Discussion of these concepts will be found in Wing (1978a).
[2] See Titmuss (1963) — it is worth recalling that the three 'acts of policy' that Titmuss suggested should be implemented, if statements about community care were to be taken seriously, were: (a) earmarked grants to local authorities; (b) central funding of specialist social work training; and (c) a Royal Commission to look into the education of doctors in social and psychological medicine.

Aims

These are important problems and the main object of this paper is to suggest that the best way to maximise the chances of resolving them is to ensure that planning and evaluation go hand in hand. (The roles of policy maker and evaluator and the principles of evaluation are discussed by Wing, 1972; 1978b.) Of course, there are major differences between the two approaches. Planners carry responsibility for decisions that often have to be made hurriedly, without an adequate basis of information. Evaluators often experience that luxury (as well as frustration) of coming to well-documented conclusions that no policy maker could dream of implementing. Each side has its own, quite separate, reference group. Nevertheless, the opportunity for creative collaboration is there.

Policy makers and workers in the field of health and social services research (HSSR), whatever their field of interest, tend to share certain basic aims. Both would like to see a decrease in the incidence and prevalence of the three main components of mental disablement—illness and/or disability, social disadvantage and personal distress—and an improvement in the quality of life. Both probably agree that people who used to be at risk of a long stay in hospital, or who still now accumulate as long-term in-patients in spite of all that is being done to prevent it, should continue to receive a fair share of resources, however these are disposed. There is general acceptance of the principles of geographical responsibility, comprehensiveness of provision and planned organisation that are supposed to underlie the health and social services.

Epidemiological basis of evaluation

If this much is agreed, it follows that epidemiological methods must be of particular importance for evaluative research since, by definition, they involve relating subgroups with specified characteristics to a parent population by calculating and comparing their rates of disorder. Thus, new methods of treatment or care or innovations in service delivery, can not only be evaluated separately, using the most appropriate and efficient designs and methodology, but they can be seen in the context of changes in other aspects of a local service. It is convenient to divide such research into monitoring, *ad hoc* descriptive surveys, and evaluation.

Monitoring: Descriptive statistics

Monitoring involves the use of relatively 'hard' indices such as bed occupancy. The trend shown in Fig. 1 is very familiar and substantial

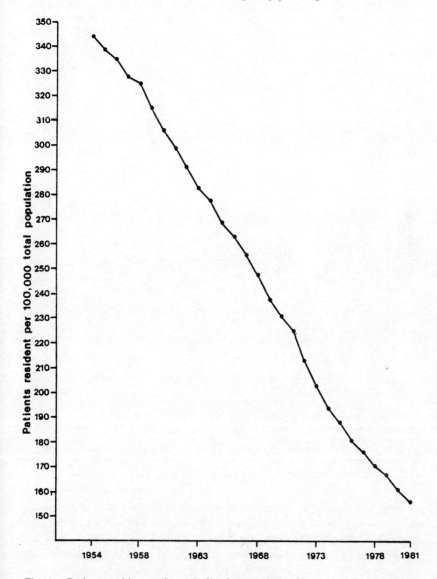

Fig. 1 — Patients resident at the end of each year 1954–1981: rate per 100,000 total population. (*N.B.* Rate to 1968 is for England and Wales; from 1969 is for England only [but the two individual rates are almost identical].)

changes in policy have been based upon it. Nevertheless, the overall rate for bed occupancy in Scotland, Northern Ireland, Eire or Holland is substantially higher. In Finland, the rate is still very little lower than that for England at its peak in 1954 (Salokangas *et al*, 1985). Administrative

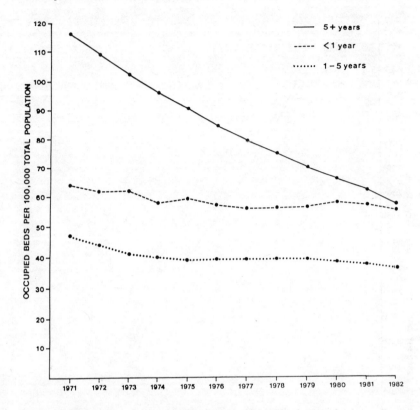

Fig. 2 — Resident in-patients on 31 December 1971–1981, by length of stay. English psychiatric hospitals, rates per 100,000 total population.

indices can be used to monitor trends, but they cannot allocate value to the policies or practices that are responsible for those trends occurring.

A more detailed breakdown of part of the trend shown in Fig. 1 is presented in Fig. 2. Here it is clear that the rundown is taking place mainly in that group of residents who have been in hospital for more than five years. Reference to the statistical sources show that this decline is mainly by death rather than discharge. The other two groups, sometimes known for convenience as 'short-stay' (under one year) and 'medium long-stay' (one to five years), seem, for a moment, to have reached relative stability at 60 and 40 per 100,000 total population respectively.

Robertson (1981),[3] who prepared a memorandum of guidance for

[3]The higher of Robertson's two estimates is used in Table I, since it is based on the assumption (correct, as it turned out, as is evident from Fig. 2) that there would be little change in the size of the medium long-stay group. The figures are substantially higher than earlier DHSS 'guide-lines'. Statistical data are taken from the annual *In-Patient Statistics from the Mental Health Enquiry for England*, which are published by HMSO in London.

regional health authority statisticians, calculated (assuming no radical changes in service practice) that, by the end of 1991, an average health district would generate 140 in-patients per 100,000 inhabitants, 80 of whom would be long-stay (over one year) including those who would have been resident since 'the old days'. This total is not much less than now. If those with a diagnosis of dementia are omitted, there would be 53 short-stay and 53 long-stay in-patients per 100,000 total population. The figures are summarised in Table I.

TABLE I
Estimated number of beds occupied in mental illness hospitals at end 1991 by age group, diagnosed dementia or not, and length of stay (England: rates per 100,000 total population)

Age group	Dementia or not	Under 1 year		Over 1 year
		<3 months	3–12 months	
Under 65	—†	A 29	6	B 32
Over 65	No	12*	6	21
Over 65	Yes		C 7	27
Total		60		80

†Dementia relatively rare
*Mainly assessment beds
Box A: Acute admission units (N = 53)
Box B: Younger and older long-stay (N = 53)
Box C: Longer-term care for dementia (N = 34)
Source: Robertson (1981)

Perhaps the key group from the point of view of government policy and of this paper is that comprising 'medium long-stay' patients. If it is not much diminishing in size, there must be a steady recruitment from the 'short-stay' to balance those moving into the over five-year group. This illustrates the problem of the 'new' long-stay[4] — recently admitted people who remain in hospital longer than a year, in spite of admission and discharge practices that are directed, some think over-zealously, at preventing such accumulation (Parliamentary Social Services Committee, 1985).

Further light is thrown on this matter by statistics from six cumulative psychiatric case registers in England and Wales. The data collected in these registers are most comprehensive and of better quality than in the English Mental Health Enquiry, and they are more readily amplified by intensive study of samples drawn for particular purposes. (The advantages and disadvantages of local case registers are discussed by Wing & Fryers, 1976.)

[4]For the origin of the term see Wing (1971). It is now often used in an administrative rather than a technical sense and has thereby lost flexibility. In this paper it is used in the original sense.

Changes in the total population of seven register areas from 1921 to 1981 compared with England and Wales are shown in Fig. 3. Table II shows the bed occupancy in these areas at the end of 1981. (The very long-stay group is omitted because of technical considerations, but its large relative size in the less attractive areas presents a serious service need.) The difference between areas that are attracting and those that are losing population is striking and reflected in other social demographic indices, particularly those measuring poverty (Gibbons *et al*, 1984).

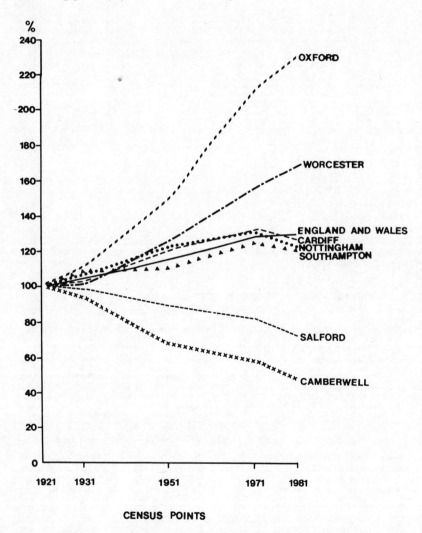

Fig. 3 — Psychiatric register areas, April 1981 (100% = June 1921).

It is probable from other evidence that the net migration into attractive areas is likely to increase the proportion of mentally healthy people, while those who seek anonymity and isolation will tend to move towards the large cities. The net migration away from unattractive areas is likely to have the opposite effects. Another important factor, not well illustrated by the register areas except for Camberwell, where there are many 'homeless single people', is social isolation. Districts such as Bloomsbury in central London (where there are three railway stations, a high proportion of lodging houses and 'single person dwellings', and a substantial transient population), are likely to have higher than average admissions to psychiatric hospitals and high attempted suicide rates.

TABLE II

Hospital beds occupied in seven case register areas (Rates per 100,000 total population, 31.12.81)

Case register	Under 1 year*	1–5 years	
Camberwell	—**	56	Inner conurban areas with
Salford	70	58	declining population
Cardiff	74	46	Medium-sized industrial cities
Nottingham	69	38	with average
Southampton	70	37	population increase
Oxford	36	16	Attractive areas with
Worcester	41	20	increasing populations
England	57	37	

N.B. The over five year group is omitted because population changes make rates non-comparable.
*For 'short-stay' beds, the ratio of upper to lower limit is 2:1; for 'new long-stay' beds, the ratio is 3:1.
**Camberwell short-stay beds are affected by special factors and are therefore omitted.
Source: Gibbons *et al* (1984)

As usual with epidemiological data, the directions of causes and effects cannot be specified without further investigations. The variations must often be due, at least in part, to differences in practice (in turn often derived from earlier local characteristics and developments), but statistical indices readily available for each district are likely to provide substantial clues to distinctive local needs.

It is not obvious from regional, district and local authority plans that such factors are being taken into account. National averages or earlier DHSS targets are still referred to as 'norms' and treated, without much reflection, as though they are absolute. There is a gap, left by the DHSS decision not to specify guidelines, that could and should be filled by national and regional authorities publicising the factors that are likely to reflect a rate that is higher or lower than average.

Descriptive surveys

The real aims of local planners, however, ought surely to be couched first in clinical and personal terms. This requires a different type of research. Data from the Camberwell case register illustrate the way this can be done (Wing & Hailey, 1972; Wing & Der, 1984). Fig. 4 shows the build-up of 'new' long-stay patients since 31 December 1964 when the case register began. By the end of 1983 the numbers had levelled off at about 100, including about 40 people with dementia. With a group of this size it is possible to interview the people involved and talk to their relatives and the staff looking after them.

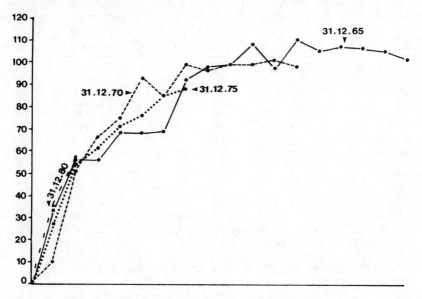

Fig. 4 — Build-up of 'new' long-stay numbers, Camberwell (non-resident > 1 year on quinquennial census days, but long-stay on subsequent annual census days).

Several such surveys have been carried out, one of them on a national scale (Mann & Sproule, 1972; Mann & Cree, 1976; Wykes, 1982). Although each person is an individual with unique problems and needs, there are features common to a substantial proportion of the group and also to other groups of people with long-term mental disablement, such as many day centre attenders, hostel and group home residents, and frequent users of centres and shelters for the 'single homeless' (those with severe mental retardation or dementia are not under consideration here). Chief among these characteristics is a record of contact with health and social services that stretches back much further than the time they have been in hospital. Very few have put down roots in a community or have recently been employed. Very few are married and in touch with their husbands or wives. Although many have relatives somewhere, contacts are exiguous or non-existent. Most are middle-aged to elderly.

The most common diagnosis is schizophrenia, but at least half have other conditions, such as short-cycle manic-depressive disorders, chronic depression or severe chronic neurosis. Personality disorders and alcohol misuse are common complications, but not common primary diagnoses. Many patients have multiple, including physical, disabilities, such as epilepsy, mental retardation, brain damage, sensory deficits, neurological disorders, heart disease and other kinds of medical complaints. The particular combination of diagnoses is not as important as an overall inability to cope with every-day life without a great deal of support, care and supervision. However, there is an important concomitant of some psychiatric diagnoses — a vulnerability to relapse with acute mental illness, suicidal attempts, disturbed behaviour or a total failure of self-care, when transferred to a less sheltered setting. This is an 'invisible' disability.

Behavioural problems can take many forms, but two types of difficulty are especially prominent. The first is less likely, in the absence of other complications, to necessitate hospital admission, except in default of alternative services, but it can be so severe, even on its own, as to require 24-hour basic nursing care. This is the 'negative' syndrome which includes slowness, underactivity, lack of initiative, poor verbal and non-verbal and social skills, inability to manage a budget or to structure time properly (so that it is never clear what activity should follow the present one), indecisiveness, isolation, wandering and even lack of awareness of common dangers. Such an individual may not take sufficient food, self-care and hygiene may be very poor, and physical health is likely to be neglected.

The other kind of behavioural problem is more serious and much less likely to be tolerated in 'normal' settings. Local authority and voluntary services are unwilling to accept people who are persistently or unpredictably 'disturbed' in behaviour. They point out very reasonably that they do not have sufficient staff, nor staff with enough training and experience, to be able to cope. Such disturbance can take several forms — persistent screaming, marked overactivity or agitation, constant pestering or aggressive teasing, violence, destructiveness, self-injury, objectionable habits such as spitting in people's faces, taking cigarettes out of their mouths, demanding money in a threatening manner, insisting on carrying out some bizarre activity to the great inconvenience and annoyance of others, and actions that would require police intervention if carried out in public. We are not concerned here with behaviours of these kinds that transiently accompany acute illness, still less with deliberate anti-social behaviour; only with persistent behaviours that are out of the individual's control due to mental illness and which have not responded to the best treatments currently available.

There is an understandable tendency to play down the severity and frequency of such problems. No one wants to increase stigmatisation. Seen in the context of a complete psychiatric service, these behaviours are uncommon, particularly in chronic form. It is tempting to deny that they occur at all or that they would cause serious difficulties to other patients, or to relatives or the general public. Another line of argument is to suggest that they are created by the hospital environment and would disappear under some other regime.

This last contention is nowadays generally wrong. The same sorts of problem can be found in people who have never been in hospital, except when these very difficulties have meant that no other agency is willing to cope. In less severe form they can be found in people who make use of any of the alternative day and residential services (Hewett *et al*, 1975; Edwards & Carter, 1979; Olsen, 1979; Wykes *et al*, 1982).

A survey of the problems of two groups of relatives of people with schizophrenia—one a representative sample from the Camberwell case register, the other from the National Schizophrenia Fellowship (NSF)—demonstrated the gaps in service with which most professional carers are familiar (Wing, 1962; Creer & Wing, 1974). The NSF group naturally described more severe difficulties, but the range of problems was much the same in the two series. What was particularly striking was that every respondent could describe some part of the service that was working well—a good day centre, a helpful community psychiatric nurse, a supportive general practitioner, a hospital ward that provided a community service entirely on its own and that responded to emergencies rapidly and effectively, a hostel that was home from home. If these excellent practices could all be put together in one responsible, comprehensive and integrated district service, there would be much less heart-searching about 'community care'.

Evaluative research

Research demonstrating the effects, for example, of poverty of the social environment on the negative symptoms of schizophrenia, carried out in some of the large hospitals of the 1950s and 1960s, also showed that these effects had been minimised in the best of them (Wing & Frendenberg, 1961; Wing & Brown, 1970). Much the same is true of 'institutionalism', a term introduced into this field in the early 1960s to describe the gradual acceptance by an in-patient of attitudes to the self and the environment that were themselves barriers to discharge; an extreme example of 'secondary handicaps'. The process can take place in any setting.

Moreover, most of the rehabilitation and maintenance techniques now used throughout the health and social services were first developed in the hospitals. They have since been considerably refined and improved and their advantages and limitations recognised. But there is no evidence that any hitherto unrecognised techniques are being used in the alternative day and residential facilities (Ryan, 1979; Wing & Morris, 1981; Watts & Bennett, 1984). There is beginning to be a substantial literature on evaluative research of the more fundamental kind that is concerned with the effectiveness with which district services 'deliver' forms of care to people in specific need.

Application to service development

Much of the research that underlies these statements has been concerned with the specific clinical and social problems of individuals and with methods of helping them to overcome or cope with those problems. Research into services must be based on the knowledge that has accumulated in this way.

Housing can be taken as an example. In general, people do not choose to live in barracks; they prefer houses. There are no obvious clinical reasons why chronically mentally disabled people should live all their lives in wards. The NHS hostels set up for 'new long-stay' patients in Camberwell, Manchester and Southampton have demonstrated that a domestic environment is compatible with intensive supervision and care, except for a small number of people who need conditions of high security. What is required, however, is not only a house providing accommodation that can be used flexibly as need arises but, ideally, sizeable grounds for recreation and facilities for day-time occupation away from the house. If a single site is not available this may involve laying on expensive transport.

These personal needs could be met in a variety of ways. The point was made in *Better Services for the Mentally Ill* (DHSS, 1975), that new experiments were needed, particularly concerning means of providing for people who needed sheltered housing, occupation and recreation, without involving the disadvantages of centralisation and bureaucracy that are associated with large complex organisations such as hospitals (or, in a different way, social services departments). Steiner communities seem to manage it, though they have the advantage of being able to select their clients. Geographical isolation is a disadvantage, but the feeling of real 'community' (as opposed to the emptiness of the term when applied to living conditions in many urban areas) is palpable (Richmond Fellowship, 1983). Havens are still needed; at least one in every district.

One of the problems of complex bureaucratic organisations is that it is difficult to disperse responsibility while retaining overall control of policy. Both elements are important and require evaluative research. On the one hand, a new NHS hostel for severely disturbed people will probably run most effectively if there is a designated 'head of house' who operates a specified budget and has authority to take on staff within the limits of the rules laid down. If a fuse needs mending it will not be necessary to wait for the hospital electrician. Meals need not be supplied from the hospital kitchen. There need be no long hierarchy of responsibility outside the house for coping with day-to-day problems. Staff and residents can decide most of these matters for themselves. On the other hand, there must be recognised operating policies so that the unit fits into an overall district plan. A management committee and an inspectorate, together with an open administration that encourages relatives and interested local people to participate in the affairs of the house, would minimise the risk of malpractice. The model of organisation would be somewhat similar to that of a school. Models of this kind need to be set up and evaluated.

The overall pattern of services which will cater for the needs of the most severely disabled as well as for the much larger majority can be visualised in terms of three ladders. (This extends an analogy first used by Early, 1968.) Perhaps staircases provide a more appropriate image because they have landings or resting-places for those who have been successful in advancing so far but, temporarily or permanently, find it difficult to make more progress. Table III illustrates the principle of the idea but it omits the psychosocial handrails or bannisters, which could represent the various forms of treatment, care and counsel that help people mount the steps and maintain their position.

Government policy is clear on three points. Large hospitals remote from the districts they serve are to close. Districts thus deprived are to build up new patterns of service that must meet the criteria of geographical responsibility, comprehensiveness and integration and be in place and working before the closure. Hospitals conveniently situated within a district

TABLE III
Stairways and resting places

Working hours	Night-time	Leisure hours
	Independent	
Can occupy self	Maintains home	Plenty of interests
Sheltered paid work	Supervised flat or lodging	Restaurant or club
IT day unit	Group home	Reserved hours in leisure activity
OT day unit	Staffed hostel/ hospital-hostel (haven)	Home OT or accompanied
High dependency day unit	Secure unit	Special recreational provisions
	Highly dependent	

can be adapted to serve that local population. In this third case, one hopes that it is the site that will mainly be used, including only those buildings with a non-institutional appearance. Such sites often carry a further advantage; the local population has become used to the idea that mentally disabled people are seen in the local cafes, libraries and other public amenities.

In order to ensure that the requirements of district responsibilities and comprehensive services are met, it is necessary to create and maintain a management organisation that is geared to attaining such objectives. This means co-ordinating several levels of service: primary care, specialist teams operating through care co-ordinators, health and social units of many kinds, an overall planning committee representing all levels, and a line of management that is geared to meeting 'grass roots' need.

All these ideas represent responses to the challenge posed by the mental hospitals, a challenge that was first presented by the pioneers of community care who worked in them.

The thesis of this paper is that the present ferment of change provides opportunities for weighing one kind of solution against another in order to determine which is more effective for meeting the particular problems of a particular community. If the alternative services are to be in place and shown to be working *before* large hospitals are closed, it is essential that multidisciplinary (including economic and administrative, as well as clinical and social) evaluation be undertaken at a local level and on a scale hitherto not considered. This is not only a matter for government departments (though there is an urgent need for initiative, guidance and sizeable central funding in order to start the process off), but for regional and district health and local government authorities which, hitherto, have not been very active in this field. Only in this way will it be possible, over a decade or two, to meet the challenge. The alternative is to muddle on as before with the result that services may actually become worse rather than better.

References

CREER, C. & WING, J. K. (1974) *Schizophrenia at Home*. National Schizophrenia Fellowship, 79 Victoria Road, Surbiton, Surrey, KT6 4JT.

DHSS (1975) *Better Services for the Mentally Ill*. London: HMSO.

EARLY, D. F. (1968) Domestic resettlement. In *Psychiatric Hospital Care* (ed. H. L. Freeman). London: Bailliere Tindall.

EDWARDS, C. & CARTER, J. (1979) Day services and the mentally-ill. In *Community Care for the Mentally Disabled* (eds J. K. Wing and R. Olsen). London: Oxford University Press.

GIBBONS, J., JENNINGS, C. & WING, J. K. (1984) *Psychiatric Care in Eight Register Areas*. Copies obtainable from Southampton Case Register, Knowle Hospital, Fareham, PO17 5NA.

HEWETT, S., RYAN, P. & WING, J. K. (1975) Living without the mental hospitals. *Journal of Social Policy*, 4, 391–404.

MANN, S. & CREE, W. (1976) 'New' long-stay psychiatric patients: A national sample of 15 mental hospitals in England and Wales, 1972/3. *Psychological Medicine*, **6**, 603–616.

—— & SPROULE, J. (1972) Reasons for a six-month stay. In *Evaluating a Community Psychiatric Service* (eds. J. K. Wing and A. M. Hailey). London: Oxford University Press.

OLSEN, R. (1979) *Alternative Patterns of Residential Care for Discharged Psychiatric Patients*. London: British Association of Social Workers.

PARLIAMENTARY SOCIAL SERVICES COMMITTEE, HOUSE OF COMMONS (1985) *Community Care with Special Reference to Adult Mentally Ill and Mentally Handicapped People: Second Report from the Social Services Committee* (Para 44), (HC 13 I,II,III). London: HMSO.

RICHMOND FELLOWSHIP (1983) Community care in action: The concept of community. In *Mental Health and the Community: Report of the Richmond Fellowship Enquiry*. London: Richmond Fellowship Press.

ROBERTSON, G. (1981) *The Provision of In-Patient Facilities for the Mentally Ill: A Paper to Assist NHS Planners*. London: Department of Health and Social Security.

RYAN, P. (1979) New forms of residential care for the mentally ill. In *Community Care for the Mentally Disabled* (eds. J. K. Wing and R. Olsen). London: Oxford University Press.

SALOKANGAS, R. K. R., DER, G. & WING, J. K. (1985) Community services in England and Finland. *Social Psychiatry*, **20**, 23–29.

TITMUSS, R. M. (1963) Community care — fact or friction? In *Trends in the Mental Health Services* (eds. H. Freeman and J. Farndale). (Reprinted from the proceedings of the 1961 Annual Conference of the National Association for Mental Health.) Oxford: Pergamon Press.

WATTS, F. & BENNETT, D. H. (1984) *Theory and Practice of Psychiatric Rehabilitation*. London: Wiley.

WING, J. K. (1962) Institutionalism in mental hospitals. *British Journal of Social and Clinical Psychology*, **1**, 38–51.

—— (1971) How many psychiatric beds? *Psychological Medicine*, **1**, 188–190.

—— (1972) Principles of evaluation. In *Evaluating a Community Psychiatric Service* (eds. J. K. Wing and A. M. Hailey). London: Oxford University Press.

—— (1978a) *Reasoning About Madness*. London: Oxford University Press.

—— (1978b) Medical and social science and medical and social care. In *Social Care Research* (eds. J. Barnes and N. Connolly). London: Bedford Square Press.

—— & BROWN, G. W. (1970) *Institutionalism and Schizophrenia*. London: Cambridge University Press.

—— & DER, G. (1984) *Report of the Camberwell Psychiatric Register, 1964–1984*. London: MRC Social Psychiatry Unit, Institute of Psychiatry.

—— & FREUDENBERG, R. K. (1961) The response of severely ill chronic schizophrenic patients to social stimulation. *American Journal of Psychiatry*, **118**, 311–322.

—— & FRYERS, T. (1976) *Psychiatric Services in Camberwell and Salford, 1964–1974*. Manchester: University Department of Community Medicine.

—— & HAILEY, A. M. (eds.) (1972) *Evaluating a Community Psychiatric Service*. London: Oxford University Press.

—— & MORRIS, B. (1981) *Handbook of Psychiatric Rehabilitation Practice*. London: Oxford University Press.

WYKES, T. (1982) A hostel-ward for 'new' long-stay patients: An evaluative study of a 'ward in a house'. In *Long-term Community Care* (ed. J. K. Wing). *Psychological Medicine* (Suppl. No. 2), 57–97.

—— STURT, E. & CREER, C. (1982) Practices of day and residential units in relation to the social behaviour of attenders. In *Long-term Community Care* (ed. J. K. Wing). *Psychological Medicine* (Suppl. No. 2), 15–27.

7 Planning a community psychiatric service: From theory to practice

JULIAN LEFF

The number of occupied beds in psychiatric hospitals in the UK has been declining steadily since the early 1950s. The data in Fig. 1 for psychiatric hospitals in the South-West, North-West and South-East Thames Health Regions show that for those with a peak bed occupancy of over 1500, the average decline between 1960 and 1980 was 1010 beds; it is also evident that this remarkable rate of reduction shows no sign of levelling off in recent years. The convergence of the individual graphs is also striking, but unexplained. Fig. 2 shows comparable data for Friern and Claybury Hospitals (North-East Thames Region); their rates of decline are very similar to those in Fig. 1. Between 1949, when records became available, and 1983 both hospitals showed a reduction of two-thirds in the number of occupied beds. It is regional policy that Claybury should close and Friern be reduced to 200 beds by 1993: in order to achieve this it will be necessary to extend the community-based services currently provided in the districts served by the two hospitals, and to develop new facilities to replace those at Friern and Claybury. This paper will consider the issues raised by the proposed transformation of the services, with particular reference to the plan to close most of Friern Hospital. I have chosen Friern because I am most familiar with this hospital and its user districts, but it is reasonably representative of the large psychiatric hospitals serving the Thames Regions (Figs. 1 and 2).

An ideal service

One of the strongest criticisms of psychiatric institutions, levelled by sociologists such as Goffman and Etzioni, is that they are designed and run more for the benefit of staff than of patients. In planning a new service, the needs of the clients should be paramount. The needs of the clients of a psychiatric service will be considered here under the broad headings of short-stay, long-stay, and dementing patients; the needs of specialised

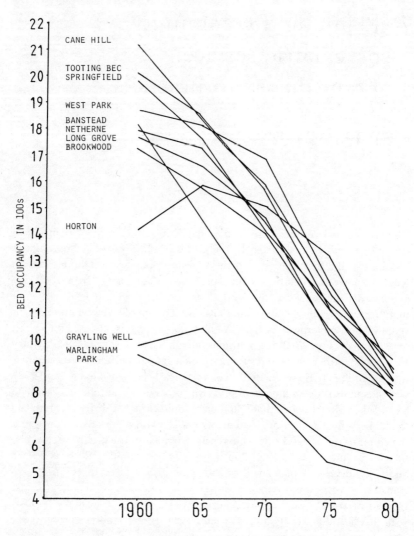

Fig. 1—Bed occupancy in psychiatric hospitals in South-West, North-West and South-East Thames.

groups, such as children, adolescents, substance abusers, or forensic patients will not be focused on, nor will mentally handicapped patients be included in this discussion.

The needs of short-stay patients

It has been claimed by the champions of crisis intervention that this form of service can obviate the need for admission, but there has been no scientific

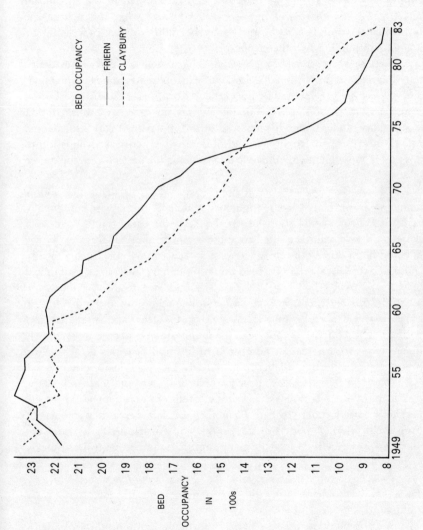

Fig. 2 — Bed occupancy in Friern and Claybury Hospitals.

study of the effectiveness of a crisis intervention team in preventing admission. The data that have been gathered suggest that crisis intervention teams have reduced readmission rates, but have had little impact on first admissions.

Nevertheless, the opinion is regularly voiced that, given an ideal community-based service, admission could be avoided in most if not all instances. It is, therefore, necessary to consider what the therapeutic functions of admission to hospital may be, and whether they could be adequately fulfilled by other facilities.

1. *Removal from a stressful environment:* There is now a body of evidence that a significant proportion of episodes of schizophrenia, mania, depression, and anxiety are precipitated by life events — abrupt and usually unexpected changes in a person's environment. It has also been established that emotional attitudes of family members towards the patient play a substantial role in attacks of schizophrenia and of depressive neurosis. Admission to hospital is consequently therapeutic in distancing the patient from the source of stress.

2. *Contact with skilled staff:* Patients who develop delusions and/or hallucinations usually become frightened, excited, or otherwise emotionally disturbed; professional staff possess the skills to reassure and calm such patients. These skills are often required at short intervals throughout the day and night during the early stages of an acute psychosis. Such a facility could not realistically be provided on a domiciliary basis for the numbers of patients involved.

3. *Shelter from the reactions of the public:* Public ignorance about psychiatric illness is still vast and results in misconceptions, fear, and stigmatising of patients. Until public acceptance of the manifestations of severe psychiatric illness is greatly increased, admission to hospital provides a therapeutic function in sheltering patients from the adverse reactions of others.

4. *Supervision of medication:* Psychotropic drugs are the mainstay of the treatment of acute episodes of psychotic conditions and depression. Many psychotic patients fail to recognise that they are ill and that they will benefit from medication. A period of stay in hospital ensures that the drugs are taken as prescribed, so that the symptoms come under control as quickly as possible.

5. *Protection against self-harm*; and   6. *Containment of aggressive behaviour:* These two problems are the commonest reasons for compulsory admission.

7. *Provision of graded activities:* This is particularly important for patients who are likely to remain ill for some months, in order to ensure that they do not lose their occupation and social skills. This function *can* be carried out in the context of a day hospital, one of the aims of which may be to provide an alternative to admission. However, it is inappropriate for severely disturbed and/or uncooperative patients.

8. Provision of a temporary home: Homeless patients pose a special problem in inner urban areas. For instance, Bloomsbury contains three major railway termini and homeless patients constitute a high proportion (20%) of admissions from this district. It is clearly only possible to treat such patients in an in-patient facility.

The functions listed above constitute a strong argument for the continued need for an in-patient facility, even assuming the existence of an ideal network of community services. The results of a survey (conducted by the author) of consultants' views on admission provide some corroboration for this; it included all consultant psychiatrists working in Friern or in the district general hospital units serving the same catchment area. Each consultant was asked to consider all the patients currently occupying his acute admission beds, and to estimate in each case whether admission could have been avoided if an ideal community-based service existed. The results were very similar for DGH units and for Friern itself. Of the total population of acutely admitted patients, numbering 242, only 16 (7%) could have been kept out of hospital under ideal conditions, according to the consultants surveyed. This may well be an underestimate, since the workings of an ideal, non-existent service are difficult to imagine. However, even if the true figure were two or three times the estimate, the new service would have to provide in-patient care for the great majority of patients currently admitted.

In-patient units should be planned to cater for the needs of short-stay patients. These are:

1. A compromise between privacy and easy observation: Acutely disturbed patients need seclusion from those who are on the way to recovery. Their rooms should be so designed as to give the patients a feeling of privacy, while allowing staff the opportunity to observe them at all times — an architectural challenge.

2. Some secure area within the facility: The survey of consultants, mentioned above, asked about the number of current in-patients who had required a secure provision at some time during their admission. Once again, the results for DGH units were very similar to those for Friern, the overall proportion being 40%. It is evident from these data that every in-patient facility needs a specially designed secure area. If this is not provided, then either potential absconders and suicides have to be individually nursed night and day — a very expensive item — or else the whole ward has to be kept locked frequently, penalising the majority of patients unnecessarily.

3. Space which gives the option of socialising or privacy: The indoor space should be so organised that patients can find privacy if they so wish it. Particularly when patients are in the throes of an acute psychosis, enforced contact with other patients, many of whom will themselves be disturbed, can be anti-therapeutic.

4. Occupational therapy and recreational facilities: Some of these should be provided on the ward, in addition to elsewhere, for the benefit of patients who are too disturbed to leave the ward.

5. Opportunity to practise domestic skills: This is important for those patients whose ability to look after themselves has atrophied, particularly those living alone.

6. Sheltered outdoor space: Many acutely psychotic patients are physically restless. This symptom can be difficult to cope with in a ward, but patients often find temporary relief if they can make use of an outdoor space; grounds are also useful for patients who need to be by themselves at times.

7. Beds: This has been deliberately placed at the bottom of the list, since psychiatric patients only need beds to sleep in. The hospital bed should not dominate the psychiatric admission ward, in the way in which it does the medical and surgical wards. For this reason, the modular design which has been adopted for medical and surgical wards is inappropriate for psychiatry. This raises the issue of where the psychiatric admission ward should be sited.

The advantages of including psychiatric admission facilities in a district general hospital are clear in terms of the reduction of stigma, the proximity to patients' homes, and the integration of psychiatric staff with their medical and surgical colleagues. But there are also disadvantages: the inflexible modular design, referred to above, and the virtual impossibility of siting the psychiatric ward on the ground floor, with a consequent increase in the risk of suicide by jumping, and the difficulty of access to outdoor space. The best compromise appears to be the construction of a separate psychiatric wing in the grounds of the district general hospital, with a design of no more than two storeys, and with outdoor space of the kind described above.

The needs of long-stay patients

The current population of long-stay patients comprises those who have been judged too disabled for the existing community services to cope with, and those who have been resettled in the community but have had to be readmitted. Innovatory services need to be developed for this group of patients, if the psychiatric hospitals which contain them are to close. In order to plan facilities for these patients, their problems and disabilities need to be ascertained in some detail. In the case of Friern Hospital, this information was obtained by a census of every patient resident in the hospital during a particular week in January 1983. Of the 839 patients included in the census, 593 had been in hospital for over one year. An arbitrary distinction was made between those in hospital for one to five years — the 'new long-stay' (n = 228), and those whose stay exceeded five years — the 'old long-stay' (n = 365). Of the new long-stay, 46% had been admitted from sheltered accommodation in the community; this is an alarming proportion, as it signifies that existing community services have proved inadequate for almost half of the new long-stay.

In terms of diagnosis, patients with dementia constituted 45% of the new long-stay, but only 7% of the old long-stay; this reflects their average life span in hospital, which is somewhat less than five years. Their needs will be considered in the next section. Schizophrenic patients comprised one-third of the new long-stay, but 74% of the old long-stay. This section will therefore focus on patients with schizophrenia: in planning services for this group, it is important to consider the possibility of 'burn-out'. This term refers to a progressive amelioration of florid symptoms over time, the 'burnt-out' patient being left only with negative symptoms, such as apathy, inertia, and restricted conversation. Using the census data, we can examine the validity of this concept of stratifying schizophrenic patients according to length of stay.

TABLE I

Florid symptoms in schizophrenic patients by length of stay

Length of stay	1–5 years	5–10 years	Over 10 years
Hallucinations	40%	39%	36%
Delusions	63%	50%	36%
Exacerbations*	63%	58%	48%

*A flare-up of florid symptoms occurring at least once in the previous year.

It is evident that delusions and exacerbations show a progressive decline with duration of stay, although this is not apparent for hallucinations. Nevertheless, over one-third of patients are still hallucinated, and the same proportion remain deluded after ten years. As a further indication of florid pathology in long-stay patients, almost one-half suffer exacerbations even after ten years in hospital. Thus, a high proportion of long-stay patients need regular professional care for florid schizophrenic symptoms.

This is reflected in the judgements made by the staff about care requirements: these decisions were made by psychiatric registrars, who discussed each patient with the nursing staff, and were checked by the consultants. Of the long-stay schizophrenic patients, continuous nursing care was judged to be necessary for 25% of those in hospital between one and five years, 42% of those with a five to ten-year stay, and 52% of those with a stay of over ten years. Only 16 (4%) out of this total group of 375 patients were considered capable of living in sheltered accommodation without resident staff. It is clear that if these long-stay schizophrenic patients are to live outside of a psychiatric hospital, the majority will need professional staff in continuous attendance. Such accommodation should be planned on the basis of the needs of long-stay patients, which are as follows:

1. *Single bedrooms in buildings of domestic style and scale:* The accommodation should look as much as possible like ordinary housing.

2. *Space giving the option of socialising or privacy:* (As for the short-stay).

3. *Sheltered garden:* Long-stay patients are subject to exacerbations of their illness, as we have found, and need outside space to move about in when restless. The space needs to be sheltered from the public gaze, while a garden can also provide horticultural facilities — work which is suited to relatively disabled psychiatric patients.

4. *Sheltered work facility within walking distance:* The work needs to be graded so as to provide for the wide range of disabilities found in long-stay patients. Problems arise if the work place is some distance from the patients' accommodation. A significant proportion of long-stay patients lack the motivation or skills to use public transport; it is possible to arrange hospital transport for these patients, but if they live in unsupervised lodgings, it is common for them not to get up in time for the arrival of the hospital bus.

5. *Sheltered recreational facility nearby:* Very few long-stay patients will attend public facilities, such as clubs or cinemas. If a sheltered facility is placed too far from their accommodation, the same problems arise as with sheltered workplaces. Ideally, normal volunteers from the community should be encouraged to join in with the patients' recreational activities.

6. *Patients involved in decisions about their home and their lives:* To avoid the accommodation becoming a mini-institution, patients should be involved in choosing menus, buying food, cooking, planning activities for the week, etc.

7. *Staff:* It is evident from the high degree of psychopathology in this group of patients, that staff should be skilled in dealing with the florid symptoms of delusions and hallucinations, as well as the negative symptoms such as apathy and inertia. However, this does not mean that they all need to be qualified psychiatric nurses, as other personnel, such as hostel wardens, can develop the necessary skills.

The siting of this accommodation requires careful thought. The provision of staff and ancillary facilities is made much easier if it is sited in the grounds of a hospital. The current development of 'hospital-hostels' is an example of this, but a more normal atmosphere, and hence less chance of institutionalism, would be produced if the building were not situated adjacent to a hospital.

The needs of dementing patients

The main issue for these patients is whether facilities and staff need to be based on a hospital-type service or not, once the initial assessment is completed. I would favour a non-hospital service, though my opinion has not been formed through direct experience of caring for this group. The

North-East Thames Regional Health Authority (NETRHA) policy statement for dementing patients is that 'residential provision will be in small, homely units of not more than 24 people'. This seems a sensible guideline, but the question remains of whether this provision should be part of a hospital, and we can also ask whether the staff need to be predominantly nurses. To answer this question, it is necessary to make a detailed enquiry into the work done by staff on a dementia ward: it is my impression that this almost entirely involves the physical care of patients, and that the demand for skills in psychological management is minimal. Thus, care assistants under the direction of a nurse would be capable of carrying out the bulk of the tasks required.

Community mental health centres

In addition to accommodation and occupation for patients, a comprehensive service requires bases in the community from which care givers can operate. The advantages of these are as follows:

1. *Accessibility to patients and relatives:* Such centres should be sited where the greatest geographical concentrations of patients are found. The proximity to patients' homes will then render them easily accessible.

2. *Reduced stigma:* Their situation within the community and away from hospital facilities will lessen stigma. This will be further reduced if they are housed in buildings with other community functions, e.g. citizens advice bureaux.

3. *Flexibility of use:* It is essential that patients be able to visit the centre whenever they like. Many long-stay patients, discharged into the community, find it difficult to adhere to fixed appointments, and few out-patient clinics can be run on flexible lines. There needs to be at least one member of staff in attendance during working hours to see to the needs of patients who drop in. Possibly a volunteer service could be run out-of-hours and at weekends. The centre would also be a useful site for relatives' groups, which have proven therapeutic efficacy in schizophrenia.

4. *Co-ordination of staff activities:* For in-patients, the ward round acts as a forum for co-ordinating the therapeutic activities of staff from a variety of disciplines. Not only do staff based in the hospital attend, but social workers operating in the community are often present. A forum of this kind is currently missing for patients living in the community. As a consequence, the activities of social workers, community psychiatric nurses, and voluntary workers are poorly co-ordinated, and communication between them is often non-existent, even when they are caring for the same client. The mental health centre should be the base from which the social workers, community psychiatric nurses, and voluntary workers for a particular area operate: this arrangement will facilitate co-ordination between them. Furthermore, the

centre should be visited regularly by psychiatrists, for two main functions. First, to ensure that their activities are integrated with those of the other care givers, and secondly to provide these others with emotional support. Staff groups are a well established method of alleviating staff 'burn-out', and psychiatrists possess the expertise to run them.

5. *Monitoring patients' needs and whether the service is meeting them:* This is essential in an innovatory service of the kind proposed, particularly as 'neglect in the community can easily remain invisible' (Kathleen Jones). Modern technology should be utilised, in the form of a central computer, located within the district, with terminals in each mental health centre. A register would include all 'at risk' patients in the community, and data would be fed in by the care givers after each visit to one of the patients on the register. In this way, an up-to-date record would be maintained of each patient's weekly activities and unmet needs should be readily identifiable. A regular review of the 'at risk' patients would be conducted at meetings in the centre, with feedback from the computer-held register. In this way, staff would appreciate the clinical value of the data they were asked to collect.

Disadvantages to staff of dispersal

There are some well-recognised disadvantages entailed in dispersing staff throughout the community. The principal ones are the problems with co-ordination, mentioned above, the likelihood of professional isolation, and the difficulties in providing training.

The location of staff from different disciplines in a common base overcomes some of the barriers impeding co-ordination, but additional remedies need to be considered. In presenting these, it is helpful to view the care worker in the community as being at the centre of three different axes:

1. *Hospital to community:* One extends from the hospital to the community. In many existing services, the social worker who is to look after the patient after discharge first gets to know him in hospital, thus ensuring continuity of care in this professional sphere. The same is not true for nurses. The nurse on the ward is quite separate from the community psychiatric nurse, who first meets the patient after discharge. Patients who have suffered a psychotic breakdown often feel strongly attached to the nurses who looked after them when they were ill, and return to the ward for social visits once they have left the hospital. A flexible system in which nurses spent part of their time on the ward and the rest in the community would improve continuity of nursing care, although it might raise administrative difficulties. The same principle should be easy to put into practice for voluntary workers.

2. *Across disciplines:* Another axis runs across disciplines, and has already been discussed.

3. Within disciplines: A third axis connects the community-based care giver with other individuals in the same discipline, including more senior and experienced people. It is essential that regular intradisciplinary meetings are held for professional advice and support. Otherwise, the care giver can readily become professionally isolated, with all the dangers and disadvantages that entails.

The remaining issue to be considered in this section is that of training. A hospital acts as a natural centre for training staff, but many of the skills needed in the community are best learned in the actual work setting. It will be necessary for trainers and for their trainees to commute around the community facilities, including visits to patients' homes. The mental health centres will be obvious places to hold training sessions. Even so, training will necessarily be more fragmented geographically than at present, and innovative administrative solutions will be required.

The reality

The above discussion has been about an ideal service. Unfortunately, the reality of current planning and practice falls dismally short of this. A number of major problems can be identified.

1. Expediency: The strong financial pressures exerted on planners have led to expedient solutions. For example, in some of the districts served by Friern, NHS buildings that are scheduled to be vacated are being proposed as the basis for the new psychiatric service. If this were to be accepted, it would mean the transfer of psychiatric patients from Victorian buildings of outmoded design to Victorian buildings that were not designed for psychiatric patients in the first place and whose structure is totally inappropriate for their care — surely a step backwards. It is of considerable interest to note that NHS buildings are falling vacant because of the policy of centralisation of medical and surgical services, while the opposite policy of dispersal of psychiatric services is being pursued.

2. Lack of a theoretical basis: Most planning in this area has been conducted on an *ad hoc* basis, without any underlying principles from which a comprehensive service could emerge. As a result, individual schemes tend to be proposed and supported in a haphazard way. There may well be major disagreements over many of the detailed points made in the proposals here for an ideal service, but the aim of planning a comprehensive service on the basis of patients' needs is incontrovertible. Where needs are not fully known or understood, empirical studies are needed before planning can proceed, as exemplified by the total census conducted at Friern.

3. A balance between buildings and people: The capital sum being offered by NETRHA for development of district psychiatric services naturally focuses the attention of planners on buildings. Accommodation for admission wards, for long-stay patients, and for demented patients certainly dictates that buildings be provided, but this is only half the picture. It is crucially important that a co-ordinated network of mental health professionals be established. There is a grave danger of unbalanced planning, with disproportionate effort and finances being invested in capital-intensive buildings, while revenue-intensive staff are neglected. It is much more difficult to demonstrate a co-ordinated network of people to outsiders as an achievement than a sparkling new building. This consideration has often led to the mis-spending of development money in Third World countries. It is to be hoped that we can avoid the same mistake.

4. *Severity of disablement:* The degree of disablement of long-stay, non-demented patients is invariably under-estimated by planners. Even psychiatric professionals involved in the planning process are rarely familiar with patients living on long-stay wards. Consequently, unrealistic plans for the care of the long-stay in the community have been formulated, particularly by those who adopt the ideological stance that psychiatric hospitals perform no useful function and should be abolished at all costs.

Conclusion

The attempts at detailed planning to date do not inspire confidence in the emergence of district-based services which will adequately replace those currently provided by psychiatric hospitals. The inadequacy of existing proposals has fuelled the doubts of staff working in psychiatric hospitals. They tend to view policy as being driven by economic considerations, at the expense of patients' interests. This lack of confidence in planners cannot be dismissed lightly, since the co-operation of existing staff is essential to the development of new district-based services.

We need to be sensible of the fact that we have arrived at a crossroads in the development of the psychiatric services. Our situation is comparable with that of the Victorians, who began building activities in the 1850s that continue to dictate the nature of psychiatric care in the 1980s. The planning decisions that are made and implemented now will set a pattern for the psychiatric services that will determine the quality of care for patients well into the 21st century.

8 Implementation of mental health policies in the North-West of England

DAVID GOLDBERG

A hypothetical DHSS official, too young to have read the papers that came out of Lancashire 20 years ago from Berlyne, Freeman, Leyberg and Silverman, and who based his views on mental health policies from diligent reading of the Department's own *Statistical and Research Reports* (DHSS, 1984a;b) might be forgiven for concluding that the North-West of England was fairly representative of the country as a whole. After all, rates for both first admissions and readmissions are both only just above the national average; the numbers for both consultant psychiatrists and nurses are also just above the national average, and the first admission rates for all major psychiatric diagnoses are broadly comparable to the rest of the country.

However, the beds we have are quite different in nature from the rest of the country: whereas only 38.7% of admissions go into district general hospital (DGH) units in the country as a whole, in the North-West a massive 82.5% of admissions are into such units. The region still has three very large mental hospitals which contain 'old long-stay' patients from many health districts, although they no longer accept such patients from outside their catchment areas. We now have the fewest number of occupied mental hospital beds of any region in England: 634/million at risk, against a national average of 1340. The only reason that we manage to come out looking average in the official tables is that official statistics for the North-West represent a rather meaningless blend of the old and the new.

Recent developments in mental health services

The purpose of the present paper is to provide a commentary on recent developments in mental health services illustrated by figures that have been divided in a way that allows planners to see the effects of different kinds of mental health service. We will examine official statistics divided into four types of service: one based solely on the mental hospital; a second with a

61

small DGH unit backed by the services of a large mental hospital; the third, the standard DGH unit without back-up, pioneered in the North-West; and finally, the service in which I happen to work, which is a teaching DGH unit without mental hospital back-up. Since there are a large number of districts with the third type of service, three have been chosen which seemed typical, and which were services used by over 90% of people who lived in the area served by the unit who used psychiatric services in 1983. The characteristics of the districts chosen for study are shown in Table I.

TABLE I

Characteristics of the districts chosen for the study

Health districts	Population at risk 1000's	% residents using local service	Number of beds	Annual admissions	Annual out-patient visits	Costs per in-patient day
(1) Lancaster Health District	245.4	98.4%	1056	1027	6392	£26.53
(2) Preston Health District	147.4	93.8%	1295	1278	8074	£36.28
(3) Salford Health District	350.1	90.6%	1572	1856	16,518	£32.92
(4) Blackpool Health District	335.1	94.9%	206	1419	10,158	£41.07
(5) Bolton Health District	246.5	91.5%	188	792	10,346	£50.94
(6) Oldham Health District	249.5	92.5%	170	1161	8873	£50.94
(7) South Manchester Health District	255.1	91.1%	243	2017	22,586	£58.43

Note: In the subsequent Tables, Districts 2 and 3 will be combined to form the category 'Mental hospital with DGH satellite', and Districts 4, 5 and 6 will be combined to form 'Standard DGH service'.

It can be seen that the DGH services (4 to 7) have a small fraction of the beds of the first three mental hospital-based services: yet they deliver almost as many admissions per year to their respective catchment areas. They can only do this by making more intensive use of their beds: so we will predict that they may be cheaper services, despite having higher unit costs, due to the fact that they participate in the 'general services' charge of the general hospitals of which they form part.

In the remainder of the paper, we will adjust all data to a standard population size, and group the seven chosen health districts according to the type of service provided. The basic service provision is shown in Table II.

TABLE II
Service provision in the four types of service

Type of service	Beds per 1000	Consult-ants per 100×10^3	All medical staff $/100 \times 10^3$	Nursing staff $/100 \times 10^3$	Other therapists $/100 \times 10^3$	Day Places $/100 \times 10^3$
Mental hospital only	4.3	2.44	6.19	286.8	17.9	22.8
Mental hospital + satellite DGH unit	5.8	5.09	13.62	324.9	25.7	59.1
Standard DGH unit	0.7	2.0	3.86	61.8	5.4	31.5
Teaching DGH unit	0.9	3.92	14.11	102.2	16.1	56.8

Note: In order to allow easy comparison, beds have been expressed per 1000 population served; and all other figures per 100,000 population served.

The most striking point that emerges from this comparison is the under-provision of professional staff to the standard DGH units, despite the intensive nature of the clinical work carried out. The larger institutions— either mental hospital or teaching hospital—each command more generous provision of professional staff. The under-provision of nurses has particularly severe consequences for the establishment of community psychiatric nurses (CPNs) in the DGH services. The standard DGH units can only spare on average $7.4/100 \times 10^3$ from their nursing establishment for work outside the wards of the hospital, while the mental hospital services are able to spare 12 to $13/100 \times 10^3$ from their much larger establishments. Yet much of the success of the DGH type of service must depend on health services making satisfactory long-term provision for those with chronic psychotic illnesses, and the CPNs are a vital component of such provision.

Finally, one must note that the combination of mental hospital and DGH satellite appears to attract very generous provision of all types: it will be necessary to look at other indicators to see whether such generous provision is justified.

In fact, the differences between the four services are dramatic, and it can be seen from Table III that DGH services are a very cheap buy for the money. The existing beds are intensively used, with a very short mean duration of stay. The admission rate for the standard DGH units is substantially below the combined rate for Preston and Salford, but it should be noted that both these services tend to attract cases in from outside their areas (41% and 46%, respectively, of patients admitted to the two services do not live in the catchment areas officially served by the hospitals), while the standard DGH units do not attract cases in from outside their areas (only 3%, 4% and 16% in the three services studied). This explains why it is

TABLE III
Clinical services provided by the four arrangements

Type of service	Mean duration of stay (days)	Admissions: per 100 beds	Admissions: per 250 thousand	Day visits per 250×10^3	Out-patient visits per 250×10^3	Cost per 250×10^3 served
Mental hospital only	264.8	97.3	1046	17,032	6511	£7.66m
Mental hospital + satellite DGH unit	256.8	237.1	1584	25,881	12,357	£14.81m
Standard DGH unit	72.9	649.7	1016	10,179	8853	£2.89m
Teaching DGH unit	36.3	830.0	1976	17,450	22,134	£4.88m

Note: The last four columns have been calculated for a 'standard' catchment area of 250,000, by making pro rata adjustment to the actual figures obtained for 1983. 'Deaths and discharges' have been used as a proxy measure for admissions, since the latter are not yet available for 1983.

that the 'hospitalisation index' for citizens from Blackpool and Oldham is only slightly below that for those of Preston and Salford, despite the fact that the admission rates for the respective services shown in Table III are very much lower.

The teaching DGH can be seen to provide a very active service for its catchment area, despite the fact that it costs very much less than the services based upon the mental hospital. This is especially commendable when one takes into account that, like Salford, 45% of the admissions are for patients attracted into the catchment area by the existence of a teaching hospital. The total numbers of medical staff are not very different in the teaching hospital and the mental hospital services with satellites, yet the teaching DGH carries out more intensive services both for in-patients and for out-patients.

The figures shown for annual costs are not really comparable, since they should be adjusted to take account of three important factors: (i) the standard DGH units do not have regional units; (ii) the mental hospitals are looking after many patients who originated from outside their present catchment areas, and such patients should be deducted from their costs; and (iii) each health district needs to be debited with the cost of any long-stay patients who are being looked after elsewhere.

The allowance for regional units is impossible to compute accurately with existing data, and in the absence of more reliable information, the assumption has been made that the cost of a patient-day is the same in each regional unit as in the remainder of the beds in that hospital. Ideally, the cost of the regional units should be distributed over the health districts in proportion to their use of such facilities: once more, the information is simply not

TABLE IV

Cost comparisons between the seven services (£m/year)

Health districts	Total expenditure on mental illness	Cost of regional beds	Cost of long-stay from elsewhere	Own long-stay in other hospitals	Balance	Expenditure per ¼ m population	% patients from outside area*
Lancaster	7.52	− 0.21	− 3.79	+ 0.03	3.55	£3.61m	43%
Preston	14.00	− 0.90	− 7.35	+ 0.12	5.87	£9.95m	41%
Salford	15.48	− 0.61	− 7.65	+ 0.80	8.02	£5.72m	46%
Blackpool	2.81	n/a	nil	+ 1.86	4.67	£3.48m	2%
Bolton	3.30	n/a	nil	+ 0.81	4.11	£4.17m	4%
Oldham	3.50	n/a	nil	+ 0.66	4.16	£4.17m	16%
South Manchester	4.98	− 0.80	nil	+ 0.59	4.77	£4.66m	45%

Note: The figures for the regional beds are difficult to calculate: we have assumed the same unit costs as the rest of the hospital, and adjusted for bed-occupancy.
*This figure refers to the percentage of admissions from outside the Unit's catchment area.

available, so the estimated costs of the units has been deducted from the district costs shown in Table IV. The allowances for new long-stay and old long-stay patients who are in hospitals outside their catchment area is easy to make, since our region publishes tables showing this information.

The cost adjustments shown in Table IV really need to be projected forwards to a time when there will be no patients at all in the mental hospitals from other districts, so that each district is, in effect, looking after its own patients. When this has occurred, the DGH services will be costing only slightly more than the figures shown in column 1, yet the two services with mental hospitals 'fronted-up' with DGH units will be costing only slightly less than the figures shown in column 5: that is to say, they will continue to cost substantially more than the standard services. Why should this be? The answer must partly be that mental hospitals are large institutions which attract substantial financial resources, but it is also probably true that psychiatrists with access to such facilities will allow more patients to accumulate in hospital than their colleagues working in DGH units.

If we look at patients who have been continuously in hospital for more than eight years by place of original residence, then Preston and Salford have a far higher rate than Lancaster, which is itself slightly higher than the standard DGH, while the teaching DGH has the lowest rate. It would be reassuring if one could report that the DGH model of service was associated with a greater provision of support services in the community, but this is far from being the case. The combination of a DGH and a mental hospital seems rather expensive—and would seem to be a way of guaranteeing that those most vulnerable to the effects of institutionalisation will be sure to be exposed to it. Yet if we were prepared to spend the difference in price between the two services on developing community facilities, we could have an enviable model service.

Threats to the DGH service

The DGH unit is a good model for psychiatric services. It is highly acceptable to patients and their relatives, and has been shown to possess undoubted advantages over the mental hospital, even in the treatment of chronic schizophrenia. Nor are its financial advantages confined to health authorities: it is cheaper for society as a whole, and it is better for the finances of the patient and his family (Goldberg & Jones, 1980; Jones *et al*, 1980). Since it is rather cheaper than the model it replaces, it might be wondered what could possibly threaten it.

The answer is paradoxical: further economic cuts. The DGH service is very easy indeed to prune, and since it must compete locally for funds with medical and surgical services, it is under constant pressure to reduce the relatively intangible benefits that it offers, especially where services in the community are concerned.

The squabbles over bed norms are because it is often appreciated that buildings mean resources: health administrators will unhesitatingly agree to heat them, feed their occupants and supply nursing salaries to support the therapeutic activities contained within them. There is a definite need for a DHSS policy document clearly setting out the desirable types of building and staff structure for community services. When job descriptions for new consultants in mental handicap and child psychiatry state that the appointee is 'expected to run a community-oriented service', all too often this means that the health authority does not intend to devote resources either in the shape of buildings or salaries of supporting staff, and that there will be no clear lines of responsibility indicating the extent to which the appointee will be supported in his work by colleagues from local authority social services, let alone by colleagues in community nursing and community psychology.

The need for flexibility in applying norms

The DHSS insists that there are no bed norms, but local planners think that there *are* such norms. Either they repeat 'half a bed per thousand' like mesmerised parrots, or they think that virtue resides in having as few beds as possible. This confusion is perpetuated by a failure of nerve of central planners, who have been unwilling to give directions on the kinds of social factors that should lead to upward or downward revision of the number of in-patient beds to be provided by district health authorities.

Two consultants now working in central Liverpool (Drs R. Philpott and

H. Egdell) had previously worked at Airedale General Hospital in Yorkshire, where they were able to give a very much better service on a bed norm of 0.3/1000 than they can give in a large city with far more beds: they estimate that they need 0.68/1000 'to survive'. The reasons are fairly obvious, but they clearly need stating: the social indicators of need should include poverty, level of family support available, proportion of single parent families, the level of drug and alcohol problems (obtainable using convictions for alcohol and drug related offences as a proxy measure), and the level of unemployment. Another factor mentioned was the lower calibre of centre-city general practitioners compared with their colleagues elsewhere.

It should be clearly stated by the DHSS that health authorities responsible for services in inner cities will need to make much more generous provision for hospital services than those in smaller towns. A constant shortage of beds means that patients are discharged as soon as the acute crisis is over, but before staff can really help patients with their basic problems, and also means that only the gravest cases are offered hospital care at all. The official statistics discussed so far cannot measure the need for hospital care that had to be refused because of shortage of resources. The very high number of admissions/100 beds associated with the DGH service (see Table III) may look like an efficient use of resources to a planner in a distant office, but to those engaged in offering the service it can become too little, offered to too few, in too much of a hurry. People with multiple social problems are likely to need longer in hospital than someone from a close supportive family with a similar psychotic illness.

The House of Commons Parliamentary Social Services Committee (1985) concluded that the DHSS should create a central bridging fund which would allow new services in the community to be created before hospital services are run down any further. There is indeed a strong case to be made for building up such services, and not merely in those areas where mental hospitals are to be closed. We have seen that the standard DGH services are poorly resourced and very cheap indeed to run.

If we are to continue with plans to dismantle the mental hospital, then there must be a credible alternative to this type of service. Indeed, even if we drift towards the millenium without closing a single mental hospital, it would still be highly desirable to give further thought to the component parts of a model community service.

Problems with community psychiatric nursing

The proper care of patients with chronic psychotic disabilities in the community requires a wide range of both residential and day care facilities if the mistakes of the previous century are not to be repeated. That we have done what we have without a sufficient supply of either is a tribute to our

TABLE V
Time trends in mean duration of stay in the teaching DGH units

	1972	1974	1976	1978	1980	1982
Annual admissions	898	1065	1227	1870	1990	2061
Mean duration of stay (days)	37	42.5	40.5	38.4	35.3	28.6
Rest of North-West RHA: mean duration (days)	312	328	264	266	210	187

Note: Our community psychiatric nursing service started in 1972 and was well established by 1978.

colleagues in community psychiatric nursing. It can be seen that before they arrived our mean duration of stay was increasing, and it reached its maximum in 1974 (the same year that mean duration of stay for the region as a whole, excluding our unit, reached its maximum: see Table V).

With the assistance of the community psychiatric nursing service, we have managed to reduce our mean duration of stay to a very low level, but recent service developments give cause for some anxiety. In the past five years community psychiatric nurses in Salford have been working in primary care settings, and we have been able to use the Salford Case Register to document the effect that their activities have on the established services (Wooff *et al*, 1985). It emerges that the effect of the move to primary care is a great increase in unsupervised work with patients with depression and other neuroses who have not been seen by secondary care services. We know from our informal contacts with community psychiatric nurses that there is greater career satisfaction in such work, and it undoubtedly eases the burden on the family doctor. However, as the community psychiatric nurses drift away from the hospital-based service, there is a risk that care of the chronic psychotic patients will take second place to work with people with minor affective disorders. The chronic mentally ill will then be left to become institutionalised in community settings.

The sort of policy statement asked for in this paper would insist that community psychiatric nurses were part of multidisciplinary community care teams with access to supervision of their work from both psychiatrists and clinical psychologists. It would acknowledge the unique contribution that community psychiatric nurses can make between primary and secondary care services, but would emphasise strongly the importance of community work with the chronic mentally ill.

The special case of the teaching units

It can be seen that the annual cost of the teaching DGH is substantially higher than that for the standard units (see Table III; £4.88m against

£2.89m/250,000 at risk/year). Much of this difference is eliminated by the adjustments shown in Table IV, but the remainder is due to the very much more generous provision of staff (see Table II). In addition to their responsibilities as teachers, it can be seen from Table III that the staff are able to admit almost twice as many patients, and to see almost three times as many out-patients, as their colleagues in under-staffed peripheral units. The Manchester schizophrenia study showed that although our service had higher unit costs than the other two services, that it was actually cheaper for society to spend more on health care (Jones *et al*, 1980). It is relatively easy to keep DGH units short of staff and short of material resources, but it can only result in a dismal and inefficient service, and one that will in the long run be more expensive, by causing very high social expenditures on social security payments and local authority welfare services, as well as more prolonged invalidism in those who should have been the recipients of proper care.

Acknowledgements

I would like to express my thanks to the officers of the North-West Regional Health Authority (NWRHA), who gave me every assistance in preparing data for this paper. The views expressed in this paper are my own, and in no way reflect the views of the NWRHA. I would particularly like to thank Ms Karin Lowson who gave me extensive details of health costs both within the Region and for England; and most of all, I would like to thank Miss Maura Noone of the NWRHA for spending many hours tabulating data for every psychiatric facility in the North West. I am especially grateful to Professor John Wing for pointing out an important error in an early draft of this paper circulated at the Conference.

References

DEPARTMENT OF HEALTH AND SOCIAL SECURITY (1984a) The facilities and services of mental illness and mental handicap hospitals in England, 1977–1979. *Statistical and Research Reports, No. 26.* London: HMSO.
—— (1984b) In-patients statistics from the Mental Health Enquiry for England, 1981. *Statistical and Research Reports, No. 27.* London: HMSO.
GOLDBERG, D. & JONES, R. (1980) The costs and benefits of psychiatric care. In *The Social Consequences of Psychiatric Illness* (ed. L. Robins). New York: Brunner/Mazel.
JONES, R., GOLDBERG, D. & HUGHES, B. (1980) A comparison of two different services treating schizophrenics: a cost-benefit approach. *Psychological Medicine*, **10**, 493–505.
PARLIAMENTARY SOCIAL SERVICES COMMITTEE, HOUSE OF COMMONS (1985) *Community Care with Special Reference to Adult Mentally Ill and Mentally Handicapped People: Second Report from the Social Services Committee* (HC 13 I, II, III). London: HMSO.
WOOFF, K., GOLDBERG, D. & FRYERS, T. (1985) Community psychiatric nursing in Salford: A case register study. Submitted to *Psychological Medicine*.

9 Mental illness services

Discussion

Mental hospital closure

There were many reasons why it was not necessary to fear the possibility of mental hospitals remaining open. For mental illness and mental handicap it could be seen that as hospitals were run down, services would not have the resources to cope with the needs of the most severely affected patients remaining. These people would therefore become more highly concentrated than at present. They were unattractive by virtue of their social isolation and their absence of roots in the community, and the advantages of moving them into another setting were not clear. The only reason for moving such people would be if the new services or settings were better.

The example of a Steiner community was given, in which, despite the institutional nature of the provision, there was a strong feeling of community. Furthermore, such a setting was protective; socially unattractive patients were more vulnerable than others, and their lot would be worse if they were left unprotected. In the end, though, it was necessary to try out different models of care in an experimental way in order to see how each worked best.

Variations in need

It was accepted that there were variations in need in different communities. However, health authorities still worked on the basis of national norms, despite the fact that it was well known that psychiatric morbidity varied with a variety of social indices. Surprisingly, even the Parliamentary Social Services Committee Report on Community Care had the word 'norm' scattered throughout the document.

A study at Springfield Hospital had shown a four-fold difference in admission rates between areas ranked high or low on social factors. It was suggested that flexible rules of guidance should be given by the DHSS to regions. Central guidance might be especially useful to the regions, it was suggested, if it provided for minimal local guidelines for a wide range of services. Most of the plans for community care were unsophisticated and did not even consider these aspects.

Alternative better services

It was quite right not to advocate advance before evaluation, but practitioners were impatient to build up alternative better services. This process took up a great deal of time, even for a relatively small-scale facility, such as a hospital hostel.

Although large institutions were clearly unsuitable, it had taken a long time to think of better ways of doing things. There were a range of alternatives to psychiatric care, but there were still great doubts about the best level and mix of service provision. We needed to ask ourselves, primarily, what local services were needed, how were they to be organised, and where they should be placed. Health districts might have some excellent features and some deficiencies, but they would inevitably be judged by the latter standards.

The enormous variability within the services was very relevant to consumers, and relatives, it was thought, would soon pick out the best facilities in their locality.

Planning decisions

The complaint was made that planning decisions tended to be taken without adequate information. For ideas that people in general would accept as good practice, it was simply a question of monitoring — since everyone 'knew what good practice was'. However, in other areas, for example with long-stay patients who were likely to accumulate further, there was a need for experiment and the evaluation of different models of care. It was thought that regions could conduct such experiments and evaluation within their districts.

Although it was acknowledged that evaluation and planning went hand-in-hand, and that account needed to be taken of demographic variability, a question remained about who was going to do the evaluation. In talking about health authorities, local authorities, and voluntary agencies, it was necessary to consider whether the relevant skills were present in every district.

The answer to this problem was thought to be complex, but evaluation might be considered as either 'every-day' or 'innovative'. The second sort of evaluation did not raise many issues. The former kind of evaluation was not being done.

DHSS supported research

It was suggested that if the DHSS were a large industrial concern, a large fraction of their turnover would be given over to marketing research. At present, consumers had to have whatever services were provided in their locality, so it was even more encumbent upon local and health authorities to look at what they provided. The proportion of the DHSS budget given to this activity was said to be small (£4 million from a total turnover of £2 billion). The problems were not tackled, even though the resources could be found.

It was suggested that only in the sphere of health and personal social services could such massive changes in social policy be considered without prior evaluation. Taking an analogy with the Ministry of Defence, it was difficult to image *them* acting in this way. A further analogy was taken with the large-scale changes in housing during the 1950s and '60s, when, following the removal of old housing stock, large housing estates were built all over Britain. The many problems associated with such housing were still present for all to see.

Implementation of the Parliamentary Social Services Committee Report

Questions were raised about how the Parliamentary Social Services Committee Report might be implemented: there had been no evaluation, and it was not clear where the necessary resources would come from. There were large numbers of patients 'walking about' who were entitled to care, but this appeared to be denied them for administrative and fiscal reasons. How was the 'mad rush' out of the 'havens' to be prevented before the new services were even organised or evaluated?

Transfer of long-stay patients

The possibility remained for regions to consider transfers of long-stay patients between hospitals. This was especially important for patients for whom 'hospital had become home', namely, the old long-stay patients. For patients losing their 'home', transfer might be a better thing than being moved a long distance to a smaller unit. The example was given of the closure of Banstead Hospital, where removal to Horton might be preferable for some patients than relocation in Victoria. Transferring patients was not always automatically wrong.

It was proposed that care givers could be 'too nice' regarding transferring patients. For example, when the long-stay patients at St. Francis/Maudsley Hospitals were asked if they might consider moving to a hostel ward, many said 'no', even though the care givers thought they were 'doing them a turn'. With persuasion, however, and within six months of transfer, the patients were saying of the hostel ward, 'we want to stay here'. To an extent, it might be argued that this response might be expected from institutionalised patients.

It might be thought that moving to another hospital was not an attractive proposition. It was certainly much easier to transfer patients elsewhere if care givers were convinced that alternative provision was better. This proposition held equally for mental illness and mental handicap patients.

The deinstitutionalisation of patients in the United States was said to be 'not planned, nor researched' and to be the product of radical reformers and fiscal conservatives. In this country, it had to be recognised that efforts to improve services must result in authorities exceeding present spending. It was not clear how acute mental health services, far less preventive services, would fare in the new developments.

The scope of psychiatry

The question had to be asked, which services were properly the responsibility of psychiatry? Should drug problems and sexual problems, which were increasingly being dealt with by psychiatrists, be part of this responsibility? How were funds to be allocated across these different clinical services? Priorities were determined largely by the public, but they were not well informed; they were unlikely to undergo a change of attitude merely because there was a change in the structure of buildings and the organisation of services.

Mental health in primary care

Most of the discussion concerned in-patient care. What about those not receiving in-patient care? They also required mental health services. If there was a shift in the referral habits of the primary care services, many more patients would come to mental health services. The conference was dealing with those who were most severely ill, but it had to be recognised that there was also an 'unseen' body of such patients contained in the community — specifically, those who were in low-grade accommodation, and those who found themselves within the prison network.

It was suggested that a doubling of the rate of referral from primary care doctors to psychiatric specialists would do little to affect general practitioners' work patterns, but would make a huge difference to the work patterns of psychiatrists.

Of general practice patients, 1.5% were chronic psychotics. However, very few general practices had practice registers and knew about these patients. If these patients were identified they would be in direct competition for scarce resources with those patients in contact with the services. It was considered that if practices with these patients were audited, they would be found to be neglected.

It was agreed that a limited register of patients at risk would be useful. In a recent study, chronic schizophrenic patients had been followed up by researchers at Northwick Park Hospital. For many of them, community care was lacking; 25% of these patients had entirely fallen through the caring network. However, some of them were doing well, some were seeing up to five different types of carers (social worker, CPN, GP, etc). These patients were not worse than the rest, but often they had young children or were able to demand services or had relatives who were able to demand services. It appeared that services were allocated by request and not on the grounds of need. A register of chronic psychotic patients could also help cope with the problem of follow-up.

Drug addiction

Two recent reports about drug addiction (concerning treatment and rehabilitation, and prevention) were mentioned. These dealt with guidelines for good practice, with emphasis on the issues of training, community services, and the likely effect on health services. The implementation of these reports had a number of resource implications.

The implications of the reports affected several areas within psychiatry and medicine, and those involved with drug addiction were likely to apply pressure for help rather than rejection.

Central pooling of evaluative information

There were a number of evaluations of pilot mental health projects taking place around the country, but this information did not seem to be pooled. There was a need for some kind of central computerised information system to store information from the many different groups who had tried different approaches and used different resources, and about which the wider caring community knew very little. Much of this evaluation was not strictly 'scientific', but it was nevertheless important knowledge.

It was suggested that the Social and Community Section of the Royal College of Psychiatrists was well placed to organise and keep a register of information about innovative research and evaluation.

Economic applications of computer technology

There was a tendency to underestimate the application of technology — for example, the use of computer simulation to help in decisions about what might be the implications if a regional or district mental health budget were to be cut. It was not beyond software manufacturers, given time and money, to produce a software package which would be generally useful in this regard.

Nursing skills for dementing patients

In relation to what had been said concerning nursing skills for dementing patients, continuing care beds were needed for 1–2% of dementing patients in each locality. It was a false observation to think that these patients did not require skilled nursing or that they did not act as a focus for training. The North-West Region had made a large impact by building local units or using small hospital sites in the care of this group of patients. These units consisted of the equivalent of two wards of 28 beds, with day hospital facilities for 50 patients, and could be housed on a district general hospital site. The essential point was that the elderly mentally ill did not have to be cared for in mental hospitals.

Interprofessional collaboration

The experience of the Worcester Development Project showed that even under ideal conditions, close interprofessional collaboration was necessary in developing mental health services. Such collaboration seemed to be the way forward. A survey of general practitioners in the area was under way and was designed to highlight faults in the existing system.

Alternative sources of funds

It was thought to be striking that at Friern Hospital less money was being provided to run the new services than was required for the old. It was also thought to be worth noting that for some patients there were other possible sources of funds. A housing association in Camberwell for patients receiving day care received sufficient funds from social security sources and from the Department of the Environment to support one manageress who was overseeing 23 patients. This was without help from the local authority and social services department.

Values systems underlying service provision

The unit for demented old people described by one of the speakers illustrated how the type of care provided was related to underlying systems of philosophy and values. Did we wish to accept certain levels of non-fulfilment of human potential or not? Certain units for 'end of the road' demented patients differed from the one mentioned. In fact, it was possible to achieve high levels of responsiveness and feedback from patients to staff. If the decision was taken that the current level of resource input was to be maintained — this might be judged to be satisfactory, but a value judgement was involved. If it was decided to set sights higher, then it was necessary to determine what level of provision would be settled upon.

It was necessary to challenge the notion that innovative treatment procedures could go ahead without more resources being provided. Annual NHS resource increases at 1% above the level of inflation would not even permit services to 'stand still'.

The quality of life provided for demented patients required society to make value judgements; there were still questions regarding the need to train psychiatric nurses to do this work, and indeed about the particular kind of training required for this work. Funding, ultimately, was a political question. It was notable that the biggest current expansion of institutional care, particularly in relation to the elderly, was in the private sector: this was a publicly funded perpetuation of old systems of care.

Advantages of district general hospitals

The apparent advantages of district general hospital units were questioned. It was suggested that Professor Goldberg had not taken into account the cost of community support in his health costs study. If community support was provided, this required staff and was more expensive. Had Professor Goldberg only presented half of the picture? Although the DHSS figures were difficult to use on account of the fact that they were conflated, Professor Goldberg maintained that his remarks stood for every single economic indicator that he had measured (the details were to be published elsewhere).

To some participants, Professor Goldberg's contribution suggested that the balance of financing might be shifted from mental hospitals to other types of service: this appeared 'to get us off square one'. The service he described resembled the district general hospital service in Kidderminster in terms of the number of admissions, the number of nurses required, and the average number of days per in-patient stay. Such a service was able to provide humane care and did not result in the accumulation of new long-stay patients at a rate that could not be dealt with.

However, this service was part of the Worcester Development Project and it was therefore difficult to generalise the experience to other areas. The DHSS has been very generous, largely with capital expenditure. Another advantage was that this was a green field site, and that it had not been found necessary to disperse old long-stay patients. However, there had been some difficulty in dealing with serious organic mental states in younger patients, and with dangerous and disruptive patients.

Professor Goldberg was said not to be comparing like with like—what caring was done between hospital stays, and who was doing it? The response was that the work was largely being done by general practitioners. It was accepted that doctors participated in this form of care, they always had, and they always would. In a similar study involving patients with schizophrenia, it was found that much of the care was indeed provided by the general practitioner. Furthermore, the social adjustment of patients appeared to be better from the district general hospital, probably because they spent less time in hospital.

Economic assessment of district general hospital services

There was surprise at the Goldberg analyses. District general hospital units appeared to be cheap. The main reasons for this were: firstly, that the mental hospital was a big organisation providing a lot of services, with a lot of ancillary staff (more than in a district general hospital), and there were also heavy maintenance and building costs. The unit cost per patient was low and the number of patients was large. Secondly, the mental hospitals appeared to be allowing a large number of long-stay patients to accumulate; the district general hospital might be said to be under-resourced, rather than cheap.

Alternatives to mental hospital

The alternatives to the mental hospitals were considered to be rather wider than had so far been discussed: for example, the community mental health centre approach (including refuge beds) had not been discussed. For certain communities, particularly rural ones, there were special problems in organising a district-based service. This was exemplified by the difficulty of organising psychiatric services for a county town and the surrounding villages.

Concentrating, in particular, on the elderly and day care facilities, clearly there was a need for a central facility. But for some geographically isolated patients it might not be possible to provide day care services every day. Geographical and financial factors affected the question of alternative service provision. The models proposed so far mainly applied to industrial Britain. It might be better, for certain purposes, to consider the provision of services from the perspective of 'the patient's living room'.

Costs of implementation of services

Considering the implementation of policies, it was necessary to separate the components of the costs of services. These could be broken down into three:

(i) the long-stay population; (ii) regional specialist services; and (iii) district services. It was crucial that a mechanism was found to sort out these components of the services in order for it to be possible to budget appropriately. Professor Goldberg's analysis had been unable, unfortunately, to provide a break-down by type of service, because the relevant figures were not provided for him.

Professor Goldberg's economic analysis might put a sum on such costs as a relative's loss of job through the necessity to look after a patient. But, could it also take account of the cost of a relative becoming depressed through undertaking such care? The response was that a modified cost-benefit analysis would estimate the costs of depressive illness in terms of the loss in family earnings and the 'soft' cost of a caring relative becoming depressed.

The needs of families caring for
mentally ill or handicapped relatives

It was important to address the question of what exactly were the needs of families caring for mentally ill or handicapped relatives. A mechanism was needed for saying to the family: 'resources are scarce—what do you feel is the greatest need in your circumstances'. Professionals made value judgements that they are not truly in a position to make.

Defrosting 'frozen' assets

It was argued that the resources tied up in mental hospitals could be 'unfrozen'. These resources could then be used for much needed community services. Society was spending quite large sums of money on mental health services (the estimates given were: £7 million in the North-West Region and £23 million in the South-West Thames Region. The district general hospital model of care appeared 'astoundingly' cheap, and if money could be spent in this way, the new services could be expected to be good.

10 Some current issues in old age psychiatry services

TOM ARIE

This paper raises issues which are currently seen as important by psychiatrists whose prime responsibility is for the care of the elderly. It derives chiefly from suggestions made by members of the Section for the Psychiatry of Old Age of the Royal College of Psychiatrists. Since the origins of psychogeriatric services, the central aim has been to help sick and disabled old people to remain for as long as is reasonable as private citizens in their own homes, and to underpin their support systems. 'Care in the community' is not new for those who work with the elderly.

The invisibility of work 'in the community'

Good services see patients at home first, and much follow-up and support is at home. However, such activity is largely unrecorded; official statistics analogous to those on out-patients and in-patients are not collected. Domiciliary visits by doctors are rarely included as part of official local statistics, while informal home visits by them are not recorded at all. Activity in patients' homes by other hospital staff is equally likely to be 'invisible'. Since referrals (as contrasted with admissions or out-patient attendances) are not officially recorded, the fact that most result in home-based forms of help does not become evident — let alone the volume of home care which is carried out independently by the primary health care team.

In our Nottingham psychogeriatric service, the single psychiatric community nurse made over 1000 home visits during 1984 — these appear nowhere in official statistics. The non-medical staff of the psychogeriatric day hospital, in addition to caring for the patients there, made nearly 600 home visits. The remedial therapists in the admission unit make one or two home visits a week, and in fact many staff move easily between the hospital, patients' homes, day centres, residential homes, doctors' surgeries, and health centres, seeing the hospital as part of its community. Such activity is 'care in the community', but is rarely identified as such; moving the mountain to Mahomet is a long-established part of our repertoire.

Without good data on the psychiatry of old age it is impossible adequately to monitor what is happening, or to see the range of variation against which local services should be measured. There has been progress, however, and this has long been the subject of discussion between the College and the DHSS. Since psychogeriatricians have no monopoly of the care of the elderly mentally ill, it is clearly difficult to identify their specific facilities and activities. But this difficulty should not be insuperable: it is compounded by lack of a rubric of 'old age psychiatry' under which such data could be collected. Yet data on the extramural activity of hospital-based staff are more telling than traditional data on out-patients, etc, in the case of psycho-geriatrics. The collaborative work of psychogeriatricians and geriatricians also goes almost wholly unrecorded, and it is not clear that these issues are adequately identified in the Körner (1982) proposals.

Data also need to be collected in relation to sub-sets of age-groups within the elderly; such data are still too often presented with a denominator of 'over-65s'. The main users of these services, however, are the 'old old', and it makes no sense to relate provision to the wrong denominator. Population projections for over-65s run in a contrary direction to those for over-75s, over-80s and over-85s, so that services must be planned and monitored in relation to the age-groups that actually use them. Similar masking of the 'old old' occurs in regard to other sources of support, notably, income: for instance, the general claim that pensioners' incomes are expected to hold up in purchasing power hides the fact that those of the very aged do not (DHSS, 1984a).

Overlaps

The overlap in the disabilities of very aged people in different care settings (notably in residential care and long-stay hospital wards, but also at home) is well documented. This is inevitable in view of the multiple degenerative disabilities of very old age, and the likelihood (even where there is careful pre-assessment) that very aged people will deteriorate further, and that the balance of their disabilities will change, after admission. (The average age of admission to local authority residential care is now nearly 82.)

Current initiatives (DHSS, 1984b) to improve pre-assessment, and to make that a collaborative function, should be supported. But even more important is that whatever compartment of the care system old people find themselves in, they should continue to have access to the whole range of facilities which, on continuing assessment, their changing needs may require — regardless of whether these facilities are primarily based in the same compartment as the old person (Arie & Jolley, 1982).

Resources

Resources for non-hospital care are actually constricting in many respects, especially when measured against the fast increasing numbers of the very aged. Local authority residential care facilities have been contracting in relation to the number of very aged (Grundy & Arie, 1982). Meals-on-wheels are not keeping pace with the increase in the numbers of their main users (the very aged); and home helps only just (DHSS, 1983a). Extreme variation is notorious: a five-fold range of variation in provision of home helps cannot be right (DHSS, 1980). The only home care facilities which appear to have increased substantially are local authority day centres, and these obviously are not often helpful to the more damaged elderly patients. Since the abandonment of central norms, reductions in local targets have become the rule. Money for improvements is not only scarce, but is at times held back by government restraints, even when it could be found—for instance, for adaptations to the homes of disabled people and for improvements to provision of residential care (Timmins, 1984).

Limits to community care

The concept of community care is beset with wishful thinking, however much, or perhaps because, we all subscribe to it. Hawks' classic review (1975) is rarely read now, but deserves to be. Nor is care outside the hospital necessarily care 'in the community': enormous time and effort (detracting from what is available for other things) is devoted to translocations of patients between hospitals and other institutional settings. When provision is short, everyone tries to shift clients to other people's compartments of the care system. This may result in a neater alignment between facilities and dependency, but it is not a triumph of 'care in the community' to shift an old person from one institutional setting to another, or to inadequately supported existence at home. Many facilities for better quality of life and stimulation are still rarer in residential and nursing homes than in hospital wards—notably, remedial and diversional therapies.

Co-ordination, appropriateness and equity

Despite often close and effective links, particularly between individuals, there is still too often only a fragmented response to the care of the aged, and particularly of the demented. Time and again, inappropriate facilities are provided simply because those are the only ones available in the compartment of care in which the patient happens (often by chance) currently to be located. This achieves the worst of both worlds — people get the wrong resources, and resources are wasted, while many patients fall between stools.

Britain still has one of the lowest institutionalisation rates of the elderly in developed countries, though with the accelerating growth of private homes since the last census in 1981, this may be changing. But ambulant demented patients at home are under-provided with services, and they (and their supporters) often do not receive the types of help that they need. One survey showed that the non-ambulant mentally impaired were 12 times as likely as those who were ambulant to receive help from the district nurse, and more than one-and-a-half times as likely from the home help (Bond & Carstairs, 1982). Provision for short-stay relief admissions is insufficiently available because the scarce places are needed for long-stay, and yet recent studies have shown how important such relief is in helping supporters to go on coping (Levin *et al*, 1983; DHSS, 1983b; Allen, 1983). Too often, short-stay care is provided only *faute de mieux*, in place of unavailable but necessary long-term care. But where local authority residential care develops special provision for short-stay clients, this has recently been shown to be largely catering for a different group of people from those who need a long stay, and so may not greatly diminish the long-stay care need. This illustrates (as does day hospital care for ambulant demented people) that what is a welcome extension of services is often only a marginal, if any, saver of long-term provision, especially if the demented person lives alone (Greene & Timbury, 1979).

The demented who live alone

The special vulnerability of persons with moderate dementia who live alone is well recognised (Isaacs *et al*, 1972; Bergmann *et al*, 1978; Arie, 1984a). Merely episodic care is usually insufficient: they need around-the-clock surveillance. The needs of solo-living demented people may be under-represented in conclusions from community studies simply because they lack those supporters who alone can give dependable interviews. Yet old people now live alone more often than ever before, including half of all women aged over 75.

Despite the current emphasis on 'community care', most psychogeriatric services (and even newly planned ones) are still forced to operate chiefly from mental hospitals, and their patients are still most often admitted there. Despite welcome Government support for access to assessment facilities in DGHs, time and again, even proposed new service arrangements are without a DGH component.

Quality of life in long-stay institutions

In spite of great improvements, life in long-stay institutions is still generally bleak; the problem of stimulus, choice, and preservation of function remains, even if Henry Miller's phrase 'a depressing mélange of deadening routine and implacably jolly attendants' hardly does justice to the attempts of staff in difficult circumstances to enrich the environment. Stimulation and choice are almost everywhere unacceptably poor; in most places, most of the time, elderly patients have no choice but to sit around doing nothing. Systematic diversional and occupational therapy, and attempts at personalisation, dignity, and choice are difficult, especially with the demented, and call for taxing personal effort on the part of staff. The implications of the changed nature of the clientele of residential homes are often pointed out, but too little recognised (Laming, 1984). Staff ratios are almost always too low and staff training still inadequate in residential care, as the Central Council for Education and Training in Social Work has long recognised. The bringing in of volunteers, and genuine engagement by local communities, has a long way to go.

Happily there are British architects and designers who are now taking interest in these facilities (Norman, 1984), but there is still little to compare with the best that is to be found in Europe, North America, or Australia. Architecture and design for the elderly, along with the exploitation of electronic technology as 'aids to living' (in Professor Heinz Wolff's phrase), need investment of brains and cash. In fact, moving from hospital to residential care is often likely to result in a poorer quality of life. It is easy to see why many old people and their families resist such transfers — leaving aside the financial disincentives. 'Local hospitals' will not necessarily be close to the locality from which residents originate; they will be chiefly where convenient buildings or sites are available, and not necessarily on convenient transport routes. Private homes aggregate in parts of cities where suitable large houses are available, and these are often most remote from where the majority of residents used to live. Whatever the advantages of the dispersal of people from large long-stay hospitals (and that there are advantages in breaking up huge institutions is obvious), this certainly does not dependably result either in bringing them nearer to their community or placing them in smaller living units. Many long-stay hospital wards are already small homely units, containing no more people than a typical home, and often run at least as intimately and 'domestically'. Many residents are without relatives or friends: where is the evidence that the community around 'local units' will take more interest in them than those associated with the hospital?

The private sector

The sudden expansion of the private sector of care for the elderly is the most significant recent development in Britain, although up-to-date data are generally hard to find (Challis *et al*, 1984; Johnson, 1984; Arie, 1984b). It seems often not to be recognised that the issues here differ fundamentally from those of private health care for episodes of illness (such as may be catered for by insurance-based schemes). What is at issue here is not treatment for an illness, but making over one's person and one's life for good.

In 1978, expenditure from public funds through supplementary benefit allowances for board and lodging in private and voluntary homes was £6 million. By 1983 it was £102 million, and by 1984 had risen to £190 million (DHSS, 1984c); recipients of these allowances increased six-fold between 1978 and 1984. Numbers of people aged 65 + in residential care have increased as shown in Table I.

TABLE I
Number of people aged 65 + in residential care

	Local authority	Voluntary homes	Private homes	All homes
		(Figures rounded to nearest 1000)		
1975	95,000	22,000	19,000	136,000
1980	103,000	25,000	29,000	157,000
1982	104,000	26,000	36,000	166,000
1984	106,000	26,000*	50,000*	182,000*

Source: Hansard, 11 November 1983
*Estimated (*Source: The Times*, 17 January 1985)

An illustration may be taken from Nottingham: between 1981 and 1985, local authority residential places for the elderly stood still — indeed, fell slightly — the entire expansion (nearly 300 more places) having been in the private sector. In addition, nursing home beds expanded by 70–80 a year over the previous four years, so that there are now 523 in the district — already almost as many as the entire complement of geriatric beds. If further applications are approved, this figure will rise by a further 300 beds. This entire development has, of course, been heavily financed (in terms of revenue) by public funds, yet it has formed no part of the planning process — it beats along in an idioventricular rhythm. This is a fundamental change in the care of the elderly in Britain.

Monitoring the 'moral climate'

No sensible person argues that the non-statutory sector will inherently provide care of poorer quality than the statutory sector. Some of the best and most imaginatively conceived institutions are non-statutory (though much more often in the voluntary than the commercial sector), but some of the worst care is also to be found there, and there is much to be painfully learnt in Britain from experience in other countries. There are special problems of quality control when commercial opportunity is the main motive, and widespread unease exists about the practicability of implementing the admirable guidelines which have been set out, for instance, in the report 'Home Life' (DHSS, 1984d). Where are the resources for the necessary intimate and prolonged scrutiny of these facilities to come from?

In inspection, neither local authorities nor health authorities are disinterested parties — if things go wrong in a private home, they have to accommodate the residents if need be, and both sectors now depend on each other. Homes can change hands rapidly. It is possible to monitor fairly adequately the space, cleanliness, fire safety, and sanitary provision, but financial exploitation is more difficult to monitor, and the 'moral climate' — whether people are happy — even more difficult: mere spot-checks are rarely adequate. Furthermore, consumer reaction cannot here be depended upon because the consumers are not primarily the frail old people themselves, but those who find it necessary or convenient to put them there. Placement, even in unsatisfactory settings, may bring relief to supporters, or even to workers in the statutory services who have been battling with an impossible domestic situation or are eager to move a patient out of a hospital bed; they are unlikely to be meticulously critical of the setting in which, to their relief, the old person has at last been accommodated. A third-party independent inspectorate, perhaps the Health Advisory Service, perhaps a new body, is surely needed.

Need to integrate the private care sector in planning and operation

No less important than monitoring standards is the need to plan and integrate private care with the other parts of the care system. There is now a bizarrie reminiscent of 'the Emperor's clothes', when local planning concerns itself meticulously with the health and local authority services, and yet largely ignores the huge private sector. One looks in vain in many planning documents and strategic plans for any attempt to measure, project into the future, or make assumptions about the contribution of the private sector: yet it is already often the largest part of the institutional facilities in any district.

Of course, planning and projections are not easy; the private sector is individualistic and opportunistic, but with its heavy dependence on public funds, it should not be impossible to find ways of integrating the private sector into the local planning process. Differential financial incentives and sanctions (such as have already been widely accepted in regulating private enterprise in relation to public needs) should be among the mechanisms that could be explored. The private sector depends heavily on the NHS sector as a longstop, and there must be trade-offs to be made here.

Many reports have occurred of selectivity on the part of private establishments, and of commitments demanded from hospitals or local authorities that they will take people over if the private home should declare itself unequipped to continue further. Many private homes pride themselves on seeing people through — and most voluntary ones do; indeed, many of the latter have in recent years greatly extended the range of facilities to enable them to do this. But too often this is not so in the private sector. Local agreements identifying the nature of responsibility which the homes are prepared to assume, and monitoring of the way in which they assume them, need to be sought — along with better mutual support. The private sector, surely, could also participate in joint pre-assessment procedures such as are currently being debated (DHSS, 1984b). There is a widespread impression that people are being admitted to private homes who could, with proper support, continue in their own homes, whilst others in great need of care are found 'unsuitable'.

Training for psychogeriatricians

We need to train doctors to fill the posts of consultant psychiatrist with special responsibility for the elderly, which are now a standard feature of district services. Yet geriatric psychiatry is not separately identified from general psychiatry in manpower planning, though the Central Manpower Committee has lately become aware that just as manpower issues in geriatrics differ from those in general medicine, so do those in psychogeriatrics from general psychiatry. Medical geriatrics could not have developed the training structure that it now has if it had been forced to expand solely with a 'frozen' pool of general medical posts. Here, psychogeriatrics is at an obvious disadvantage, compared not only with geriatrics, but with other officially recognised branches of psychiatry, such as mental handicap or forensic psychiatry.

The main problem is at senior registrar level. It has lately been shown (Wattis & Arie, 1984) that only 14 posts offer training on a regular basis in the terms required by the Joint Committee for Higher Psychiatric Training, and that these need at least to be doubled to meet the demand for new consultant posts; there is a clear unmet demand at present by trainees. The Joint Committee has pressed for redistribution of training slots, and for making training available in old age psychiatry in all large rotations, for doctors who seek it. The evidence is that these injunctions are not yet making much impact.

The continuing help of the DHSS with special arrangements to institute and maintain seven extra posts has been invaluable. But with so few higher training posts, how are we to reach the target of one or two psychogeriatricians in each district? In 1983, 34 consultant posts were advertised, but 50 per cent could not be filled, for want of adequately trained candidates. Worse, it would appear that some inadequately prepared candidates are being appointed, through zeal to make such appointments (Jolley, 1984).

A unified local service for the aged

Psychogeriatrics and geriatrics have been shown to be capable of being married together (Arie, 1983), along with orthopaedics (Boyd *et al*, 1983) and the other related professions, as one unified local department for the elderly. Why are we not planning such unified local departments which bring together all the main local services? There could, at the very least, much more often be a district unit of management, covering services primarily for the aged.

Needs, characteristics, and attitudes of old people are changing, and will no doubt go on doing so. Cross-sectional studies can yield misleading data, so that for services, as much as for basic research, we in this country need comparative cohort studies. Existing single surveys could be followed up as cohort studies. The Douglas (1948) or the 1958 Perinatal Cohorts (Butler & Bonham, 1963) would, if enabled to continue into the old age of their subjects, be unique investments in the study of ageing.

References

ALLEN, I. (1983) *Short-Stay Residential Care for the Elderly*. London: Policy Studies Institute.
ARIE, T. & JOLLEY, D. (1982) Making services work: Organisation and style of psychogeriatric services. In *The Psychiatry of Late Life* (eds. R. Levy and F. Post) Oxford: Blackwell.
——— (1983) Organisation of services for the elderly: Implications for education and for patient care — experience in Nottingham. In *Geropsychiatric Diagnosis and Treatment* (ed. M. Bergener). New York: Springer.
——— (1984a) Dementia: Implications for services. In *Senile Dementia: Outlook for the Future* (eds. J. Wertheimer and M. Marois). New York: Alan R. Liss.
——— (1984b) Current themes in the care of the elderly. *Hospital and Health Services Review*, September, 233–236.
BERGMANN, K., FOSTER, E. M., JUSTICE, A. W. & MATHEWS, V. (1978) Management of the elderly demented patient in the community. *British Journal of Psychiatry*, **132**, 441–449.

BOND, J. & CARSTAIRS, V. (1982) *Services for the Elderly. Scottish Health Services Studies No. 42.* Edinburgh: Scottish Home and Health Department.

BOYD, R. V. *et al* (1983) The Nottingham Orthogeriatric Unit after 1000 admissions. *Injury*, **15**, 193–196.

BUTLER, N. R. & BONHAM, D. G. (1963) *Perinatal Mortality.* Edinburgh: Livingstone.

CHALLIS, L., DAY, P. & KLEIN, R. (1984) Residential care on demand. *New Society*, 5 April, 34.

DEPARTMENT OF HEALTH AND SOCIAL SERVICES (1980) *Personal Social Services. Local Authority Statistics. Home Help Service, 1979–80, England.* Statistics and Research Division.

—— (1983a) *Health Care and Its Costs: The Development of the NHS in England.* London: HMSO.

—— (1983b) *Elderly People in the Community: Their Service Needs.* Essays based on a seminar sponsored by DHSS at the University of East Anglia in 1982. HMSO.

—— (1984a) *Population, Pension Costs and Pensioners' Incomes: A Background Paper for Inquiry into Provision for Retirement.*

—— (1984b) *Assessment Procedures for Elderly Persons Referred for Local Authority Residential Care.* Working Document for DHSS Development Group Seminar, Leicester.

—— (1984c) *Supplementary Benefit Board and Lodging Payments: Proposals for Change.* Consultative Document issued by Secretary of State for Social Services.

—— (1984d) *Home Life: A Code of Practice for Residential Care.* Report of a Working Party sponsored by the DHSS and CPA (Chairman: Lady Avebury). London: Centre for Policy on Ageing.

DOUGLAS, J. (1948) *Maternity in Great Britain.* Joint Committee of Royal College of Obstetricians and Gynaecologists and Population Investigation Committee (Director: J. Douglas). London: Oxford University Press.

GREENE, J. G. & TIMBURY, G. C. (1979) A geriatric day hospital service. *Age and Ageing*, **8**, 49–53.

GRUNDY, E. & ARIE, T. (1982) Falling rate of provision of residential care for the elderly. *British Medical Journal*, **284**, 799–802.

HAWKS, D. (1975) Community care: An analysis of assumptions. *British Journal of Psychiatry*, **127**, 276–285.

ISAACS, B., LIVINGSTONE, M. & NEVILLE, Y. (1972) *Survival of the Unfittest.* London: Routledge and Kegan Paul.

JOHNSON, M. (1984) *Residential Care for the Elderly: Present Problems and Future Issues.* London: Policy Studies Institute.

JOLLEY, D. (1985) Further developments in psychogeriatrics in Britain (Correspondence). *British Medical Journal*, **290**, 240.

KÖRNER, E. (1982) *Steering Group on Health Service Information, First Report.* (Chairman: Mrs E. Körner).

LAMING, H. (1984) *Residential Care for the Elderly: Present Problems and Future Issues.* London: Policy Studies Institute.

LEVIN, E., SINCLAIR, I. A. C. & GORBACH, P. (1983) *The Supporters of the Confused Elderly at Home.* Report to the DHSS.

NORMAN, A. (1984) *Bricks and Mortals: Design and Lifestyle in Old People's Homes.* London: Centre for Policy on Ageing.

TIMMINS, N. (1984) *The Times*, 18 July.

WATTIS, J. & ARIE, T. (1984) Further developments in psychogeriatrics in Britain. *British Medical Journal*, **289**, 778.

11 Mental health services for the elderly

Discussion

It was generally not appreciated, at present, that much of the work done with the elderly was not recorded formally. However, it was very necessary to collect this data in order to make comparative studies about which services worked well, what the contribution of different members of staff was, and what the range of variation in need and provision was around the country. The basic data concerning different models of psychogeriatric care did not exist, and before embarking upon new services it was necessary to evaluate those in existence. Particularly, since it was always necessary to prove to the professional community that certain practices were worth pursuing.

This argument could be generalised to include the recording of ward referrals seen by psychiatrists working in general hospital settings, and also much of the psychiatric emergency work which was done, as well as liaison–consultation between physicians and psychiatrists — who often worked closely together in the same department in the care of the elderly.

Working role of the psychogeriatrician

The issue of 'invisible' work raised questions about the working roles of psychogeriatricians. It was sometimes believed that the main role of the psychogeriatrician concerned the management of elderly severely mentally infirm wards in mental hospitals. In fact, the picture was quite different: there were many new patients to be seen; teaching to be done; medical, orthopaedic and geriatric ward referrals to be assessed; old people's homes to be visited (planned and unplanned); there was collaboration with social workers on planning services — often involving consultations on individual cases; and efforts had to be made to support families. Indeed, elderly severely mentally infirm patients constituted a tiny part of many psychogeriatricians' working responsibilities. This was held to be a serious misperception by psychiatrists of the role of the psychogeriatrician, which led to unrealistic job descriptions being written for psychogeriatricians at district level.

The example was given of a draft job description for a post in Northumberland, for a consultant to run a general adult psychiatric service for a town of 28,000 people in a deprived area, and also to provide psychogeriatric services for a population of 23,000. Either job was thought to be a challenge for a full-time consultant. In such job descriptions there was often no comment made about day hospitals, assessment beds and the composition of the multidisciplinary team. Altogether, such posts were unlikely to attract psychogeriatricians, though they might attract general psychiatrists. Sometimes insufficiently trained people were appointed to such posts, and the result was to the detriment of psychogeriatric care.

The private sector in the care of the elderly

The private sector had been mentioned. There was some ambivalence about this. It had been suggested that their activities needed inspection. But, alternatively, there was a case for suggesting that they ought to be nurtured, and invited to apply themselves to certain types of care. In view of the recent and continuing massive development that had taken place in the private sector, there was evidently a great need for some integration of public and private services. The private sector currently functioned more or less independently from public health services, and a negative clinical selection process was in operation. It was frequently suggested, for example, that people were cared for in the private sector who did not need such care. It was emphasised that a *modus operandi* had to be developed between the two sectors.

The elderly and the closure of mental hospitals

One of the themes of the meeting was the thrust to reduce the size of, and to close, mental hospitals. The decrease in the numbers of the old long-stay appeared to be due mainly to deaths in this group. Nevertheless, there was a threat that the decline in numbers would not continue, based on the observation that, of the new long-stay, more than half were elderly. The experience of some psychogeriatricians was that these elderly patients did not need to be in mental hospitals, they could be housed in smaller units, preferably as in-patients with access to day care facilities.

It appeared to many to be possible to provide an entire psychogeriatric service outside the mental hospital. Psychogeriatricians were one of those groups which did not need such beds. The district general hospital component was said to be satisfactory — provided there was full access to geriatric medical services, a long-stay unit, and sufficient supporting personnel.

The remedial professions

The role of the remedial professions (occupational therapists, physio-therapists, and speech therapists) was acknowledged to be highly important in the running of psychogeriatric services. Clinical psychologists also had a part to play in this. It was reported that an innovative course on remedial treatment in the care of the elderly was being run in Nottingham.

Training of psychogeriatricians

Regarding the training of psychogeriatricians, the main problem seemed to be at the senior registrar 'bottleneck'. Judging by the experience of those on the Manpower Committee of the Royal College of Psychiatrists, all districts wished to provide proper comprehensive psychogeriatric services and to appoint suitable consultants responsible for psychogeriatric care. However, surveys showed that there were only 14 suitable training posts at the senior registrar level in the country. It was important to stress that the number of posts at this level needed to be increased. But there was no mechanism to do this. On the other hand, there was a pool of 'frozen' posts in psychiatry. It was suggested that there was a need to support more 'one holder' posts, as was the case in surgery and medicine. In that case, a post would only be filled if there were specific manpower requirements for it.

12 Changing services for disturbed, severely retarded adults: Problems and opportunities

LORNA WING

The findings and comments in this paper are based on the MRC Social Psychiatry Unit's study of the effects of the closure of Darenth Park Hospital (Wing, 1981–84), but can be generalised to any hospital for mentally retarded adults.

The term mental retardation covers a wide range of patterns of handicaps and behaviour, due to an equally wide variety of causes. There are many different ways of subgrouping mentally retarded people, and each has its value depending upon the purpose for which it is intended. For the present paper, a subdivision based on quality of reciprocal social interaction will be used.

Mental retardation, by definition, involves impaired development of cognitive skills, and often motor skills also, as well as sometimes impairment of the skills underlying sociability (Wing & Gould, 1979; Wing, 1981b); these are the instinctive recognition that human beings are the most interesting and important of all the things in the environment, the ability to give and receive non-spoken as well as spoken social signals, an innate desire to take part in social communication and social situations, and empathy for other people's feelings. The majority of retarded people, particularly those with Down's syndrome, have these skills at least up to the level to be expected from their general intellectual development. But there is a minority who, as well as their cognitive problems, are severely impaired in these areas. Certain other problems are closely associated with this pattern. Language development tends to be affected, varying from, at one end of the scale, total absence of understanding and use of speech, to, at the other end, a large vocabulary used in a repetitive stereotyped way without regard to comments made by others. Non-verbal communication is also severely impaired. In childhood, imaginative play is absent or severely limited. The pattern of activities is dominated by repetitive pursuits, varying from simple stereotypies such as finger flicking, or twiddling pieces of string, to more complicated routines such as arranging objects in lines, or asking the same question on the same topic over and over again. Strong resistance is shown to attempts to change these repetitive activities. Finally, certain types of difficult behaviour are strongly associated with impairment of reciprocal social interaction—namely, aggressiveness, destructiveness, screaming or other unacceptable noises, temper tantrums, running away, aimless wandering, unpleasant personal habits, disturbance of others at night, throwing objects around and creating general chaos, and, more rarely but distressingly, self-injury (biting, scratching, eye-poking, head-banging). All these problems are due to the lack of understanding of the rules governing social behaviour and social interaction, and the inability to cope with changes in the environment or routine.

Almost all people with these impairments have, in addition to their general mental retardation, a history of early childhood autism or a related condition. Such syndromes are similar to other forms of mental retardation in that they are disorders of childhood development beginning from birth or the early years, and are irreversible. But they are like mental illnesses in that the behaviour problems fluctuate markedly in severity over time, though the underlying impairments remain the same, and the behaviour pattern is strange and difficult for people to understand. The puzzling quality is due to the marked discrepancy between the very poor social interaction skills and the apparently higher level of intellectual ability. This contrasts with, for example, Down's syndrome in which social interaction skills are relatively unimpaired in comparison with intellectual performance (Wing & Gould, 1979).

Owing to general lack of awareness of the autistic spectrum of disorders before the 1960s, these conditions in retarded people who are now adults have usually not been formally diagnosed, but the Darenth Park Hospital study has shown how common they are in the retarded population (Shah *et al*, 1982). In this hospital, in August 1980, there were 890 adult residents, of whom about 80 had a history of childhood autism, and a further 200, a history of social impairment and marked autistic features—i.e. about one-third of the population at that time were socially impaired. Darenth had over 2,000 residents in the early years of this century, and the population has gradually declined to its present level. From Darenth's history and present state, it should be possible to estimate the numbers of socially impaired people to be found in other mental handicap hospitals. This group is numerically larger than the non-ambulant poulation in Darenth, of whom there were 122 (14%) in August 1980; about 40% of these non-ambulant people were socially impaired in addition to their general mental retardation and physical disabilities.

The socially impaired group can be further subdivided into those with and those without useful practical skills, and then again into those with and without major behaviour problems. As emphasised earlier, behaviour problems are especially common in socially impaired people, but a minority are amenable: these are to be found especially among the middle-aged or elderly. Those who are amenable and who have useful practical skills obviously present the least problems, and manage reasonably well as long as they can follow their usual routines. But, in the Darenth study, some even in this subgroup became more obsessed with their repetitive activities when moved to hostels, where there was little structure to the day and not much provision for occupation.

However, as would be expected, the really severe difficulties are presented by those with few or no skills who also have marked behaviour problems, and this is the subgroup to be dealt with here. People of this kind are to be found in the wards of mental handicap hospitals and in mental illness hospitals as well, since some are incorrectly labelled as suffering from schizophrenia. These wards tend to be understaffed, poorly equipped, dreary, and depressing; episodes of aggressive and destructive behaviour are frightening to inexperienced staff. The reports of investigations of ill-treatment in mental handicap hospitals (e.g. DHSS, 1969) contain accounts of people of this kind who cannot express their own needs and who are difficult to manage, and upon whom individual members of staff have vented their exasperation and frustration.

In Darenth Park Hospital, in the 1980 survey, there were 183 adults in this subgroup—i.e. approximately 20% of the total hospital population and 65% of all the socially impaired people. These figures can be compared with those from a survey carried out in 1971, of all mentally handicapped people aged 15 + in the former London Borough of Camberwell, in which 26 people out of a total of 414 (6%) were severely socially impaired, disturbed in behaviour, and had few or no skills. This latter survey included all those with home addresses in Camberwell, whether they were living at home or in residential care (including hospitals) anywhere in the country.

The problems of large, understaffed, hierarchically organised institutions for mentally retarded people have been described by King *et al* (1971). Some workers believe that all mentally retarded people can benefit from placement in small living units, in ordinary houses, dispersed in ordinary streets, as opposed to clustered on a campus (Thomas *et al*, 1978). The problems of the socially impaired, severely retarded disturbed subgroup have been attributed to the effects of institutional care (Oswin, 1978; 1981) with the implication that, if placed in small community units, they will lose their stereotypies, develop higher levels of skills, become more amenable and easier in behaviour, and enjoy the opportunities of taking part in local community activities.

To date, the only new place to which such people have been moved from Darenth is another mental handicap hospital, smaller than Darenth, but more restrictive. NHS, local authority, voluntary, and private hostels will rarely accept them. For example, one young man with these problems was on the list for transfer to an NHS hostel, but the supervisor of the hostel decided not to take him because he was notorious for running out of open doors; the hostel front door opened on to a main road—unlike the Darenth wards, which are surrounded by large grounds.

Units planned by district health authorities which will presumably take this socially impaired group are not yet open. In order to carry out a comparative study, the MRC Social Psychiatry Unit team investigating Darenth Park tried to find, in 1983, some non-hospital units that did cater for this type of person. Despite enquiries made in all parts of the country, only two local authority and one voluntary home could be found with residents whose handicaps were severe enough to be comparable to those in the relevant hospital wards, and only one of those homes was in an ordinary street. Thus, it still remains an open question whether all or most of the adults in this subgroup can be successfully accommodated in small scattered units in ordinary houses in ordinary streets.

In the study mentioned above (Rawlings, 1985a;b), 12 socially impaired, severely retarded, and difficult young adults in hospital wards were compared with 11 young adults, matched for level of handicap and severity of behaviour problems, in three non-hospital units. One unit was a sheltered rural community in a country house with large grounds, while another was an apartment in a building on a campus, which also contained a house for retarded children and other houses for children in care; this was situated in a suburban area. The third was an ordinary house in an ordinary street in an urban area. Though the study was limited in scope, some findings emerged.

Compared with those in the hospital wards, the staff in the non-hospital units had more autonomy of action, including financial budgeting; they organised most of their own services such as cooking, laundry, transport, and provided care that was more orientated towards the residents' needs.

Looking at the residents' behaviour, the most positive differences in favour of the non-hospital settings were, firstly, that the residents in all three units spent more time in activities that were socially acceptable, though at a very low level. These included looking at picture books, being guided through simple domestic tasks by the staff, responding to staff approaches, being engaged with staff help in self-care, etc. Secondly, their repetitive activities were of a less urgent and obtrusive kind than those seen in the hospital wards. Thirdly, they were kept cleaner and tidier by the staff, and were 'nicer to be near'. On the other hand, the hospital and non-hospital groups did not differ in their level of self-care or practical skills. The total time spent in stereotyped repetitive activities did not differ significantly, but in the non-hospital units, stereotypies more often occurred at the same time as appropriate activities, such as looking at a book while flicking fingers. In general, in the hospital wards, stereotypies were often the only activity. Disturbed behaviour (screaming, aggression, etc.) was sporadic, was not recorded very often in either type of unit, and showed no significant differences in the two settings.

Compared with the wards, the non-hospital units had far fewer residents in each living unit, better staff ratios (on average 1:3 compared with 1:7), better physical accommodation, and more and better equipment and facilities for occupation and leisure.

Comparisons between the individual units were also of interest (Rawlings, 1985b). The findings for the hospital wards suggested that, despite the low level of staff autonomy and the bureaucratic system of management, there was still scope for individual initiative on the part of the person in charge of a ward, which could make a sizeable difference to the life style of the residents. Perhaps the most important point to emerge was that geographical location made little difference to the socially impaired, severely retarded residents. The quality of life of those in the rural community was as good as for those in suburbs or town (see also similar findings by Baker *et al*, 1974). In fact, the ordinary house in the ordinary street had the major disadvantage that its front door opened on to the street: the staff always had to be on the alert in case one of the residents ran out, because they had no road sense. The staff in the rural house and in the suburban campus did not have this worry because of the large grounds surrounding the living unit. Outings were simpler to arrange from the town house, but transport was available to the other non-hospital units, and all the residents had a variety of outings to a wide range of local community facilities.

In evaluating these results, it must be emphasised that, with the exception of the rural community (run by a voluntary body), the non-hospital units (run by local social service authorities) were at least twice as expensive in weekly costs per resident than the hospital wards. If the same financial, personal, and physical resources, and the same degree of staff autonomy could be provided in a hospital, there seems no reason why the life-style of the residents here should not be as good as in the non-hospital units.

As things are at present, however, many socially impaired severely retarded adults are among the most underprivileged people to be found in the mentally handicapped population, and they may well be among the last to leave the hospitals. If they do move, it may be to accommodation that does not meet their needs. There is the danger that the expense of providing good alternative living units will be too great, and that the money and enthusiasm for community care will run out before this group have been provided for.

From experience gained in the Darenth survey and from close contact with the small number of homes for socially impaired people run by a voluntary body (the National Autistic Society), it is possible to list the characteristics that are important in units for this group.

Firstly, the numbers living together should be small. Severely socially impaired people, by definition, have no concept of friendship or co-operation with peers. Noisiness, restlessness, or aggression in one will exacerbate such behaviour in another, so that living groups of, e.g., four people are easier to care for than those of larger size.

Secondly, autonomy for each living unit, so that the direct care staff can organise the daily activities, is essential. A good staff ratio is necessary, but to be most effective, requires appropriate deployment of staff (Tizard, 1975). At busy times (getting up in the morning, meal times, etc.) one-to-one may be needed, whereas at quieter times, it is possible to manage with less intensive staffing. A system in which staff have responsibility for their small 'family', and look after all their needs, works much better than a hierarchical system in which specific tasks are allocated by the senior person and roles do not overlap.

Thirdly, there should be an organised routine, giving a predictable shape to each day, but, within this framework, there should be sufficient flexibility to allow for the individual, idiosyncratic needs of each resident. Staff need to be able to spend enough time with each resident in their care to allow him or her to carry out, or at least to assist in self-care. This requires great patience and a real understanding of the nature of the handicaps of socially impaired people, so that the right amount of assistance is given in the right way, and at the right time. The senior staff should have the right personal qualities, viz., common sense, patience, physical endurance, self-confidence, the ability to be both firm and warm, a real liking for the residents, tolerance of their peculiar behaviour, and last but not least, a sense of humour. They also need experience in this particular aspect of mental retardation, so that they can guide and teach junior staff. Ready access to support and advice from medical, psychological, and other professionals with knowledge of the social impairment syndromes is also essential. Caring for socially impaired people is difficult and tiring, and it sometimes seems that there is no return for all one's efforts. However, access to information about the nature of the handicaps and opportunities for training within and outside the unit help to make the work more interesting and rewarding.

Fourthly, the residents need occupation each day: one of the advantages of staff autonomy and the organisation by the staff of day-to-day services within the home is that residents can take part in the domestic work, however small their contribution. The opportunity to attend a day centre providing appropriate activities should also be available.

Fifthly, leisure activities have to be organised and should include regular physical exercise of the kind that socially impaired severely retarded people can enjoy, such as walking, running, trampolining, use of other simple gymnastic equipment, swimming, and horse riding. This occupies time, improves health, and helps with sleeping problems.

Sixthly, most socially impaired people like music, so that moving to music, musical games, and even singing are suitable leisure activities. Outings to parks, or the seaside, coach rides, and picnics, and use of community facilites such as eating places, bowling alleys, and local social clubs for handicapped people should all be on the agenda. Whenever such outings are organised, the expedition should never last too long, and enough staff should be available in case a member of the group becomes disturbed and a rapid exit has to be made.

Finally, the home should be comfortable, with sitting room, dining room, kitchen, and bedrooms like an ordinary family house, and should not look like an apology for a hospital ward. Most socially impaired people find it hard to be with others all the time, and need to be able to escape to be on their own when the pressure becomes too much, so that provision should be made for this. They also find relief from the tension induced by social pressures in wandering or running around in the open air; this can be done safely only if there are reasonably sized grounds around the house. Life is easier for staff and residents if the front door does not give immediate access to a road with traffic, or other dangers, to people with no instinct for self-preservation.

When deciding the site of the accommodation, the neighbours have to be considered. It is unreasonable to expect people with no special involvement in the field of mental handicap to take kindly to being kept awake at night by noises from next door, to have objects (mentionable and unmentionable) thrown over the fence, or to see large adults of either sex stripping themselves in the garden, to mention only a few of the possible problems. When considering the needs of the residents and those of the general community, the most suitable setting for this particular group of severely socially impaired, retarded, and difficult people is in a small homely living unit, on a sizeable campus, with other living units for handicapped people also needing this type of sheltered provision. The idea of a 'normal community' is meaningless to socially impaired people with this degree of handicap. The presence of other people is a source of distress and disturbance, and can only be tolerated if carefully planned and experienced for short periods of time. A campus setting would allow residents to walk without danger, and would give the staff easy access to fellow professionals, but each living unit should be autonomous and organise its own day-to-day services. Various bodies could set up homes on the same site — NHS, social service department, and voluntary organisations. The campus would be managed by an overall management committee, with members from the local community and the direct care staff, as well as other relevant professionals. A system of independent inspection should be organised to ensure that high standards are maintained, while the mixture of different administrative bodies using the site would also help to keep up standards. A social club and some leisure facilities should be provided on site, and active encouragement given to people living in the surrounding neighbourhood to make use of them. In this way, good relationships and patterns of informal mixing can be built up, while avoiding the stresses caused by living in close proximity to people with difficult behaviour.

Four separate points must be emphasised in conclusion. Firstly, that severely socially impaired and retarded people of the kind described here cannot be expected to change much, if at all, in their level of skill, however ideal their environment. Pressure to acquire skills beyond their capacity (which is rarely above the two or three year-old level, and often well below this) causes marked exacerbations of aggressive, noisy, destructive behaviour. Staff need to know and accept this before taking up work with this group: the justification for improving the life style for these people is humanitarian. Secondly, providing a good life style for them is very expensive, and costs at least twice as much as the usual present standard of accommodation and care in hospital. Thirdly, the greatest expertise in this field is to be found in the National Autistic Society. Co-operation between statutory and voluntary bodies is likely to lead to the best quality of care for handicapped people. Finally, the life-style in any residential accommodation depends on the quality of the staff and way it is run, not on the type of administration or the geographical location. Where the site is suitable, the grounds of existing hospitals could be used for the type of campus described above, with new small houses replacing the old unsuitable buildings.

References

BAKER, B. L., SELTZER, G. B. & SELTZER, M. M. (1974) *As Close as Possible: Community Residences for Mentally Retarded Adults*. Boston: Little Brown.

DEPARTMENT OF HEALTH AND SOCIAL SECURITY (1969) *Report of the Committee of Inquiry into Allegations of Ill-Treatment of Patients and Other Irregularities at the Ely Hospital, Cardiff*. Cmnd 3975. London: HMSO.

KING, R. D., RAYNES, N. V. & TIZARD, J. (1971) *Patterns of Residential Care*. London: Routledge & Kegan Paul.

OSWIN, M. (1978) *Children Living in Long-Stay Hospitals*. London: Heinemann.

—— (1981) The short-term residential care of mentally handicapped children. In *Assessing the Handicaps and Needs of Mentally Retarded Children* (ed. B. Cooper). London: Academic Press.

RAWLINGS, S. A. (1985a) Behaviour and skills of severely retarded adults in hospitals and small residential homes. *British Journal of Psychiatry*, **146**, 358–366.

—— (1985b) Life-styles of severely retarded non-communicating adults in hospitals and small residential homes. *British Journal of Social Work*, **15**, 281–293.

SHAH, A., HOLMES, N. & WING, L. (1982) Prevalence of autism and related conditions in adults in a mental handicap hospital. *Applied Research in Mental Retardation*, **3**, 303–317.

TIZARD, J. (1975) Quality of residential care for retarded children. In *Varieties of Residential Experience* (eds. J. Tizard, I. Sinclair and R. V. G. Clarke). London: Routledge & Kegan Paul.

THOMAS, D., FIRTH, H. & KENDALL, A. (1978) *ENCOR: A Way Ahead*. London: Campaign for the Mentally Handicapped.

WING, L. (1981) *Evaluation of New Services to be Provided for Residents of Darenth Park Hospital.* MRC Social Psychiatry Unit. Unpublished Report, No. 1.

—— (1982) *Ibid.* No. 2.

—— (1983) *Ibid.* No. 3.

—— (1984) *Ibid.* No. 4.

—— (1981b) Language, social and cognitive impairments in autism and severe mental retardation. *Journal of Autism and Developmental Disorders*, **11**, 31–44.

—— & GOULD, J. (1979) Severe impairments of social interaction and associated abnormalities in children: Epidemiology and classification. *Journal of Autism and Developmental Disorders*, **9**, 11–29.

13 From institution to community services

HOWARD GLENNERSTER and NANCY KORMAN

It is now 24 years since a Conservative Minister of Health announced the demise of the mental illness hospital (National Association for Mental Health, 1961) and 16 years since a Labour Secretary of State set in train a process that was to lead first, to proper inspection, and improved standards; and, ultimately, to the closure of the large institutions for the mentally handicapped (Crossman, 1977). Since then few closures have taken place, and so far as we can tell, no large institutions for the mentally handicapped have closed. Though the total size of the resident population has fallen by about a fifth in ten years, the proportion of long-stay residents (over five years) has increased (Jones & Fowles, 1983). Why has so little happened? Political motivation to avoid a damaging succession of scandals was certainly present. The institutions faced considerable difficulties in attracting adequate staff. It was believed that other solutions would be cheaper. The climate of opinion turned against the institutions in the wake of damaging social research (Robb, 1967; Morris, 1969).

In consequence, the pressure for closure has grown. The deterioration in the fabric of these old buildings has led to demands for expenditure which is not seen as justifiable in terms of the type of care provided, let alone possible in terms of the funds available for new capital expenditure. The continuing exposure of conditions which seem unresponsive to changes in resources and management effort has led to growing pessimism that more modern forms of care could be developed in these institutions. Further contributions to the climate for change came from radical criticisms made by voluntary organisations and professional groups who looked to a time when all mentally handicapped people could pursue an ordinary life (King Edward's Hospital Fund for London, 1982). Cash constraints on the National Health Service have made the potential capital gains from these hospital sites far more attractive. However, despite these incentives, little has actually been achieved.

Most of the popular explanations for this failure are only partially convincing — professional and trade union resistance, lack of genuine political concern, local community opposition, the absence of feasible alternatives. Overall, we believe there has been genuine political concern and relatively little purely negative professional or local opposition (perhaps because so few schemes have actually got to the point of closure) — at least until recently. Our explanation is different and is drawn from our own research in the London Regions and especially on an in-depth study of the planned closure of Darenth Park Hospital. Policy makers, whether at the DHSS or at regional level, simply seemed to have no conception of the complex political and administrative tasks involved. Neither the traditional planning role of the region nor the financial machinery were appropriate. Nor has the Government appreciated the interim costs involved. Short-term constraints have made it difficult to realise what may be long-term gains. That is the disheartening side. The heartening aspect is that we can see a process of 'political and administrative learning' at work. Over a long period, administrators and planners have found ways round some of the obstacles and shown some inventiveness and political skill in doing so, but even more is going to be necessary to achieve the closure of this one hospital.

The Darenth Park Project

Darenth Park Hospital is a large institution for mentally handicapped adults. It was one of the first public institutions built for those suffering from mental handicap, and opened in 1878 with places for 500 children as the Darenth School; within 20 years it was accommodating about 2,000 adults and children.

In 1973, the South-East Metropolitan Regional Health Board announced its intention to work towards the closure of Darenth Park Hospital, following adverse reports from Health Advisory Service visits to the hospital. However, little progress followed, and five years later, when an approach was made to the region by an industrial firm wanting to buy the hospital land for the chalk which lay under the buildings, the region saw the means of gaining enough capital to achieve its objective of replacing the hospital by local services in each district of the catchment area. It therefore set up the Darenth Project to plan the new services. A public inquiry was held for the granting of permission for excavation; the result was refusal, so the sale of the hospital fell through. By that time, considerable momentum had built up in planning new services, and the region decided to carry on, despite the loss of external capital.

The hospital is now scheduled to close by the end of the financial year 1987/88. Local authority officers, regional and district health authority officers, and members of voluntary organisations all believed that a distant and large hospital could never provide a personalised service designed to meet the needs of varied individuals. Despite the acceptance of the ends to be achieved, it will nonetheless have taken 10 years, at least, to bring about this change. In our view, this was not due to the absence of political will to bring about the change, nor even the absence of a spirit of co-operation. The difficulties lay in the new attitudes to and techniques of planning and financing which this type of service development requires. The authorities involved needed to unlearn lessons of planning which the NHS had traditionally undertaken and to invent new financial incentives.

Learning a new style of planning

In the past, the regional health authorities' planning has been primarily concerned with capital planning and has not involved other statutory or voluntary agencies to any substantial extent. Both traditions were a poor preparation for planning a move from institutional to community-based services. The new NHS Planning System begun in 1976 did envisage a wider consultative role, including other services, but it was firmly based on what political scientists term the 'strategic co-ordinator' concept of planning, i.e., some superior body seeks the views of all the subordinate tiers and interested parties, finds a compromise view and sets down a common pattern for all the participants to follow (Lindbolm, 1965).

In the Darenth Project, the South-East Thames Region drew on these approaches to planning. Understandably, officers were concerned to ensure residential accommodation, and, in some cases, day care facilities were established. Without these facilities, the hospital could not close. Providing purpose-built facilities would achieve that objective, particularly if the level of provision made in each district matched the norms proposed in *Better Services for the Mentally Handicapped* (DHSS, 1971). Reaching this kind of conclusion was made easier because the region was already involved in planning two capital schemes to take residents from Darenth. It was aware of the speed with which the hospital buildings needed to be vacated and of the inexperience of planning at district level.

The region was required to consult areas on their plans. A steering group for the Darenth Project was set up, and had as members a chief officer from each of the four area health authorities of the catchment area, two directors of social services departments, as well as regional officers concerned with planning and finance and observers from the DHSS and social work service. Areas were given weeks rather than months to produce agreed joint plans with the local authorities for comprehensive mental handicap services at the local level. In the end, the process took months rather than weeks, and the results showed that a much greater diversity of facilities was wanted locally than the region had anticipated. So the region produced a compromise model; it responded to consultation with areas by introducing further residential options into its pattern of service provision, whilst attempting to retain what its officers saw as advantages of economy, and of planning and design time and costs by producing a standard model suitable for each district.

Some districts agreed with the model, and planned on the basis of those guidelines. But other districts did not: some produced their own model of services and began developing these; others went on discussing what kinds of services they wanted without reaching conclusions; and others, originally agreeing with the region's guidelines, changed their minds later on and began seeking other ways of developing a different style of service. After initial progress, there followed a period of three to three and a half years in which no further movement was made towards eventual closure. There was no evidence of joint planning for new facilities with local authorities.

This exercise in planning was failing. First, local authorities saw the hospital closure as the health service's problem, not theirs. They had no real incentive to participate. Many of the people in Darenth had not even distant links with the catchment area: on the contrary, increasingly stern financial constraints made them wary of taking on any long-term commitment, and they saw the hospital's refusal to admit new patients as withdrawal of support for their families in most need. District health authorities saw their first priority as developing services for their existing communities. Providing services for people from Darenth would, within a given budget, make that more difficult. Moreover, some disagreed with the compromise strategy the region had adopted, and none were committed to it as their very own. Yet other practical and political problems, such as finding scarce sites in salubrious neighbourhoods, demanded very strong commitment and new expertise on the part of districts. It was the local 'actors' who held the effective veto power. What was called for was complex local political bargaining by people who had a strong organisational and professional interest in seeing results. That did not exist: and neither districts nor region were used to that kind of activity.

Districts had to learn new approaches to planning. For a start, they could not assume that local services for mentally handicapped people would be seen as desirable, and thus they had to learn the art of political persuasion. Secondly, districts had to learn that they could not claim sole planning responsibility, even for the health service contribution to comprehensive services for mentally handicapped people. Parents and relatives, voluntary organisations, social services and education departments, and even mentally handicapped people themselves all claimed a say in what was being planned.

New planning structures had to be created to allow for participation for these different groups or interests. In this way, mental handicap services planning provided a model for the joint planning of services for other client groups.

High interim costs

What no one foresaw either was the fact that whatever the eventual costs and benefits of closure, the interim costs were going to be high. We can summarise these costs as follows:

(i) *Transaction costs:* a significant amount of senior officer time was devoted at regional level to maintaining momentum, keeping the project high on the agenda of diverse bodies, and managing a bewilderingly complex set of interconnecting, not to say duplicating, procedures. Less senior but important technical advice and support to districts on site acquisition, capital planning, finance and service planning was also needed.

(ii) *Compliance costs:* other bodies whose collaboration was crucial — districts, local authorities, housing associations, voluntary bodies — would not

TABLE I
Actual and estimated financial costs of transition

		1983/4	1984/5	1985/6	1986/7	1 April 1987
Hospital budget allocation	(£)	7,119,439	6,549,067	5,526,331	3,736,543	2,025,427
Number of residents leaving during the year		58	104	182	174	—
Savings target (for following year)	(£)	570,372	1,022,736	1,789,788	1,711,116	—
Variable costs	(£)	355,489	451,365	1,416,042	1,696,312	—
Non-recurring support required (i.e. fixed costs)	(£)	214,883	571,371	373,746	14,804	—
Number of residents in hospital at start of year		724	666	562	380	206
Actual costs per resident	(£)	9,833	10,156	10,850	10,817	9,704

(i) *Hospital budget allocation* is the 1982/3 out-turn updated to 1983/4 pay and price levels reflecting the hospital's share of the district efficiency, RAWP and Lawson cuts. The budget allocation is reduced annually by the savings target based on the previous year's loss of residents.

(ii) *Savings target* is the number of residents leaving the hospital each year multiplied at present by the actual expenditure per resident of 1982/3 at 1983/4 out-turn level (£9,833).

(iii) *Variable costs* are those portions of the savings target, including the hospital's share of the estimated district decrease in allocation for RAWP, liaison and efficiency costs, which it is thought the hospital will be able to save through a decline in the number of residents of the previous year.

(iv) *Non-recurring support required* is that remaining part of the savings target which the hospital will not be able to realise because of the increasing dependencies of remaining residents.

(v) *Actual cost per resident* is based on the hospital's budget allocation for that year and the non-recurring support required for the year.

respond if other services were to suffer as a result. The region came to see that a specific monetary inducement would be necessary to get compliance.

(iii) *Transition costs:* although some costs at Darenth declined as people moved out, many did not, and some increased — e.g., the intensity of nursing care, the scale of training and the sheer infrastructure costs of maintaining civilised life in a large institution not designed for easy dismantling. Average costs per patient were estimated to rise before they fell (see Table I). On top of this, expenditure in the receiving districts would be incurred long before patients moved there. In the face of these costs no one had the incentive to move. To embark on change meant taking away from existing activities.

Some lessons learned

In the end, two new approaches were adopted — a more flexible planning approach and financial incentives from the region, and the creative tapping of Central Government resources from the DHSS. Despite its initial disruptive effect, NHS restructuring in 1982 was a positive influence. The region came into district working relationship with districts; this eased communications and misunderstandings that had arisen between region, areas and districts. The region was able to demonstrate how it would be possible to close the hospital. Thus, a closure date could be identified, and this gave an additional impetus to the project. Districts themselves became more active in planning mental handicap services because NHS restructuring had brought new personnel at the unit level where such expertise had been missing before. The region gradually moved towards a greater degree of flexibility in its attitude toward the nature of service provision by districts, and began to evolve techniques to make it more difficult for districts to opt out of the project and also, to support district planning activities.

The region found a means of unlocking the resources tied up in hospital care by essentially telling districts, 'if you produce a viable scheme to take people out of Darenth, we will give you a regular addition to revenue', i.e., so much per person transferred (currently £11,180 a year — the average annual cost of keeping a patient in Darenth long-term). This sum could be transferred to local authorities or voluntary bodies.

The region's new planning role amounted to:

(i) Its commitment to the closure of Darenth Park Hospital never wavered and it used every opportunity to remind districts that the closure was its top priority;

(ii) It developed a firm framework for the planning of the project so that districts had a clear understanding of what their responsibilities were.

The framework included a date for the closure of the hospital; a statement of the revenue level of resources each district could expect to receive by taking residents out of the hospital; and an agreement on the number of hospital residents each district was expected to take;

(iii) It appointed (jointly with Kent University) a Regional Staff Training Co-ordinator, who provided courses for staff planning new services and who involved himself in some of the new ideas for joint training of local authority staff and mental handicap nurses;

(iv) It appointed a Mental Health Service Development Co-ordinator to keep in close liaison with all districts involved in the project and to propose solutions to particular problems which arose; and

(v) It approved a regional task force to speed up the legal and financial aspects of house purchasing which needed to be completed at the regional level.

The region learned how to support new developments, leaving enough room in plans for local interests to have the diversity of service provision thought appropriate, while still ensuring that the main objectives (hospital closure and development of complementary local services) were achieved. The delay, then, was a consequence of the failure of the NHS planning system to give adequate recognition to the diversity of relationships existing at the local level — professional, consumer, administrative and political. Moreover, by identifying the mental handicap portion of the RAWP target expenditure, the region attempted to protect the total mental handicap budget.

A great many diverse and innovative arrangements have been developed in districts: e.g., a consortium including local authorities, housing associations and voluntary bodies, has been established to provide residential accommodation; and a joint identification and assessment of residents in particular wards of a local authority has helped to draw agencies together in joint planning for individuals, as well as to establish aggregated levels of service needs. Thus, after a long delay, changes and collaboration began to take place at the local level, a prerequisite for success in this endeavour.

The process of managing hospital closure is difficult. Planning for that must begin as soon as a firm decision to close is taken. It began too late at Darenth. Although we have devoted the last chapter of our Report to that subject, unfortunately we have no space to explore it here.

Extending the lesson?

The experience of the Darenth Project suggested that giving local districts more freedom, some financial incentive to develop services and a separate allocation for the mentally handicapped began to produce results. Can the principle be extended? We believe it can, though just how far is more difficult to say. What this region (and now others) has done is to create a separate NHS budget for the mentally handicapped, with money tied to residents as the responsibility for their care passes from one district to another, or from the NHS to a local authority or voluntary body. In practice, however, there are a great many limitations to this freedom of allocation. Local authorities are still suspicious, despite reassurances that money that comes under the 'care in the community' heading will not run the risk of forcing them into rate-capping difficulties or penalties. This fear is not surprising, because if money comes under the 'joint finance' heading, for example to provide a day centre not alternative residential care, it does count towards penalties or rate capping. How long will this money be guaranteed? Moreover, there is the paradox that if the health service opens a hostel in its own grounds it must pay the full costs. If it gets a housing association or voluntary body to open sheltered housing or residential facilities over the fence, it can get supplementary benefit funding.

As a first step, the government should remedy this kind of anomaly by making similar kinds of benefits available for similar types of service provision. Next, it could go further and consider making a single allocation to a joint service for the mentally handicapped at local authority level (Glennerster *et al*, 1983).

Where there are large hospitals to be closed, the region, with special Government help, should provide the initiative, expertise, bridging finance and support to the district having to handle closure, as it has done in the South-East Thames Region.

Should we take the logic a step further and devolve responsibility for the budget to interprofessional teams of specialist workers, as has been done with the elderly in the Kent Community Care experiment, giving them the power to spend the budget as they wished, after discussion with the relatives, on domiciliary and social support, or intensive care? Or should we go to the next step, as Nicholas Bosanquet (1984) suggests, and give the money (tied quasi-money or voucher) to the relatives who could spend it in private or public care? There will no doubt be divergent views on this as well as on the other steps we have suggested.

References

BOSANQUET, N. (1984) *Extending Choice for Mentally Handicapped People: The Case for Service Credits*. Discussion Paper No. 1. London: MIND (National Association for Mental Health).

CROSSMAN, R. H. S. (1977) *The Diaries of a Cabinet Minister, Vol. 3* (especially entries for March 11–27th, 1969). London: H. Hamilton and J. Cape.

DEPARTMENT OF HEALTH AND SOCIAL SERVICES (1971) *Better Services for the Mentally Handicapped*. Cmnd. 4683. London: HMSO.

GLENNERSTER, H., KORMAN, N. & WILSON-MARSLEN, K. (1983) *Planning for Priority Groups*. Oxford: M. Robertson.

JONES, K. & FOWLES, H. J. (1983) People and institutions: rhetoric and reality. In *Yearbook of Social Policy, 1982* (eds. C. James & J. Stevenson). London: Routledge and Kegan Paul.

KING EDWARD'S HOSPITAL FUND FOR LONDON (1982) *An Ordinary Life: Comprehensive Locally-Based Residential Services for Mentally Handicapped People.* (King's Fund Project Paper No. 24). London: King's Fund Centre.

LINDBLOM, C. E. (1965) *The Intelligence of Democracy.* New York: Free Press.

MORRIS, P. (1969) *Put Away.* London: Routledge and Kegan Paul.

NATIONAL ASSOCIATION FOR MENTAL HEALTH (1961) *Annual Conference Report.* London: MIND (National Association for Mental Health).

ROBB, B. (1967) *Sans Everything: A Case to Answer.* London: Nelson.

14 Developing services for the mentally handicapped: Some practical considerations

KEN DAY

This paper is written from the perspective of a service practitioner with a firm belief in the concept of community care for the mentally handicapped. However, in the light of present financial constraints, I am concerned about our ability to match principles with practice, and about idealistic attitudes that have given rise to unrealistic proposals for certain aspects of care, which if implemented, would have disastrous consequences.

Improvement in the quality of life of mentally handicapped people is the essential goal of new patterns of care, but whilst this has undoubtedly been achieved for some, others have suffered a deterioration. There are increasingly numerous accounts of unhappiness, discomfort, breakdown, and readmission to hospital—problems well known to field workers, but which are rarely exposed in evaluations of well-resourced pilot projects and which rarely reach the ears of policy makers and service planners in a coherent form. Recently, this anecdotal evidence has been supported by the work on the monitoring of the run-down of Darenth Park Hospital, Kent, where out of the 1500 patients discharged over the past ten years, one-third have been judged to be worse off and one-third no better off, while the most disturbed and handicapped groups have yet to be discharged (Wing, 1984 — personal communication).

Main barriers to successful community care

Uncertain policy, ineffective joint planning, lack of mandatory responsibilities, and inadequate funding are the main barriers to the successful implementation of new patterns of care.

Lack of a clearly defined policy

It might be argued that there is a clear national policy, but between the assertions that mentally handicapped people should be able to lead as normal and independent a life as possible in the community, and that only those requiring medical and nursing care on a day-to-day basis should be in a hospital setting, lies an enormous grey area of uncertainty, into which has crept dispute, disagreement, and unrealistic idealism.

Lack of a clear policy in key areas is causing concern to parents, provoking confusion and sometimes disagreement amongst service planners and providers, making a nonsense of manpower planning and staff training, and worst of all, threatening to leave certain groups of mentally handicapped people bereft of essential services. They are then falling between the stools of dwindling traditional services and non-existent community provision. There is an urgent need, for example, to settle which agency should have primary responsibility for services for the severely mentally handicapped and how provision should be made for the psychiatrically and behaviourally disturbed and other groups with special needs.

Uncertain policy, coupled with a sense of frustration at the slowness of local authority developments, has led to some health authorities developing community services themselves. The argument then is that it does not matter who provides, so long as provision is made. But if this trend were to become widespread, there would be a danger of establishing a new style health service for the very people who, professionals and parents alike have been arguing cogently and apparently successfully for the past decade, need a social educational model of care and not a health model. Such developments take with them all the disadvantages of the health service model, while the argument that they can be handed over to social services departments in the fullness of time is naïve and simplistic.

It is particularly important where so much new ground is being broken and evangelical zeal abounds that policy and service developments should be properly informed by evaluative research. A dangerous tendency in recent years has been for developments to depend mainly upon fashion and belief; for example, some health and local authorities are planning services on the assumption that severely mentally handicapped people exhibiting behaviour disorders can be managed in regular community facilities. There is, however, no evidence to support this, nor the accompanying belief that providing a more normal environment will reduce the level of disturbance. On the contrary, numerous studies have demonstrated how persistent such behaviour can be, and the relative ineffectiveness of a range of behavioural and other treatment approaches. The placing of a severely disturbed individual in a small group home with other non-disturbed individuals not only does not help the former, but can have a serious deleterious effect on the lives of the latter, restricting their freedom, exposing them to physical attacks and emotional upsets, depriving them of staff time, preventing group activities, and generally working against the very purpose for which the home was established in the first place. It also seriously overstresses the staff.

Innovation and experimentation in the development of services are essential, but new patterns of care must be properly evaluated before acceptance and implementation of them on a large scale.

The mildly mentally handicapped are a particularly vulnerable group, in the absence of a clear policy; in fact, they pose the greatest challenge for future caring services. Numerically, the problem is two or three times greater than that of severe mental handicap; there is an association of factors rendering them more prone to all forms of social pathology and less hope of a substantial reduction in numbers through preventive measures. As life becomes increasingly more complex, more and more individuals from this vulnerable pool are emerging as in need of special provision.

Ineffective joint planning

It was recognised from the outset that the transition from institutional to community care would be highly dependent upon effective joint planning between concerned agencies. Yet despite repeated guidance from the DHSS, this is still conspicuously absent in many areas, as successive reports of the Development Team for the Mentally Handicapped attest. Urgent consideration needs to be given to the ways in which this process can be strengthened. The knock-on effects of unilateral planning can be enormous, and in the case of the mentally handicapped, are further exaggerated by the lack of a clear policy. One serious consequence can be a reduction in the overall pool of resources if a hospital service runs down faster than the development of community provision. Serious problems can also arise where there are differences between the philosophy and goals of the various concerned agencies, particularly between the health district, which is currently the main provider of services, and its related local authorities.

The present emphasis on the transfer of hospital residents to the community is in danger of taking precedence over the development of services for those mentally handicapped people already living in the community. It is not uncommon for a hospital to be negotiating the discharge of substantial numbers of residents on the one hand, whilst at the same time still having to admit patients for long-term residential care because of a shortage of local facilities. It could be argued that enabling those already living in the community to continue to do so should be the first priority: there are large numbers of middle-aged mentally handicapped people living with ageing parents who are on the verge of needing residential care.

Lack of mandatory responsibilities

Lack of mandatory responsibilities is another potent barrier to the establishment of satisfactory community care, leaving developments subject to the vagaries of local authority spending and planning priorities, in which the mentally handicapped and their families as a minority group are at a considerable disadvantage. Comparison between the high quality of educational provision for the mentally handicapped (which is mandatory) and local authority provision for the adult mentally handicapped (which is not) provides a clear illustration of the benefits of legislation, and leads to the conclusion that these latter responsibilities should be obligatory rather than permissive.

Under-funding

Improving the quality of services for mentally handicapped people and their families must cost more, whatever form it takes: there are many years of neglect and under-funding to make up. Community care can never be a cheap option, but present financial constraints are creating an ever-widening gap between the many excellent well resourced, showpiece 'pilot projects' and the reality of services for the majority of mentally handicapped people. Local authorities, which are subject to financial uncertainty and constraint, and have substantial and widely ranging responsibilities, cannot possibly fulfil their commitment to the mentally handicapped properly without a substantial injection of earmarked funding. Joint financing and other strategies for transferring funds between agencies, whilst helpful, are not enough. A fundamental problem is that the financial calculations for new patterns of care have to a large extent been based upon the costs of inadequately funded institutional care.

Funding of community developments must not be at the expense of hospitals, which not only will remain the main providers of residential care for some years to come, but also have a long-term responsibility for developing specialised services. As community care programmes expand, hospitals are becoming increasingly concerned with the care of the more highly resource-intensive groups — the profoundly and multiply handicapped, the elderly, and behaviourally disturbed; they must be adequately funded to carry out this task properly and to provide satisfactory standards of care.

The financial equation relating to the transfer of hospital residents and their funding to the community is proving more complex than was initially appreciated, and has sometimes led to misunderstanding between health authorities and local authorities as to exactly how much money might be available. The amount released can vary from as little as £1,000 if only one resident is discharged, up to £15,000 or more if a group of villas is closed. However, the process of transfer takes time and bridging funding is essential. The amounts quoted are 'average', and do not take account of the cost differentials of different types of mentally handicapped people, both in hospital and in the community; sums transferred are for the total care of the individual and not just residential provision.

Community care — problems and needs

Successful community care depends on meeting all the needs of the individual — residential, occupational, leisure, and domiciliary support — but all too often, one of these vital elements is missing. Few social services departments have been able to provide the full range of options needed, with the result that certain individuals either cannot be accommodated or are inappropriately placed.

The capacity of a mentally handicapped person to cope in a particular environment can be overestimated. In our enthusiasm to help mentally handicapped people make the most of their limited abilities, there is a tendency to push them to their limits, assess them at this level, and expect peak performances thereafter. Crucial factors like motivation, common sense, resilience, and an ability to get on with others are rarely assessed adequately before placement is made.

Currently, we expect the least able money managers to cope and enjoy life on a well below average income. How many of us could? Insufficient funds not only increase the overall stress of living, but act as a potent barrier to integration, restricting leisure activities and intensifying loneliness and isolation. In those countries whose community care programmes we so rightly admire, the income of mentally handicapped people nearly equals the national average, with plenty to spare for holidays and luxuries.

A too rigid application of the principle of locally-based services can act against the best interests of the individual. It has in my experience sometimes led to groupings of people with such widely different abilities and needs as to have prevented the development of a true family unit, and restricted the lifestyle of residents. In some circumstances, grouping according to ability levels and needs is more appropriate and advantageous.

There has been a dramatic increase in the life expectancy of mentally handicapped people during the last 50 years, with a correspondingly increasing number of elderly mentally handicapped people, both in hospitals and the community. The commonly held view that elderly mentally handicapped people should be catered for by generic services for old people fails to take account of the fact that they need this provision somewhat earlier in their lives, and for different reasons. Whilst some elderly mentally handicapped people are certainly able to benefit from sheltered housing and warden-supervised provision, the majority of those requiring staffed accommodation are physically active and mentally alert, and would be wholly out of place in an old people's home alongside dying, dementing, and severely incapacitated residents, 20 years their senior. To condemn them to this would be a flagrant contravention of normalisation principles. What is needed is special day and residential provision for 'retired' mentally handicapped people, which takes account of their need for a slower pace of life, but enables them to remain active and involved.

The large numbers of elderly mentally handicapped people currently resident in hospital should surely be allowed to live out their lives in what has been their home for many years. It would be grossly unfair and inhumane to subject them to a major upheaval at this time in their lives, and to discharge them to what could well be less adequate accommodation, for the sake of a principle.

Meeting general medical needs

It is generally agreed that the medical needs of mentally handicapped people can and should be met as they are for the normal population, through the primary health care team and acute services. By and large, this is working well, but clinical experience has highlighted certain problems.

Mentally handicapped people are generally rather poor at self-reporting illness, often lacking the ability to recognise when they are ill and an understanding of what to do if they are. Insidiously arising conditions like anaemia and neoplasms easily go unnoticed until they have reached an advanced stage, minor problems go unrecognised and untreated, and in other conditions, diagnosis may be delayed until the individual has become acutely ill. Improved health education will help, and should be an integral part of all social training programmes, but for many, a regular health screen is the only realistic measure, and consideration needs to be given as to how this can best be provided.

Severely mentally handicapped poeple who are admitted to a general hospital, away from their familiar surroundings, experiencing extreme discomfort and unable to comprehend their situation, can become extremely disturbed. Such cases are comparatively rare, but when they do occur, have a devastating effect in an acute medical or surgical ward or paediatric department. At the moment, these cases can be admitted to sick bay facilities in mental handicap hospitals, but what will happen when these no longer exist? The situation needs careful monitoring, as community care programmes expand, to ascertain the size of the problem and what special provision is required.

Account must also be taken of the capacity of community residential facilities to cope with physically ill residents and the position of mentally handicapped people living in unstaffed accommodation, either alone or with other mentally handicapped people, who could not be expected to look after themselves or their companions in the same way as non-handicapped people in similar situations. There is likely to be a greater demand for admission to acute services in these circumstances.

Services for the psychiatrically and behaviourally disordered

Nearly one-half of mentally handicapped children and adults suffer from associated psychiatric disorder. Amongst mental handicap hospital populations, the prevalence is between 30% and 60%, and over two-thirds of recent admissions have been for this reason. Over half the problems presented are behaviour disorders, ranging from emotional instability and anti-social behaviour in the mildly mentally handicapped to a wide repertoire of severe and often intractable disorders in the severely mentally handicapped. Schizophrenia is two to three times commoner, and neurotic and alcohol-related disorders, previously of reportedly low incidence, are on the increase as the implementation of community care exposes more and more mentally handicapped people to the stresses, strains, and temptations of every-day life (Ballinger & Reid, 1977; Corbett, 1979; Day, 1983; Primrose, 1971; Spencer, 1976; Williams, 1971).

It is imperative that facilities for these groups of patients are developed in parallel with the implementation of community care. Currently, they are very inadequate, with few specialist units, and there is a very real danger of their being overlooked in the massive drive towards community care. Yet the success of the latter will be in no small way dependent upon the availability of the former.

It has been argued, on normalisation principles, that psychiatrically and behaviourally disturbed mentally handicapped people should receive their care and treatment from the general psychiatric services. There are, however, many cogent arguments in support of a specialised service, with appropriately trained and experienced doctors, nurses and other staff, and special facilities. The diagnosis of psychiatric disorder in the mentally handicapped is complicated by communication difficulties and atypical presentation; unusual responses to drugs and atypical side-effects are common; therapeutic interventions have to be tailored to take account of the level of intellectual functioning, and additional resources are needed to deal with other aspects of handicap; furthermore, many of the behaviour disorders presented are relatively unique, and require a highly specialised approach to assessment and management.

Specialised psychiatric services will in the main need to be provided on a supra-district basis, since a wide range of treatment settings are required for comparatively small numbers of individuals, and few health districts are of sufficient size to enable them to establish a fully comprehensive viable unit. On the basis of running such a service for the past eight years, I have calculated that a 140-bedded unit for adults and young people is required to serve a catchment population of 500,000 (Day, 1983; 1984). A detailed breakdown of bed requirements is given in Table I. Special rehabilitation facilities in the community (20 residential and 30 day places per 500,000 catchment population) are also needed, as experience has shown that these groups of patients, particularly the young offenders, are not always able to manage immediately in regular community facilities for the mentally handicapped.

TABLE I

Estimated psychiatric bed requirements for the mentally handicapped — population 500,000

Acute psychiatric beds — mixed	30
Long-stay psychiatric beds — mixed	30
Offenders/anti-social behaviour: Male	20
Female	10
Rehabilitation — mixed	10
Disturbed severely mentally handicapped adults — mixed	40
Total	140

There is an equal need to establish specialist psychiatric treatment beds for mentally handicapped children. Many mental handicap hospitals no longer have children's wards, child psychiatric services are rarely able to cope, and in the absence of alternative provision, children requiring assessment and treatment on an in-patient basis either cannot be admitted or have to be admitted to adult facilities. Ten beds for severely mentally handicapped children and ten for mildly mentally handicapped children, for a catchment population of 500,000, would appear to be needed.

Adequate provision must also be made for the dangerous and potentially violent mentally handicapped of all intellectual levels. The present restrictive policy relating to admissions to special hospitals, coupled with the inability of many mental handicap hospitals to cope, is creating serious hardship for numbers of mentally handicapped offenders who have to endure long periods of remand, be admitted to unsuitable facilities where it is difficult to provide humane care, or worse still, suffer imprisonment. The Butler recommendations that they might be accommodated with the mentally ill do not appear to be working in practice. Special regional medium secure units are needed, which include provision for the small, but significant number of severely mentally handicapped people exhibiting gross behaviour disorder who cannot be cared for in an ordinary mental handicap hospital unit.

Staff training

Much attention has been paid to the preparation and training of all groups of staff for community care — and rightly so. But insufficient thought has been given to the training needs of staff who are caring for the mentally handicapped with special problems. Of particular concern is the present mismatch between the current training syllabus for mental handicap nurses, with its minimal emphasis on medical and psychiatric aspects of care, and the types of patients nurses are increasingly having to care for in hospital — a paradoxical consequence of changing services, but one which needs to be speedily rectified. Some nurses will undoubtedly wish to move with patients into the community, and to assume the role of carers. Others will be needed to care for the physically and psychiatrically disturbed, and this must be reflected in training programmes, both at basic and post-basic levels.

Conclusion

The success of community care for the mentally handicapped will be judged not by its principles, but in its practice. I have tried to highlight some issues whose consideration and resolution are, in my view, a prerequisite to success. The closer community care comes to being a reality on a large scale, the clearer the attendant complexities become. There is already growing scepticism among parents and professionals — the very people who campaigned so strongly for change in the first place — about the real benefits for mentally handicapped people. It is essential that poor practice and under-funding in the early stages do not compromise the principle in the eyes of these people and of the general public, for ever.

Fortunately, changes in service provision have only just begun in the UK. We are thus in a position to benefit from the Darenth Park experience and from the alarming reports of disastrous experiences in the United States and Italy, before it is too late.

References

BALLINGER, B. R. & REID, A. H. (1977) Psychiatric disorder in an adult training centre and a hospital for the mentally retarded. *Psychological Medicine*, **1**, 525–528.

CORBETT, J. A. (1979) Psychiatric morbidity and mental retardation. In *Psychiatric Illness and Mental Handicap* (eds. F. E. James and R. P. Snaith). London: Gaskell Books, Royal College of Psychiatrists.

DAY, K. A. (1983) A hospital based psychiatric unit for mentally handicapped adults. *Mental Handicap*, **11**, 137–140.

—— (1984) Service provision for mentally handicapped people with psychiatric problems. In *Care in the Community: Keeping it Local*. Report of MIND's 1983 Annual Conference. London: MIND.

PRIMROSE, D. A. (1971) A survey of 502 consecutive admissions to a subnormality hospital. *British Journal of Mental Subnormality*, **32**, 25–28.

SPENCER, D. A. (1976) New long-stay patients in a hospital for mental handicap. *British Journal of Psychiatry*, **128**, 467–470.

WILLIAMS, C. E. (1971) A study of the patients in a group of mental subnormality hospitals. *British Journal of Mental Subnormality*, **17**, 19–41.

15 Future health services for mentally handicapped people

G. B. SIMON

As Director of the National Development Team for eight years up to November 1984, I had the opportunity of seeing services at first-hand and listening to opinions up and down the country, and in this paper I will attempt to give you some idea of the differing views and services I encountered. It is not comprehensive, but covers a wide range of services.

In the past 25 years, there has been considerable discussion on the most appropriate way in which services should be provided to mentally handicapped people and on whether or not they require any form of health service at all. The principles of the White Paper of 1971, *Better Services for the Mentally Handicapped*, are generally accepted, although there are differences of opinion on the detailed form in which services should be provided and on who should be responsible for them.

I believe that the National Health Service has a necessary contribution to services for mentally handicapped people, but also that its responsibility should be confined to those mentally handicapped people with medical and psychiatric problems, most of whom will be severely and multiply handicapped, and many of whom would receive none of these services if they were not provided by the National Health Service.

Frequency

The frequency of severe mental handicap is between 3.5 and 4.0 per 1000 of the population. Not all will require services from the National Health Service, but many will—some over long periods, others for short periods (as will be the case for acute psychotic episodes). Surveys (Development Team for the Mentally Handicapped, 1979) have shown also the prevalence of additional handicaps in hospitals at present (Table I).

TABLE I

	White Paper 1971 estimate (in hospital)		National Development Team (actually in hospital 1978)	
	Children	Adults	Children	Adults
Vision and hearing	20%	20%	Blind or almost 11.4%	3.9%
Epilepsy	33%	20%	No hearing or almost none 7.6%	3.2%
Speech defects	Not known	33%	Lack of speech, no words 66%	21%

	White Paper 1971		National Development Team (actually in hospital 1978)	
	Children	Adults	Children	Adults
Non-ambulant	25%	6.5%	14%	8%
Behaviour difficulties	14%	13%	20%	18%
Severely incontinent	13%	6%	25%	8%
Needing assistance with feeding, washing, or dressing	25%	14%	52%	22%

Several surveys indicate that the prevalence of severe mental illness (psychosis) in mentally handicapped people is between 11% and 13% of hospital residents.

Some views on the future

Most people agree that as many services as possible should be provided locally, while many go further, and state that every requirement could, and must be met locally in every district. There are few who would disagree today with the proposed reduction in the size of the large institution, and that in many instances they should be abolished.

There is little doubt that many of the extreme views being expressed about large hospitals for mentally handicapped people are the result of years of stagnation in such institutions and a lack of specific measures there to increase the competence of their residents. In addition, most large hospitals still contain people who should never have been admitted in the first place, but whose discharge is now most unlikely. It would be wrong to assume that because hospitals were often used for the wrong purpose, every service they provided was unnecessary and that they could be abolished without any of their services being replaced. This would cause considerable unnecessary hardship to mentally handicapped people and their families.

There is also a strong feeling in some regional health authorities that any form of medical and psychiatric care should be provided by general practitioners and by psychiatrists working in mental illness. There is no doubt that this view in some authorities may have been brought about by the difficulties they have experienced in obtaining consultants in mental handicap, although there is also considerable support for this view from certain pressure groups. The latter are undoubtedly influenced by their dislike of the 'medical model', whatever form it takes, rather than the real needs of the mentally handicapped themselves. Regions which experience most difficulty are usually those which are not convinced that they should provide services, and very little change and updating of their services for mentally handicapped people has taken place recently.

Mentally handicapped children

Ministers have, over the past five years, repeatedly stated that the long-stay hospital is not appropriate for children, and as a consequence, have made sums of money available for the purpose of getting children out of hospital. Consultants in mental handicap have been exhorted not to admit children to hospital for long-term care. The Development Team were frequently told of considerable hardship being experienced by families as a result of this, and in more than one instance, of several hostels which had been forced to 'take turns' in admitting a difficult child for two-week periods, because the local mental handicap hospital could no longer admit children. This is a good example of the closing down of a service before any alternative care has been made available. Mentally handicapped children do require respite, care, and residential assessment with close observation from time to time, and this usually applies to the most difficult children. If there is no other situation where this can be done, is the child to be deprived of treatment or short-term care?

Essentials of all future services

Community mental handicap teams (CMHT)

The establishment of these teams is now regarded as a priority for any local mental handicap service. Each team should include two full-time members (a community nurse in mental handicap and a social worker) with the part-time services of a consultant in mental handicap (two sessions), clinical psychologist (two sessions), and any other specialist as and when required. Each such team should serve a population of 60–80,000.

Nine years ago, there were about 50 community nurses in mental handicap: today, there are over 500, but unfortunately, only about 100 are matched by a social worker (Development Team for Mental Handicap, 1979, Second Report, paras. 102–106).

Community units

If a community mental handicap team is to function satisfactorily and achieve any credibility at all with families, it must have easily accessible residential care; this must be available immediately and on demand, when necessary. The Development Team suggested the community unit for this purpose. There are now over 70 such units, which vary in size from 8 to 30 beds. About one-third of the beds in each unit are used for the 'on demand' service, one-third for observation and assessment, and about one-third for long-term care for people from families residing in the neighbourhood. Each 24-bedded unit, like the community mental handicap team, should serve a population of 60–80,000.

The concept of the 24-bedded unit has been questioned. In some parts of the country, for instance in parts of the North-West, the use of normal housing is being promoted, with nurses and others being paid special allowances to provide 24-hour care. However, in Gloucester and Kidderminster Districts, there are community units which provide the form of service described above.

The 'core and cluster' scheme is now being promoted in many parts of the country; in essence, it consists of a core house, supporting seven or eight other residences, with from two to six residents in each. There are a number of other schemes which use the same principle, for instance, the Bath District Health Authority and the Wessex Region offer a number of variations of the same basic idea.

In Cornwall, the planning team for mental handicap have decided that because of the scattered distribution of their population, they will need to invest in a greater number of smaller units, appropriately located to ensure services to every family. In Devon, community units of 20 to 24 places are now established in every district, and plans are being made for those mentally handicapped people who can, to move into normal houses. Here, the initial establishment of community mental handicap teams was regarded as a priority, and was followed up with the necessary residential element in the form of community units. Ordinary houses are also being used now, and in this way they hope to close one of their two large hospitals by the end of 1986.

These statutory provisions have been accompanied by a considerable increase of accommodation in the private sector, where people can be quite comfortably maintained on their social security benefits. Much of the latter has been through the initiative of nurses. However, at present, because of the rapid increase in the private sector, the problem of ensuring the maintenance of standards has been greater than most local authorities can cope with.

Whatever form residential care takes, the aim must be to meet all or as many of the needs of the mentally handicapped person and his family, the most important aspect of which is the on-demand respite care service, and as families become less able to cope, to provide local long-term care if required.

Services for mentally handicapped people with special needs

The incidence of various additional handicaps is shown in Table I. Severe mental illness will require the attention of a psychiatrist, and he is at present, in most instances, the consultant in mental handicap. This service could be provided by general psychiatrists if they were available and willing to work with mentally handicapped people.

Severe epilepsy is present in 30–35% of severely handicapped people, who will need the services of a specialist, at least from time to time in most cases, and more frequently in those who are more difficult to control. This could also be provided by general physicians and practitioners, but from past experience, such an arrangement is never very satisfactory.

Behaviour problems which are not amenable to behaviour modification or environmental change, in my experience, usually become the responsibility of the psychiatrists. However, the work of the clinical psychologist is also essential to the proper management of many severely mentally handicapped children and adults, especially those with behaviour problems. In the other handicaps listed, the National Health Service and its staff will be involved in varying degrees while in many, the main responsibility may be elsewhere, although the NHS should be available as a right when its services are required.

A question which is being continuously debated is how, where, and by whom these specialised services should be provided. Some regions are now suggesting that a specialised service for mentally handicapped people is not necessary, as the generic services can meet all these needs. This, of course, is possible in theory, but most unlikely in practice. Services for some of these disabilities are in short supply to the general population, and so would be unobtainable for mentally handicapped people in most areas if not specially provided for them.

The West Midlands Regional Health Authority have published a detailed document on the 'special services' required for mentally handicapped people, and to date have succeeded in establishing subregional units for mental illness, blind/deaf people, and a semi-secure unit for mentally handicapped people. Several other regions have also succeeded in establishing some specialist services; a blind/deaf unit, for instance, now exists in Colchester; Professor Bicknell has also established some specialist services at St Ebba's Hospital. Dr Day (1983) described a hospital-based psychiatric unit for mentally handicapped adults at Northgate Hospital, Northumberland.

Attempts at establishing a single management team

In Sheffield, the district health authority has decided that all its resources for mental handicap will be handed over to the city social services department, who will take over responsibility for the care of all mentally handicapped people.

Attempts in other parts of the country to pool resources and establish a joint management team for mental handicap services have not met with much success, however, as the treasurers have not been able to agree that the funds they allocate to the pool should be managed by an independent body, over which they will have no control.

The Sheffield proposal is, of course, a novel one, as only one authority would in fact manage the services. There are, however, a number of details which have still to be agreed, and ultimately there will be the question of who, for instance, will care for the mentally handicapped with special needs?

Transfer of funds and residents to achieve the closure of hospitals

Many district health authorities which have responsibility for mental handicap hospitals are now offering to transfer 'marginal costs' to neighbouring districts, if they will remove people from hospital who came from those districts originally. However, there are some problems which have arisen in connection with these 'marginal costs'. Most hospitals understandably are not prepared to transfer an 'average' cost, because they say, quite correctly, that not every resident costs the same. The hospital in which I work bases the marginal cost on dependency, which ranges from £2500 per annum for the least dependent to £9500 for the most dependent; it has also stated that no money will be paid until over 12 people leave the hospital, so that a ward may be closed completely. Most local and health authorities receiving people from hospital usually choose them carefully, and they are invariably from among the least dependent. There are therefore a great many problems to be solved before hospitals can be emptied, especially as no extra funds are being made available for this operation in most regions. Where it is decided to close a large hospital completely and move all the funds to provide an alternative, the problems will no doubt be of a different kind.

Conclusion

There is some evident progress in bringing about the changes in services which are generally accepted as required, but the present financial restrictions and the difference in the methods of funding between health and social services are factors which will inevitably slow up the process. It is essential, however, that these changes do not cause mentally handicapped people and their families unnecessary hardship.

References

CORBETT, J. A. (1979) Psychiatric morbidity and mental retardation. In *Psychiatric Illness and Mental Handicap* (eds. F. E. James and R. P. Snaith). London: Gaskell Books, Royal College of Psychiatrists.

DAY, K. (1983) A hospital based psychiatric unit for mentally handicapped adults. *Mental Handicap*, **11**, 137–140.

DEPARTMENT OF HEALTH AND SOCIAL SECURITY (1971) *Better Services for the Mentally Handicapped*. London: HMSO.

DEVELOPMENT TEAM FOR THE MENTALLY HANDICAPPED (1979) *Second Report, 1978–1979*. London: HMSO.

TIBBITS, J. C. N. (1978) Major mental illness in mentally handicapped adults. *Journal of the British Institute of Mental Handicap*, **6**(2), 24–26.

16 Services for the mentally handicapped

Discussion

The various presentations had given participants a 'feel' for the practical problems involved in changing from institutional care to community care for the mentally handicapped. The main question was, how was it possible to get everyone to stand up and say 'we want to go forward despite the difficulties and painful decisions involved'? The DHSS, local authorities, districts and regions had the solution in their hands; the Royal College of Psychiatrists had people who had initiated and organised services; but, it was argued, unless new money was forthcoming, the whole process could founder.

The Darenth experience

It was said to be wrong to be pessimistic about the Darenth experience. Administrative learning had taken place. Also, the project had incorporated a monitoring function which others could learn from, once the results were made available. The more that was done and passed on, the more that we could learn from each other.

The leadership of the Regional Nursing Officer in the Darenth project was emphasised: because of his contribution, no one was allowed to forget the closure plan. The determination of such individuals was a key factor in promoting the project. Similarly, contact with the local authority directors of social services was important. They were brought in from the beginning, and were able to have their say, in a collective voice. Thus, people were encouraged to apply themselves to the project. The importance of leadership in this whole area was again emphasised: the problem was, how could appropriate people be identified? Did such a person 'emerge', or was it possible to identify them at an early stage, in a more rational way?

Residential care for disturbed, severely retarded adults

The voluntary sector home was shown to be cheaper than the other community facilities, but not the hospital. However, there were conflicting ideologies in the community about what mix of residential services to provide. It was as well to remember that although the evils of institutionalisation were known, we still did not know what the evils of community care were. The pain felt by the Darenth residents, the anxiety and distress of those left behind (who did not wish to leave) should neither be forgotten nor underestimated.

The reason why the smaller homes cost about twice as much as hospital care was probably because the staffing levels were so much better in the smaller homes. In addition, all the day care and the transport were provided there, and day activities were provided by the local authority (except for the voluntary home). On the other hand, the residents in hospital had the on-site hospital facilities.

On the issue of whether any of the residents in the smaller homes had regular intensive individual treatment programmes, it appeared that some residents had, at least at some stage, received such treatment, sometimes in a small hospital unit but, in general, they did not receive such care. It was pointed out that these patients were some of the most seriously disturbed of all patients in this broad group. The question was asked whether or not some change might be expected in the less disturbed type of patient: did they do any better with such care? In reply, it was stated that not much change in the level of skills of patients was observed during the study. In the good non-hospital units, the patients were encouraged, for example, to do their own domestic work and so on. It was the quality of life and the opportunity presented rather than ability that was important.

In relation to this, it was regarded as not only quite possible, but also desirable to provide more autonomy to the staff looking after these patients — the barriers to this seemed to be largely traditional. It appeared that very few hospitals allowed staff much scope for initiative and autonomous functioning. This was said to be because 'it didn't occur to them to organise themselves in this way'.

Hospital specialist units

The forecast was made that hospital services remaining after the transition to community care would be highly specialised. In the past, mental handicap hospitals had been 'homes for life'. In the future, they would be akin to psychiatric units or acute services. Moreover, there would be a need to maintain some empty beds for crisis intervention purposes and short-term admissions.

Furthermore, there was a need to ensure that there were facilities for the behaviourally disordered and for those with forensic problems. There was a tendency to admit only 'nice' patients, and there was also a pressure to exclude certain groups of patients. It was argued that psychiatrists only had a minor role with the handicapped, but this was clearly an untenable view. Psychiatric facilities, including secured provision, were necessary for such patients.

Training of general practitioners, paediatricians, community physicians and psychiatrists

The papers and discussion raised important issues regarding the training of general practitioners in vocational training schemes. Six-month posts in hospital did not equip trainee general practitioners for the work described. There was much room for innovative six-month attachments in the community with psychiatrists and community psychiatric nurses. Joint planning between psychiatrists and those responsible for the approval of posts for vocational training seemed to be required. Young general practitioners were surprised and shocked when they saw the problems of this nature that they had to deal with in the community.

Community care for the handicapped would mean changes in the training of other types of doctor: paediatricians and community medical officers had a role, and there might be a need for general and child psychiatrists with an interest in mental handicap to be appointed to some posts. Those in other relevant medical disciplines might also have to redefine their roles to some extent. This was happening already over the country, and was particularly seen in the role of community physicians who were providing health screening services for the mentally handicapped.

It was argued that although there was a need for joint appointments, as described above, there was also a pressing need for the appointment of specialists interested primarily in the problems of the mentally handicapped. It was emphasised that these appointments should form the main body of the psychiatric input to the speciality of mental handicap. Where there were joint appointments there were split loyalties, and experience showed that mental handicap lost out under these circumstances. The need for joint appointments had arisen because there were problems with recruitment to mental handicap, but these problems had improved now.

'Normalisation'

In some regions, mental handicap services had adopted the policy of 'normalisation' without advice from psychiatrists, and in some cases there had been no discussion with the local authorities. In planning, no account had been taken of the need for beds for mentally handicapped patients with psychiatric illness, and these patients were expected, presumably, to be treated in mental hospitals, though this had not been made explicit. If there was a district mental handicap service there would undoubtedly be a need for district units for this purpose.

Estimated number of hospital beds needed for a health district of 500,000

If it were assumed that the prevalence of severe mental handicap in the community was 3 per 1,000 population (and this estimate might be low), this meant that 1.5 per 1,000 might be expected to have serious psychiatric illness, compared with about 110 per 1,000 of the non-mentally handicapped population. On this basis, it was suggested that about 2.5 beds per 1,000 population would be required for the mentally handicapped. Overall, a health district of 500,000 people could provide a comprehensive mental handicap service with 160 beds for acute patients, long-stay patients, offenders, patients needing rehabilitation, and those with severe behavioural disorders, including facilities for children.

Residential services — community units

Some speakers stressed that residential services were required for only a small section of the mentally handicapped group. Their first priority was for community units to accommodate 16 to 20 persons. In one development, such a unit consisted of four completely self-contained flats. Many such developments were taking place in large old houses. However, even with special adaptation these were sometimes unsuitable. On the whole, these developments were successful, but, of course, they did not provide for every need.

Family support services

It was maintained that insufficient consideration was given to the practical problems of families and the family support services required. It had to be remembered that nine out of ten mentally handicapped people were already living with their parents in the community. Very little reference had been made to the needs of these parents in official reports and circulars. The question remained about how the support services, which were already inadequate, were to manage when this community group was further enlarged.

The amount and pattern of support given was undoubtedly greater than 10 years ago, and the current model of home support involving practical support, financial support, counselling services, and respite care seemed satisfactory: but there was need for much more of it.

MENCAP's worries about family support were also stressed. In their view, the vast majority of the mentally handicapped were living in the community and the services were falling short of needs. A number of plans for future services were being put forward, but it was not at all clear which plan would be followed. Whatever strategic plan was accepted and put forward, it seemed likely that little would happen unless mandatory responsibility was placed upon local authorities. The present 'Byzantine' financial structures gave local authorities great opportunities not to do things. If this conference would recommend that the Government look closely at the Parliamentary Social Services Committee Report, and back mandatory action, this would help to make certain that a cohesive strategic plan for the future would be implemented.

It was pointed out by a psychiatrist that the bulk of support for the mentally handicapped was for families. Experience has shown that about 90% of the current work was done with mothers and children at home — and district-based services were needed to accomplish this work. Local community services based on small-scale units were required, with small numbers of personnel trained for this purpose. For the purposes of in-patient care, a supra-district unit might be necessary.

Making use of social security funding

Inadequate attention was said to be given to the possibilities provided by making imaginative use of the funding provided by social security. Thirty-five billion pounds of funds were currently available. A great deal of the evidence presented merely highlighted the complexities and snags of using these resources. This was a pity, because social security funds were dismissed rather than accepted as an opportunity and a challenge. The Government's views on this resource were shortly to be issued for comment: if they received the message, in return, that there were only overwhelming problems, their response might merely be to remove this 'irritation'.

Community nurses

Of the 500 or so community nurses working with the mentally handicapped around the country (and the numbers had risen from 50 in the past few years), about a half had gone through a course and were conversant with the special skills necessary for treating mentally handicapped patients. Many of these nurses were able to use behavioural modification techniques, and were going into homes and doing things that people had said could not be done in the past. Nevertheless, specialist back-up services for such developments were necessary, and districts had to consider how best to provide them.

Inadequate take-up of services

The problem of the inadequacy of take-up of services was highlighted, and this was said to be especially the case for the mentally handicapped in the community. There was a need for community services for the large numbers of mentally handicapped already treated in the community, but speakers maintained that it had to be recognised that the prevalence rates quoted by the DHSS and other sources appeared to be underestimating the problem. In addition, this prevalence was likely to increase, since the life span of the mentally handicapped was also increasing.

In this connection, allowance had to be made for the fact that of the severely mentally handicapped, 50% had psychiatric impairment, not the 11–13% quoted in Professor Simon's paper. The overall picture was not being painted, attention was only given to people given services, not the total number who were in need. And, along the same lines, education for the mentally handicapped did not stop at the age of seven. After this age, educational aid was only provided if services were requested. If there was no demand, the need was neglected.

The extent of the true need was reflected in the numbers of patients found 'underneath the arches' and in the prison population. There was an underestimation of need, both at the top end and at the bottom end of the scale.

It was pointed out that the percentage of mentally handicapped patients with psychiatric disorder referred to by Professor Simon only referred to psychotic illness; when lesser degrees of psychiatric disturbance were included, the percentage indeed rose. A psychiatric unit for such patients had recently opened in the West Midlands, partly because it was so difficult to get general psychiatrists to admit such patients to mental hospitals. The unit had been in existence for about two years, and the 18 beds had a turnover period of about nine months.

Problems of mixing short-term and long-term patients in community units

A question was raised about whether or not there were problems about mixing together children for whom the community unit had become a home with those who required intermittent care — severely disturbed mentally handicapped children who required interim provision, the so-called 'home wreckers'? The response was that these patients were sometimes admitted to community units in the short-term, though the time scale was relative, sometimes the admission might last for nine months. Some of these children then turned out to need long-term care. It was important to note that such children did get better and might be discharged at a later date. They were admitted if it appeared to be essential, and if the community unit was thought to be able to cope with them.

The National Development Team

The role of the National Development Team was queried, and, in particular, whether or not this would change in view of the various findings described. In College approval exercises, it was the educational policy of the College which was at issue, not personal views: was this also the case for the National Development Team? In reply, it was stated that the National Development Team made their comments on the basis of previously decided policy. The view had been taken that such teams were there to give guidance, to listen and to try to persuade professionals to change their views, if this appeared to be appropriate. A permissive approach was adopted, but if it appeared that professionals were 'going down the wrong road', it was equally necessary to be frank in criticism. It was hoped that, in the future, the National Development Team would take a problem-solving rather than an inspection-minded role.

Services for the multiply handicapped and the sensorily deprived mentally handicapped

The vexed issue of providing services for those with multiple handicaps and the sensorily deprived mentally handicapped was raised. It was generally agreed that this group had been neglected. Nevertheless, experience had shown that it was possible to care for such patients in small-scale homely units. Funds had been provided for such children and adults, it was true, but it had to be recognised that these were amongst the most severely handicapped of all patients. The special needs of this group constituted a problem that the DHSS should be giving urgent attention to, it was stated.

There were not thought to be enough services for these patients, though, in fact, they could do exceptionally well. There was a hostel for the blind, the residential charges for which were met by the British Institute for the Blind. Such facilities should be developed in every region. The number of day places and special units could be estimated, and it should be borne in mind that some of these patients were capable of living in sighted facilities without specialist help at all. Thereafter, another problem was that it was often difficult to find places for them to progress on to.

Prospects for community care under resource constraint

It appeared that the accumulated wisdom presented at the conference and in the Parliamentary Social Services Committee Report all pointed in the direction that there was unanimous commitment to the development of community services. However, it was found necessary to state, yet again, that more money was needed to do this properly. In the meantime, professionals would be required to do the best they could without such resources. Much had been heard about national policy, but there was wide scope for experimental approaches and evaluation at the local level. It was important to document these activities and share the accumulated information.

There still remained serious doubt about what were the right services. National policy for the closure of mental hospitals should not proceed until the current services were adequately researched and that was a prior task to the development of new services. The directives from Central Government also needed to have more punch—and this depended upon the documentation of current efforts and impressing ministers of the current great deficiencies in health and social provision.

Hospital facilities for children with mental handicap

It was reported that in the North-West Region no children with mental handicap were to be admitted to hospital. There were apparently to be no special beds for the handicapped in that region at all. The National Development Team was invited to advise, but had made few comments. No one at the present conference had suggested that it was possible to run a service in this way. The policy appeared to fly in the face of experience, and it was uncertain what could be done to influence matters.

In response to these remarks, it was stated that there appeared to be some misunderstanding by psychiatrists about regional policy in the North-West regarding mental handicap. The major drive was that people should live wherever it appeared that they were most appropriately placed. There was no barrier to hospital treatment for those that required it—there were hospital beds if they were required. However, it was often possible to provide nursing care when this was required outside hospital.

It was repeated that specialist psychiatric services were needed for children and adults with mental handicap, and that there was a high prevalence of psychiatric disorder in this population—was it being argued that this problem did not exist? If this was the case, the evidence should be provided. Some services appeared to be going along on the assumption that they did not need such psychiatric facilities for the mentally handicapped. What was going to happen if they were required? This problem had to be tested. It should be possible to evaluate the effect of a hospital-based service against a purely community-based service. This would be the only way that the problem could be settled. Otherwise there would be no place for the most difficult and unattractive patients to go. Community care would be compromised if provision was not made for such patients.

Amalgamation of mental handicap with other medical units

In some districts, general managers were considering amalgamating mental handicap and mental illness units into one unit, with one leader. Alternatively, mental handicap might be linked with some other medical discipline. Was this a good idea? Experience had shown that when mental handicap services were linked with other services, mental handicap came out of such arrangements the worse off every time. Mental handicap had to fight for its share of the budget at every turning. It was said to be stretching imagination to think that uncommitted people would argue for wallpaper on mental handicap house walls when there were competing demands for operating theatre air-conditioning or kidney machines.

17 Multidisciplinary and consumer views

**TESSA JOWELL; JAMES ROSS;
CHRIS CULLEN; PETER MELLOR;
BEN ESSEX; STUART ETHERINGTON**

1. Tessa Jowell (MIND— National Association for Mental Health)

The overriding reason for developing policies for the community care of mentally ill people is to enrich, not diminish, the quality and potential of their lives. However, the volume of rhetoric about community care has been disproportionate to the amount of achievement. Effective community care presupposes access by a mentally ill person to a range of services which support and enhance his or her citizenship, and offers the opportunity for satisfying social relationships and a socially valued life style. Service planning should start, therefore, by seeking to implement these objectives.

The radical re-casting of our mental health services will be achieved only by effective partnership between the major agents of care—the statutory health and local authority services, the voluntary sector, and, increasingly, the private sector of care. Accountability and monitoring of standards of care are crucial in each sector. While these standards should be relatively easy to establish in the public sector, they are much more difficult to establish consistently in the voluntary and private sectors of care.

The general rule which the development of district-based mental health services must observe is to give absolute priority to the most disabled—people whose mental illness has become of a chronic and severely handicapping form. Against this general background, what is the key role of the voluntary sector in developing district-based mental health services? There are three major functions: as innovator, as advocate, and as service provider.

Innovation

Voluntary organisations must be provided with the freedom and the resources to set-up, run, monitor and evaluate low-cost projects which develop, demonstrate and disseminate alternative methods of support for mentally ill people and their families.

Advocacy

The voluntary sector represents, publicly, politically and professionally, the needs for service improvement for mentally ill people and their families. In acting as an advocate, the voluntary sector can represent collectively or individually the needs and wishes of mentally ill people and their families.

Service provision

Voluntary organisations can complement the service provision of the statutory services. MIND's local associations have a fine tradition in this regard, through the development of group homes and other forms of supported accommodation and day services.

Clearly, present Government policies in relation to local authority spending pose grave threats to the partnership between statutory and voluntary sector. Too often the constraints imposed by financial stringency on local authorities is misinterpreted as reluctance to collaborate by health service staff. This is profoundly destructive of the essential partnership which is crucial for the effective planning and development of locally-based services for mentally ill people and their families.

2. James Ross (MENCAP—Royal Society for Mentally Handicapped Children and Adults)

Since MENCAP gave evidence to the House of Commons Parliamentary Social Services Committee enquiring into community care for mentally handicapped people in May 1984, we have had the opportunity of examining many of the regional health authority and district health authority strategic plans which have been prepared at the request of the DHSS. We have also looked at the local authority plans — where they exist — in an attempt to measure what has been the response to central government policy by the authorities responsible for providing services for mentally handicapped people.

MENCAP — an organisation founded by parents for parents — has good reason to be worried about the findings from these recent enquiries. To emphasise the point, I refer to this year, 1985. I stress this year because we have to set MENCAP's position in the context of Government policy, promises, plans and priorities over the past 15 years, since the publication of the White Paper, *Better Services for the Mentally Handicapped*.

Thousands of parents have died bitterly disappointed that they have not lived to see Government promises implemented. Many parents grow old, forced to accept inappropriate care for their mentally handicapped children, and many die suffering the agony and torture of inappropriate facilities and the shortages of services provided for mentally handicapped people. The vast majority of parents are desperately worried about the future for their sons and daughters. Few parents see signs of the services or the kind of care they want.

The lack of progress

The law was changed in 1959 in order to launch the great new concept of 'community care'. Unfortunately little happened during the next 10 years. In fact it was 12 years later, when Central Government produced the 1971 White Paper, *Better Services for the Mentally Handicapped*. The overall aim was to develop co-ordinated health and social services in each locality, and to advise a major shift from institutional health care, according to individual needs, with increasing responsibilities and resources for local authorities. The programme was envisaged to be implemented over a period of about 20 years. The 'half-term' report (*Mental Handicap: Progress, Problems and Priorities*) at the end of 1980 was prepared by a team of officials from the DHSS. Chapter 10 of this report, in particular, confirms MENCAP's disappointment and the enormous problems experienced by parents coping at home — struggling to get help and support.

Ten years on, progress had been pathetically slow and in some areas there had been little or no progress. In some areas health and local authorities have completely ignored Central Government policy. MENCAP asks: What has Central Government done about it? What are they doing about health and local authorities who ignore the needs of mentally handicapped people? Fifteen years on, in 1985, what has happened? The clarion call of the DHSS has gone out again, and mammoth amounts of money and staff resources are being used to produce yet another set of strategic plans. Three-quarters of the way through a 20-year plan — and we are still planning.

Parents are sick and tired of hearing about plans. MENCAP appeals to Central Government and the statutory authorities responsible for the provision of services to put the plans into operation. We are pleased to see that the recent Parliamentary Social Services Committee Report confirms our view: 'The stage has now been reached when the rhetoric of community care has to be matched by action'.

Of course, progress has been made in some areas, and we are pleased to recognise and pay tribute to the commitment and determination shown in the places where services have improved. But they are few and far between. Ministers, and those writing conference papers, often quote the same examples — because there are so few models of good practice. MENCAP has good evidence and good reason to be concerned about the lack of progress.

Lack of resources

Parents are deeply worried about the deterioration in both the quantity and quality of services. MENCAP has a large network of local groups where the lack of family support is felt, most of all, by parents. I have, regretfully, to report to this Conference that parents do not, and are not, receiving improved family support service. According to the policy papers on care in the community, family support services have the highest priority. The fact is that they are extremely sparse, except in a few areas.

According to a DHSS review in 1980, 'up to nine-tenths of severely mentally handicapped children now live at home'. But the Parliamentary Social Services Committee Report provides undeniable evidence that health and local authorities fail to provide the help and support families need. These fears of parents are increased as we read in reports from the Association of Directors of Social Services on community care who: '. . . draw attention to the growing sense of crisis which is emerging from many local authorities in relation to the planning and funding of these services'. Later in their report to the Parliamentary Social Services Committee, they go on to say:

The ADSS attempts to draw attention . . . to the growing sense of financial crisis which is seriously undermining the development of community care services. . . . There is a growing sense of crisis in relation to the mechanism for funding much-needed service developments essential for care in the community — Joint Financing. This sense of crisis is exacerbating a widening range of variation between the levels of service that are available in one area of the country and another, and often between one part of an authority's area and another.

Parents have good reason to be extremely worried about the lack of resources. The list of shortages is enormous — from the desperate lack of respite care and residential provision through to the alarming dearth of trained professional people in most areas — health visitors, social workers, community nurses, special therapists, psychologists and residential care staff.

The response to our enquiries to health districts and local authorities clearly shows that they are seriously underfunded to provide the services envisaged in the Government's community care programme.

Lack of joint planning

According to the National Association of Health Authorities: 'The planning and management of community care requires close collaboration and co-operation between many individuals and agencies. Therefore, *joint planning* and *commitment* on the part of officers and members of health and local authorities and members of voluntary groups is seen by the Association as being essential.' As we compare that statement, and we fully agree with it, with the Association of Directors of Social Services' report, you will understand why parents are deeply worried.

The Association of Directors of Social Services says:

In some parts of the country strategic planning initiatives are being pursued by regional health authorities, without the full involvement of the local authorities who will be directly affected by the plans produced. In some such areas health authorities are pursuing detailed plans to establish community-based systems of care for people who are disabled by mental handicap or chronic mental illness, without any significant development of community-based services by the involvement of the local authority.

The fact that such plans appear to be implemented with the approval of regional health authorities highlights the need for a structured, collaborative and integrated planning and decision-making arrangement.

There is a danger of services being developed in a competitive rather than a collaborative way.

The consumers — mentally handicapped people and their families — have good reasons to be alarmed when they are at the receiving end of this conflict. The lack of joint planning must be of very real concern to all of us.

Lack of legal direction

Finally, I want to draw attention to what we in MENCAP, in consultation with thousands of parents throughout the country, see as the major problem. It is the lack of legal direction or, to put it more clearly, the failure of the Government to strengthen its policy with mandatory responsibilities.

MENCAP believes that community care and all that it implies in resources and services for mentally handicapped people must be legally enforceable. Current legislation allows individual authorities to respond as and when they choose — if they choose to at all. All the evidence proves this is unsatisfactory, and the people who suffer most are the mentally handicapped people and their families. Can we, and should we, allow health and local authorities to decide for themselves whether or not to accept and to implement Central Government policy on community care for mentally handicapped people? MENCAP believes this to be the most important question in this context.

Is it right to allow the decision as to whether or not community care policy is implemented to be at the whim of local politicians, on the one hand, and to the interest or commitment of health authority members on the other?

MENCAP believes that this is the enormous cost we cannot and never should ask mentally handicapped people to bear.

I finish by quoting what a father said to me the other week. He is a civil servant and in his mid-forties:

> My wife and I are both worn-out with caring for our 22-year-old mentally handicapped son. We are emotionally drained; we are socially isolated, and we struggle to meet all the extra costs. We have had to fight for everything and we have little left to fight with. What is to happen to our son? We worry constantly about the future.

3. Chris Cullen (British Psychological Society)

It has been pointed out during the conference by several speakers that, since community services are already in existence and in many places are considered to be insufficient to meet the needs of people leaving long-stay hospitals, as well as those people living in the community, the emphasis ought to be on improving community services rather than replacing them. The basic axiom of service delivery is that more important than where a person lives is what happens to the person. This is not to deny the importance of the appropriate siting of services and dwelling places, but is to assert that simply moving people from one place to another does not result in a better service. There is obviously a relationship between the kind of service which can be delivered and the place in which it is delivered, but there is an important need for research into patterns of care. It is not enough to hope that value statements alone will result in good services — what is needed are clear statements of objectives and the contingencies whereby those objectives will be realised and maintained.

What is the current pattern of service delivery? In general, residential services, hospitals and hostels vary little in their practices from area to area. Without going into too much detail, of which plenty is available in the literature, residencies range from appalling through the stunningly mediocre to the occasionally good. On the whole, though, we have very little to be proud of.

Day services are similarly variable, although the common pattern of occupying mentally handicapped adults with demeaning, boring tasks still prevails. It has never been clear to me what value a mentally handicapped man gains from sitting flicking through last year's copy of *Woman's Own* or an out-of-date catalogue.

Parental support is acceptable in some areas and non-existent in others. I work with a number of families and I am acutely aware of my inadequacies in providing the kind of of psychological advice they need. Sometimes we are successful and problems are overcome. At other times we are not, and the necessity for increasing our professional sophistication is emphasised. What is needed to change this level of service? The answers are undoubtedly complex, as many speakers throughout the conference have emphasised. One thing, though, seems to have become clear, and this is that we have to become rather more sophisticated and stop relying on rhetoric and platitudinal statements. The following directions will be worth pursuing·

(i) We are in danger of slipping into the belief that mentally handicapped people can be cared for by a deprofessionalised service. Some people seem to believe that large numbers of mentally handicapped people need only the opportunities and they will develop, normally, a multitude of new skills. There is no doubt that increasing opportunities is crucial and often results in a person being able to engage in an activity which he or she has previously been prevented from doing by circumstances. There are, though, many disadvantaged people who will need professional help from skilled care staff to develop appropriate behavioural and social repertoires. These range from basic self-care routines through to activities such as job finding, using normal leisure facilities, claiming welfare rights, and so on. It will not be enough to hope that simply allowing people the opportunity to do these things will be sufficient. This mistake has been made in the United States.

Andrew Scull (1981) has pointed out that asserting a person's negative rights, i.e., specifying those things they do not have to do, is relatively easy. For example, we can easily assert that people do not have to attend day centres, they do not have to live in hospitals, and they do not have to have their lives regulated by someone else. The end result of a service plan which revolves around the assertion of negative rights is a population which is at the mercy of those in society who are more capable and who can take advantage of opportunities. Scull points out that much more important, but also much harder to achieve, is the assertion of positive rights; that is, the setting up of a social system in which people receive from society services which are appropriate to their needs.

(ii) It is this latter problem which should be exercising the minds of service providers and service planners. How can we set up management systems within services which will insist on the implementation of individual programme plans rather than concentrate on trivial things, such as whether the linen cupboards are tidy or the beds made? How can we ensure that mentally ill and mentally handicapped people will receive the services of a clinical psychologist or a social worker or a psychiatrist when they are needed? How can we prevent the all too common situation where disadvantaged people do not receive medical and dental care of the same high calibre as more influential members of the community? Further, how are we going to develop professional skills so that we

implement procedures of known effectiveness to help handicapped people acquire adaptive and desired behavioural and social repertoires?
(iii) It is clear that research is needed to enable us to set up good services. There are very few examples of Government spending on the scale of health and social services where procedures are not evaluated. What, though, is the evidence that a full-scale closure of long-stay institutions is going to result in a better standard of life for mentally handicapped and mentally ill people? A few pilot projects exist, often with rather inconclusive results, but we are contemplating here a massive social movement which demands a more thorough research basis than it has so far received. The Government has set up a small research project to evaluate some community care schemes in different parts of the country whilst, at the same time, pre-empting the possibility of their findings having much influence on public policy by going ahead anyway with the hospital closure programme. It is to be hoped that the advice of the Parliamentary Select Committee is heeded.

In the 1950s and 1960s a comparable social problem was tackled. It was widely agreed that the slum areas of our cities were disgraceful and something had to be done. The proposed solutions of building tower blocks and huge housing estates miles from the cities resulted in the destruction of communities and the alienation of old and young alike. The problems we have now of vandalism and psychological and psychiatric disorders are, in part, a consequence of this ill-considered massive social programme. I hope that we are not making a similar mistake in our desire to close out-of-date Victorian institutions.

To pursue these avenues will require concerted action on a multi-disciplinary basis. It will not be sufficient to hand over resources to a single agency. Table I of John Chant's paper (page 19) makes it clear that the structure and organisation of health and social services are so different that the likelihood of them being able to work together in any meaningful way is very small. Since local authorities do not have a history of a multidisciplinary approach to care, a new and major initiative will be needed to enable various professional disciplines to make a proper contribution. That initiative must come from Central Government and, until this nettle is grasped, the danger will remain of a fragmented service; a badly co-ordinated service; and, in the final analysis, an inadequate service.

Reference

SCULL, A. (1981) The institutionalisation and the rights of the deviant. *Journal of Social Issues*, **37**, 6–20.

4. Peter Mellor (Society of Psychiatric Nursing, Royal College of Nursing)

Less than 5% of all psychiatric nurses work in community services. This small proportion represents 10% of all qualified psychiatric nurses and 15% of all registered mental nurses. There are clear implications from these percentages for the ratio between trained and untrained staff in the provision of nursing care in institutions.

There are still considerable variations in both the size and structure of community psychiatric nursing services and, in addition to those nurses who are part of a community nursing unit of management, there are other psychiatric nurses working in specialist units who spend the major part of their time working in the community. This is particularly evident in units for children and adolescents and from secure units. Those involved with substance abuse and care of the elderly mentally ill may work either in a specialist unit or within the general community team. This latter group of community psychiatric nurses comprise the greatest proportion of those in specialist practice.

Although community nursing services are an integral part of the total psychiatric services, many are now at least partially attached to health-centres and general practitioners. The Royal College of Nursing does, however, believe that the management of community psychiatric nursing services should remain as part of the overall psychiatric nursing service, on the grounds that the knowledge base of all the staff in the service is primarily psychiatric nursing. This issue is important in the context of the increasing run-down of psychiatric hospitals. Whilst most services formally operate on a 9am–5pm basis from Monday to Friday, there are both formal and informal developments outwith this framework.

Referral patterns also vary, with hospital-based services tending to be more restrictive. The Royal College of Nursing is frequently involved in advising in conflicts where consultant psychiatrists wish to restrict a more open referral system; however, our College's advice is that the referral pattern is and must be a nursing decision, and will be based on skills available within the nursing teams and manpower ability to cope with additional demands. Further variables within services include direct access to short-term beds and, in some parts of the country, a need to provide support to the private sector.

With the anticipation of increases in community psychiatric nursing services, our College has noted with interest the comments and recommendations of the Parliamentary Social Services Committee Report. Whilst most of the regional strategic plans refer to the development of community psychiatric nursing services, there are considerable assumptions about the ability and/or willingness of psychiatric nurses working in the community.

Very little reference is made to the need, in some places, to make provision for relocation of staff.

At present there is a financial disincentive to working as a community psychiatric nurse, not so much in terms of the psychiatric lead and superannuation status, as referred to by the Parliamentary Social Services Committee, but more in respect of the loss of special duty payments, which can lead to a loss of up to 15% of gross salary.

Nursing education is likely to change significantly over the next decade with, hopefully, a much stronger commitment to community care, especially in the basic training of psychiatric nurses. A new specialist syllabus for community psychiatric nurses, which is much more directed towards skills training, has now been produced by the English National Board for Nursing, Health Visiting and Midwifery. The Royal College of Nursing in principle supports the concept of mandatory training for community psychiatric nurses, but recognises the practical problems associated with the idea. Currently, less than 25% of all community psychiatric nurses have undertaken the English National Board post-basic course (or its Joint Board of Clinical Nursing Studies predecessor). Even if a specific date were to be set for all new entrants to community psychiatric nursing, the lead-in time for those currently in service would probably take some 15 years, at least.

What will be important over the next few years will be that community psychiatric nurses evaluate their work to a much greater extent. The need to assess and quantify the value of nursing interventions is likely to assume even greater significance in the post-Griffiths era.

Finally, on the consequences of being a priority service, I can do no better than quote a friend and colleague, Jim McIntegart, Director of Nursing Services in Canterbury: 'If what we have received over the past decade or so is the consequence of being a priority service, then the sooner some other parts of the health service become priorities and we move out — the better.'

5. *Ben Essex (Royal College of General Practitioners)*

Caring for people with chronic mental illness is a life-long commitment. It involves patients, families, health personnel and voluntary carers in a continuing responsibility. These patients have physical, psychological, social, and occupational needs which can only be met if all concerned are able to plan how to make the best use of scarce resources. This means that district planners and general practitioners (GPs) have to: identify needs of patients and relatives; identify goals which are acceptable, feasible, and measurable; identify available resources; select cost-effective options; plan and organise care efficiently and effectively; and evaluate outcomes.

There is now general acceptance of the idea that mentally ill patients should be transferred from hospital into the community for long-term care. However, there is no agreement on how this can best be achieved, as the problems differ greatly from one district to another.

Variations between districts

The great variations between districts make it difficult for one district to learn from the success or failure of another. Transfer of care from hospital to community will be affected by the following factors which differ in each district: objectives; resources presently available, i.e. hospital, community (workshops, day centres, housing, hostels) and personnel; needs; demands on services; time limits; budget (available now, proposed for the future, and transfer of funds from health sector to social services); private sector involvement; priorities; and political decisions. All these variables interact with each other and change over time. Planning needs to take this into account at every stage.

Asking the right questions

Planners need to ask a series of 'what if' questions in order to decide how to implement the new policy in the most effective way. Such questions include: (i) What are the financial implications if closure takes place over different time periods? (ii) What personnel and resources are needed if those patients presently receiving occupational therapy in hospital are to continue to receive it in the community? (iii) What extra out-patient facilities will be needed by psychiatrists if differing numbers of chronic schizophrenics are transferred to the community? (iv) What back-up hospital services will be needed if x number of families caring for patients are to be given short-term admission facilities once, twice, or more times a year? (v) What community and hospital resources will be needed if x % of elderly parents presently looking after their mentally ill offspring, will not be doing so in five or ten years' time? (vi) What are the implications for manpower and training if follow-up care is to be provided by GPs or community psychiatric nurses (CPNs). (vii) What problems may arise if decisions about x precede decisions about y?

These are examples of the sort of 'what if' questions that need to be asked before making important decisions about the transfer of care from hospital to community.

Computer assistance

There are two ways in which computer technology can help us. First, computer simulations can help to answer a wide range of 'what if' questions, enabling decision makers to identify the possible outcomes when different assumptions are made about goals, resources, and time. Such methods are widely used in business management, defence, economics, and operations research. It is now time such techniques were applied to increase the effectiveness of planning within the health service.

The second way in which computers can be of use is in helping us to learn from each other. Much experience has already been gained by different regions in planning the transfer of care from hospital to community. However, this is not readily available to those about to start such programmes. There is an urgent need to record the advantages and disadvantages of different approaches to facilitate learning from the experience of others.

This sort of data needs to be centralised to enable it to be immediately accessible and continuously updated. Its availability could decrease the costly repetition of planning errors and omissions, and enable the multidisciplinary groups of professionals to learn with and from each other. This is a most appropriate use of computer technology and could provide a feasible and cost-effective aid for planning teams throughout the country.

Deciding what to do

When patients with chronic mental illness are discharged from hospital to community, they need long-term care and follow-up. They are registered with a general practitioner who is responsible for continuous provision of medical services to all patients registered with the practice. This may involve many members of the primary care team, including GP, CPN, social worker, health visitor, and occupational therapist.

The first question that must be asked is: What are we trying to do? Our management objectives are to: (i) identify all psychotic patients in the practice population; (ii) prevent disability in the patient, stress in the family, self-injury, institutionalisation in the community, default, relapse, failure of compliance with treatment, and breakdown of family or social supports; (iii) identify needs of patient and family; (iv) provide management that is acceptable, cost-effective and capable of meeting needs that change over time; (v) reduce stress in patient and family; (vi) maintain occupational functioning; (vii) identify early signs of relapse; (viii) educate patient, relatives and other voluntary carers in long-term management, alongside members of the primary care team; (ix) ensure good communication between all involved in patient care; and (x) evaluate outcomes.

Who does what?

After deciding what needs to be done, the next task is to decide who should do it. Because the provision of long-term care is multidisciplinary, it is

Background details (name, details about relatives, consultant, addresses, admission and discharge dates, diagnosis, present disabilities, special needs)

Work Prognosis
At-risk groups
Lives alone
Single parent
Little family support
Young children
Housing problems
Poor compliance
Multiple admissions
Multiple relapses
History of self-injury
Drug/alcohol addiction

Discharge to:
Family
Hostel
Part III
Sheltered accommodation
Other

Management responsibilities

Management	Relatives	GP	CPN	Social worker	Health visitor	OT	Voluntary carers	Psychiatrist	Psychologist
Medication									
Family support									
Follow-up									
Retraining									
Rehabilitation									
Behavioural therapy									
Occupational therapy									
Day centre									
Default follow-up									

Next Follow-up (person, place, date)
Medication (details)
Information (given to patient and relatives)
Outcome(s) (date, observations, personnel)

Fig. 1 — Model of a co-operation card

essential to allocate responsibilities for different tasks amongst members of the primary care team. The use of a co-operation card (Fig. 1) helps us to identify who does what.

Lack of resources

Some of the difficulties that make it impossible to provide effective community care at present include: (i) lack of resources, such as hostels, homes, day centre placements, and occupational therapy; (ii) shortage of personnel, e.g. CPNs and occupational therapists; (iii) inadequate short-term readmission facilities; (iv) poor communication between GPs and others involved in care, including psychiatrists, CPNs and relatives; and (v) absence of practice disease registers, without which long-term follow-up and evaluation are impossible.

Rationing

Communication can be improved; practice registers can be created, but lack of resources means rationing. At present, resources are just not sufficient to enable us to meet the needs of all our patients. Psychotic patients known to the practice and rarely admitted to hospital are in direct competition for scarce resources with those recently discharged from long-term hospital care. Uncomfortable questions must therefore be asked. Who should get a day centre place or receive occupational therapy when so few places are available? Which patients should be assigned to the community psychiatric nurse? Who should be routinely visited by the GP when they default from follow-up or therapy? Who should get priority for the few short-stay readmission beds?

The present 'first-come first-served' policy is unacceptable. Care should be provided on the basis of need. The criteria for establishing this must be made explicit, and should be selected with maximum consumer participation. They might include such things as age, severity of disability, presence of dependants, amount of family support, accommodation, prognosis, risk factors, previous response to treatment, amount of stress in family, statutory duties, etc. Rationing must be seen to be fair. We must enable patient groups such as MIND and the National Schizophrenia Fellowship to participate in selecting the criteria used to allocate scarce resources and identify priority groups.

Working together

Co-operation cards are now widely used to improve communication between GPs, hospital specialists, and others involved in shared care for certain groups of patients e.g., in antenatal care and diabetic patients. What might be the advantages of using such a co-operation card for patients with serious long-term psychiatric disorders? It would enable all those involved in shared care to: (i) identify at-risk patients, the needs of patient and family, dependencies, and management objectives; (ii) allocate responsibilities; (iii) indicate what services have been mobilised; (iv) improve communication between hospital and community personnel; and (v) evaluate outcomes.

A card designed to facilitate these tasks might contain the sort of information shown in Fig. 1. Such a card is a prerequisite for working together efficiently and effectively. It helps us to allocate responsibilities and audit the quality of long-term care.

Evaluating outcomes

The Royal College of General Practitioners is committed to a policy of audit in which GPs assess the quality of care they are providing. This is especially important for patients who have chronic illnesses which require long-term care and follow-up. The first step is to define measurable goals. It then becomes possible to identify whether or not these have been achieved.

In order to find out how well we are caring for these patients we must try to answer the following questions: (i) Have we identified all patients in the practice with past or present psychotic illnesses? (ii) How many patients are on long-term medication? (iii) How many have defaulted from treatment? (iv) How many relapses could have been identified and treated earlier, perhaps avoiding readmission? (v) Is the co-operation card providing the data it is designed to record? (vi) Are allocated responsibilities and tasks being carried out effectively? (vii) Are patients allocated to day centres or occupational therapy receiving these services? (viii) Do families feel they are getting adequate support?

The concept of audit as an integral part of general practice is new. Yet it has profound implications for teachers, trainers, and course organisers responsible for vocational training. The challenge is to motivate young general practitioners to see the care of the mentally ill as an exciting and challenging task utilising all the skills upon which good general practice is based.

6. Stuart Etherington (British Association of Social Workers; Director, Good Practices in Mental Health Project)

The recent industrial dispute over the implementation of the approved social worker within the Mental Health Act and the loss of specialist mental health skills are now well documented, and I do not need to emphasise the problems which this has caused within social work itself. Perhaps, against this backdrop, it is even more problematic to make out a case for social work intervention with mentally ill people, and to suggest that this is a distinctive contribution within a new community mental health service. However, this is what I intend to do.

I will argue that the social work task relates to three areas. In this I do not want to confine social work purely to local authority social service provision, although inevitably this will play an important role.

There are three primary tasks for social work with mentally ill people. The first of these is to do with case planning, the second with advocacy, and the third with counselling. In some of these areas there may be a functional overlap with other professional groups. For example, most groups working with mentally ill people would argue that they provide some form of counselling service.

Case planning or case management

When mentally ill people spent a considerable amount of time within psychiatric hospitals, the accountability for the care that they received was clear. Services were being provided in one place by several groups of professionals. With community care representing care from a variety of sources, this single accountability for services is no longer appropriate. Indeed, as we try to 'normalise' the services to people with long-term psychiatric problems, we are in fact dictating that services should be provided from a number of different areas. We receive services from a number of different sources. Our housing is provided from one source, leisure activities from a variety of sources, work from another, and so on. This is fine, except where there is a level of vulnerability and a possibility of exploitation.

Not only are a variety of different types of resource involved, but these are also provided by different areas of welfare (voluntary, statutory and private). Co-ordinating packages of care therefore becomes more important in the community mental health service than it is in an institutional service.

Given an increase in pluralism, both in service providers and types of service, we could do worse than reflect on North American experience in co-ordinating discharge policies. In relation to this, case planning or case management has become of crucial importance. Essentially, a case planner co-ordinates a variety of services following an initial assessment. It is his or her job to monitor the effectiveness of the service provision and to ensure that the clients are satisfied with the services that they are receiving. So individual assessment, planning and evaluation fall primarily on those involved in case management.

This task could well be performed by a social worker. The social workers' basic training equips them to understand well the variety of service provision available. However, a problem that faces social workers in fulfilling this role is their organisational position. From outside the health service, it is difficult for them to co-ordinate services which are primarily health service resources. One of the changes that will be necessary to enhance this role for social workers will be to provide more social workers within the health service, and perhaps, eventually, a combination of health and social service provision.

Advocacy

Since the passing of the new Mental Health Act, considerable emphasis has been placed upon the rights of mentally ill people. Of course rights do not only relate to the legal position of mentally ill people, nor only to their representation in front of tribunals. Welfare rights advice and information is an essential part of the comprehensive mental health service: indeed, income support provides for one of the basic needs faced by people being discharged from hospital. There are many projects which involve advocacy work both in the strict legal sense and in the broader welfare rights sense. Social workers have played a leading role, particularly in the latter.

A problem for social work in this area is its association with service provision. It may be difficult for those who are responsible for planning and co-ordinating services to also advocate on a client's behalf. Social workers who wish to perform advocacy tasks may best do so from outside the statutory services. Clearly, the change in role from mental welfare officer to approved social worker has an impact upon this situation. The need for the approved social worker to become aware of local resources and to suggest alternatives to hospital admission would tend to describe the social workers action, even at the point of crisis, as being one more related to case planning than to advocacy. Several advocacy projects are based in citizens advice bureaux. Advice and information workers in this setting may prove to be better suited to advocacy; though some social workers may also wish to become involved in this work as a primary activity, since the interpersonal skills which they possess may be of value to clients suffering from mental disorder.

Counselling

Social workers do not have a monopoly on counselling skills. General practitioners, community psychiatric nurses, psychiatrists, occupational therapists and others all claim some counselling expertise. This is acknowledged in several post-qualification courses; and within psychiatric nursing, one course particularly equips nurse therapists to use behaviour modification techniques. The crucial issue is to clarify for the client who is providing this service.

Undoubtedly, some form of multidisciplinary approach is best in the assessment of a particular client's needs. But the appointment of key workers to work with clients over time is also important. Any team, or loose therapeutic network, needs to be sure that key workers are appointed with declared and agreed responsibilities. The main problem in developing a community mental health service may not be in deciding upon the desirability or otherwise of providing services outside of institutions, it may well be in clarifying the confusion amongst professionals as to what their individual roles should be.

Social work has a role to play in developing community services for mentally ill people. It will be clear from what I have said that the most important role that I see emerging is that of case planner or case manager. This is certainly prescribed by the Barclay Report (National Institute for Social Work, 1982) on the roles and tasks of social workers, and their training equips them well to undertake this particular form of care. Other roles and tasks may be performed by other professionals, but I would argue that the case management role is crucial in the development of service provision, and is one which social work must perform.

It is necessary to consider the detailed staffing requirements of the new services and to put both in-service and external training to work to ensure that professionals are able to develop their roles along commonly agreed lines. More work has been done on this aspect of mental handicap than in mental illness services. In mental handicap there are now joint nursing and social work courses at post-qualification level; and in mental handicap, in the long term, there may be no distinction between the roles of nurses and social workers. Nursing is moving to encompass a more socially oriented role, seeing the actual provision of nursing care as something which is incidental to the role of care workers for mentally handicapped people. With maintenance medication being required by mentally ill people, the nursing role in this area may still remain a distinctive one; although it is likely to develop also to encompass counselling. What is necessary, however, is that professionals clarify the roles that they are performing within the new services and reach agreement on aims and objectives with individual clients.

The Good Practices in Mental Health Project

The Good Practices in Mental Health (GPMH) Project was established in 1977 by the International Hospital Federation in order to discover what local initiatives were being undertaken in mental health services. To date, there have been some 50 local studies which have detailed good practice initiatives in existence. Although the service has expanded and the Project has now become an independent charity, the basic method remains the same. Local professionals and volunteers draw together in a core group to examine local mental health services. The core group holds a 'springboard' meeting where particular projects, both large and small, identify themselves as potential good practices. The core group then appoints an information gatherer who writes up descriptions of the projects. Projects are then selected for inclusion in the final which is published, and which provides a local information resource. The process of the GPMH study not only creates a resource, but also enables local professionals and volunteers to draw together to focus on good practice. The resulting local communication networks are also useful once the study is completed.

The local studies are then collected together to produce a national information bank. Currently, GPMH possesses some 7,000 items of information which describe good practices in mental health services. This information service is available to practitioners and planners in the mental health services. GPMH is able to provide information either on single projects or on a particular dimension of service delivery. In addition to the information service, the Project also provides information packs on particular aspects of mental health services. A housing and day care pack are currently in production, and future packs will include a pack on advocacy, services for the elderly mentally infirm, primary health care and community psychiatric nursing. The Project also produces a bi-annual newsletter which describes current developments in service provision. Details of the information service or advice on how to start a local study is available from Good Practices in Mental Health Project, 380–384 Harrow Road, London W9 2HU (telephone: 01-289 2034).

Reference

NATIONAL INSTITUTE FOR SOCIAL WORK (1982) *Social Workers: Their Roles and Tasks.* London: Bedford Square Press.

18 Problems in community care

Discussion

Fragmentation of services for individuals

The crucial issue appeared to be the fragmentation of services which were designed for individuals. Mental health services were provided by a diversity of organisations and had arisen for historical reasons. However, the various organisations had different values and priorities, and they did not always see each other's point of view. At the individual (rather than the organisational) level, many patients could easily fall between the services provided. Much more thought needed to be given to the mechanisms of care, for example, referral procedures. The case manager approach, with one person orchestrating care, or the multidisciplinary team structure, worked quite well. But which was more effective, and in which circumstances?

One remedy was the opportunity that has arisen for the joint management of services, with the shared objective of providing for the person receiving the services — in particular, because there was an opportunity for incremental support (in hostels, and care and cluster models), and a need for innovation and a fundamental change in the provision and receipt of services.

It was reported that the Dorset area had been supporting community services successfully for several years. Training centres were provided by the local authority but were used by patients cared for by the community health team. There was wide local support for the development of community services, within which individual programmes were the key theme. Unfortunately, having got so far, it was not going to be possible to go further, mainly for financial reasons. There was a need to reduce the staff in caring establishments.

This experience led to the suggestion that penalties were being imposed even on authorities who were trying to implement the appropriate mental health policies. 'Care in the community' money was said to be the rock on which the whole process of community care might eventually founder, and this remained true even for those who had achieved progress so far.

New ideas in the care of mentally retarded in ordinary dwellings

The NIMROD scheme (new ideas in the care of mentally retarded in ordinary dwellings) taking place in Wales was mentioned. Joint management of services was taking place and although there were problems in joint financing, success in compromise had been achieved. Problems over the employment of staff had been resolved without health authority or local authority members giving up the base of their employment. Problems over autonomy for staff had also been overcome.

Welsh mental handicap strategy

In Wales, there was also a mental handicap survey with the support of the Secretary of State. All interested parties had taken part in the discussions, and resources were linked to the scheme. Progress was still variable, but broad guidelines had been given and resources had been provided. The speed and variations in competence in taking up the resources on offer appeared to be due to the lack of skills of local authorities and health authorities in working together.

Role of social workers

It had been said that social workers should be involved in crisis settings, with an emphasis on their statutory role. However, it was pointed out that, frequently, part of their statutory role was to ensure that there were no alternative sources of care — and this necessarily involved going into the background of each patient. The key to success was the notion of the social worker detecting alternative sources of care than the hospital. However, resources were distorted in the local authority setting. For example, training might absorb more resources in one area than in another. There was clearly great variability in the range of services provided and it was only to be hoped that better developed services would come about in the future. The district nature of local authority services (including out-of-hours services) largely determined what the social workers duties might be.

On the question of long-term care, it had been suggested that work with families was a low-key operation. This was a questionable judgement. In reply, it was stated that the term low-key was being applied in relation to the professional skills needed. A contrast was being made between 'staying' skills and assessment skills. Nurses, for example, had both these sorts of skills. What would the implications be for mental health services when large numbers of nurses were trained for working in the community?

Furthermore, what evidence was there that advocacy services were likely to be independent? It was thought that advice regarding benefits was distinct from that on statutory work/rights to service, and that advocacy services, as had been described, might develop as an unplanned independent service. Indeed, there were already some welfare schemes along these lines in existence.

Role of general practitioners

General practitioners also had skills in the long-term management of patients with mental disorders. The GP was the one who had to do the job — he had the interprofessional linking function. Having a social worker attached to the practice was a good idea, but in planning a mental health service, it was a luxury.

If in general practice there was a clear statement of need, the general practitioner found it easy to say, 'We'll discuss this at the primary care team meeting'. Current patients could be discussed in this kind of forum. This enabled the relevant professionals to get together with less risk of the 'fragmentation' which was mentioned above. Such communication structures were well developed within general practice, and the model could be generalised within the new mental health services. One speaker made the point that 'learning to talk to each other did not require excessive money or thought'.

Citizenship

On the notion of citizenship, it had to be recognised that although people had rights, these implied duties and responsibilities, too. Mentally ill people had behaviour which was not the norm, and although the most disturbed were secluded, to what extent were the public prepared to accept these patients back in the community? It was thought that there would be a lot of public distress at such an unqualified proposal.

This was a difficult question. It was not now thought that the general public were prepared to accept the severely mentally handicapped or mentally ill in the community, as they had been expected to do in the past. It appeared that there was more acceptance when such patients were placed in the community in small numbers and in natural units: for example, using ordinary housing stock, with two or three patients per house or flat. Under these circumstances, there was usually no objection from the public whatsoever. If the numbers were increased, then there tended to be objections.

Other speakers were more optimistic than the evidence on public attitudes which had been presented might suggest. The pessimism about the hostility of the community was not borne out by the MIND 'group homes' programme, the housing association initiatives, and the impact of the Homeless Persons Act. Where there were problems, this was often because the 'front-line' staff were not trained to provide help when problems arose with patients. The progress and achievements to date should not be underestimated.

Day centres

There were great fears in relation to the provision of local authority services provided after the closure of hospitals. Many were especially concerned to ensure that day centres did not see their role as providing psychotherapy to those who were severely socially disabled. It was important to ensure that the most disabled got the best and most appropriate service. The services were not provided for the needs of the people providing them.

Community psychiatric nurses

A question was raised about a statement which had been made to the effect that community psychiatric nurses should decide what referrals they took. This might not fit in with the notions of a district manager. There could be many problems — as had arisen when people were appointed according to specified job descriptions, and then took up special interests for which there was no budgeting. The management budgeting system might be the only way in which this problem could be handled. It might be that a given district manager would conclude, for example, that community nurses would be provided after hours and at weekends. It was important that the nursing skills were used in the best possible way. There was a need for specific objectives to be outlined. The individual nurse's role in this area was to decide about, and set nursing priorities for his or her patients.

Public education

On the theme of public education, one of the few studies which had been undertaken had shown, somewhat paradoxically, that such education increased public hostility. If this was the case, what should be done to educate the public? A speaker suggested that the bulk of education was done when people met the services through their personal experience of illness in the family. Otherwise, there was little effect. Involvement in local developments was also thought to be of educational value. MENCAP reported that television was an effective influence: recent episodes of a popular television series had shown a young person with Down's syndrome and this had met with an unexpectedly large supportive and positive response from the public.

19 Summing up

KENNETH RAWNSLEY

The process of running down the mental hospitals began in the 1950s and was not the result of a Government decision, but the reflection of a revolution in current attitudes and practice at that time. Mr Enoch Powell in his Hospital Plan of 1962, imprinted what was probably a somewhat over-optimistic seal of approval on the policy of shift to district general hospital units and closure of mental hospitals.

The evil consequences of over-zealous discharge policies have been well documented and we were reminded to have a look in the prisons, as well as underneath the arches, for psychiatric derelicts. To quote from paragraph 30 of the recently published Parliamentary Social Services Committee Report on community care (1985): 'Any fool can close a long-stay hospital: it takes more time and trouble to do it properly and compassionately. The Minister must ensure that mental illness or mental handicap hospital provision is not reduced without demonstrably adequate alternative services being provided beforehand, both for those discharged from hospital and for those who would otherwise seek admission.' Certainly the Conference was not against the philosophy of care and treatment, which places less emphasis on the traditional mental and mental handicap hospitals and more on the development of a range of facilities — including well-designed district general hospital units. However, I detected a deep sense of unease, both in the conceptualisation and the implementation of this strategy, and I would like to indicate the roots of this as I see it.

Planning

There is the daunting, sheer complexity of designing a service to cater for the needs of a heterogeneous collection of patients and their families. Many authorities, including both statutory and voluntary, have to be involved, and the ramifications run far and wide. Consultative machinery may be set up, but implementation may founder on a lack of motivation — for example, in the local authority sector — or because of uncertainty and lack of direction in the absence of a clearly specified, universally acclaimed model for a comprehensive service. We hear a good deal about the need for flexibility and the undesirability of national norms, and I am sure that is right, but it does imply that each area must work out its own destiny and must make decisions on the basis of imperfect knowledge.

Can the Department of Health take a further lead in this field — despite poor relations generally between central and local government — to facilitate the commitment of local authorities to this endeavour, by whatever means? Would it be useful for someone to publish a compendium of actual service — to serve as a model, a kind of shopping list — to see the variety of places involved and circumstances prevailing?

Policy

Planning, of course, must wait upon policy, and although the broad thrust of policy is clear, it has also become apparent in the course of this meeting that there are many areas of uncertainty in policy which need resolution.

Lord Glenarthur reminded us that 'money does not grow on trees', but one of the speakers thought that it might grow on the trees of mental hospitals, which, having been run down could liberate large sums of money by sale of land and property. But then we heard that both in the field of mental illness and mental handicap the hospital campus might remain as the locus for a variety of specialised units, including even a residence for the remnants of the old long-stay populations, and maybe for some of the new long-stay patients who are getting older. Well, as they say in Lancashire, 'Tha' can't 'ave bun and t' penny', and a difficult decision may have to be made as to whether the campus 'bun' or the more liquid asset of a few million pounds is the best option.

There is also a policy issue which was not explicitly declared, but which was implicit in certain patterns of care. That is, the extent to which psychiatry is to again become isolated and separated from other branches of medicine. The district general hospital concept had the virtue of bringing psychiatry back into the medical fold. There is now a tendency to step up the centralisation of medical and surgical services, but to decentralise psychiatric services. We heard talk of community mental health centres with refuge beds: Victorian buildings in Bloomsbury are being evacuated by physicians and surgeons, who could be replaced by psychiatrists.

Another example of policy dilemmas lies in the optimum deployment of community psychiatric nurses. Should they be anchored firmly to the specialist multidisciplinary team and stay very much with the care of severely disabled chronic patients, or should they be allowed to spread into the field of primary care — dispensing comfort, solace and support to the infinite multitude of the 'working worried'?

Chronic disorders

Much conference time has been spent in discussing these conditions. We saw remarkable curves, with steep descents, showing the decrement in mental hospital beds. We then discovered that this was mainly brought about by the death of the old long-stay patient fraction, whereas the new long-stay patient numbers were depressingly constant. The view was expressed, and certainly would warrant further scrutiny, that the district general hospital system was less likely to produce chronicity than was the mental hospital.

It was said that people tended to underestimate the disabilities of long-stay patients. The Friern Hospital survey bore this out, showing that only 4% of their schizophrenics in this category could manage in residential accommodation without supervision. On the other hand, it was clear that many chronic patients could live in a more domestic setting with a good deal of supervision and care. It seems to me that it is in this area of chronic mental disorder with substantial disability that the main challenge to the new policies arises. It is also here that the opportunities for innovative experiment lie. There has been talk of the 'quality of life', and the avoidance of a new form of institutionalisation. The schizophrenic sees the world in ways which are fundamentally different from his normal brother, and I believe it requires much imagination and empathy to freshen an environment for the comfort and support of a disabled schizophrenic. There is no universal narrow formula for success, and here resides an exciting challenge to planners and evaluators.

Finance

This provided another major cause for concern. Health economics is to me an arcane and difficult subject — the hidden costs of community care might be difficult to fathom, e.g., how to estimate the cost of the development of depressive illness in the relatives of discharged patients. It occurs to me that we do not know the answer to some very basic sums, thus it has been asserted that the new policies are inevitably going to cost more than the old, and yet, seemingly in some parts of the country, notably the North-West of England, they appear to cost substantially less.

Psychiatrists and other professionals cannot in all conscience endorse a policy for change which they believe cannot be funded: implementation would be disastrous. Maybe I am expecting an answer to this question which would be universally applicable, and maybe this is a naïve and simplistic view, but we really need to know whether we can afford to live in the new house before the removal men arrive. Incidentally, I detected a spirit from some of the speakers—which I heartily endorse—not to accept meekly the particular mess of potage which is doled out to us. I am a great believer in fighting a corner, and I think we must press very hard within the health service and in local authorities for a better share of resources.

Old age

Some clear points emerge from our consideration of the psychiatry of the elderly. I was struck by the fact that the entire psychiatric service for the elderly in Nottingham exists outside mental hospitals, though it does, of course, include a district general hospital long-stay unit. It seems also that elderly people in the mental hospital new long-stay patient category can be looked after in other settings, i.e., other hospital provision, or homes. The striking development is the rise in private residential resources, which now rival statutory provision in some areas, but which are, of course, indirectly financed by public funds—social security payments. These generally are not included in planning, monitoring, or inspectorate arrangements.

The notion of an integrated service between psychiatry and geriatrics has a great deal to commend it, and would deserve close attention from planners.

Mental handicap

We heard a *cri de coeur* that the parents of the mentally handicap are sick and tired of hearing about plans, but observing very little action. Much of what I said about policy and planning applies also to mental handicap services. It seems to me that although in the field of traditional hospital residential care we think we know what is bad, we cannot yet confidently draw up a blue-print for alternative residential resources which is patently good. Again, I point to the lack of clear policy, the lack of joint planning, and the failure of the Government to strengthen policy by making local authority obligations mandatory. Policies should be clarified in broad terms nationally, and local initiatives should be developed within broad guidelines.

In conclusion, I do not believe that this Conference has produced any answers, but it may have clarified some of the questions. We have been discussing a radical reorganisation of psychiatric services in a country where public expenditure is in decline—as in other fields of medicine, expectations arising from new approaches, new insights and new technology, must await realisation in a priority queue.

Reference

PARLIAMENTARY SOCIAL SERVICES COMMITTEE, HOUSE OF COMMONS (1985) *Community Care with Special Reference to Adult Mentally Ill and Mentally Handicapped People: Second Report from the Social Services Committee.* (HC 13 I,II,III). London: HMSO.

Appendix:
DHSS Background Policy Papers

*I. Mental Illness: Policies for
Prevention, Treatment, Rehabilitation and Care*

Introduction

1. This paper, prepared by DHSS Mental Health Division in consultation with professional colleagues, was originally intended to meet a request from Regional Health Authorities for a brief consolidated note on the mental illness policies advocated by the Department in various circulars and notes. (It was envisaged that it might be particularly helpful in the preparation of papers for Regional Reviews.) It does not describe any new policies; nor does it seek to specify the detail of good professional practice, or to prescribe the precise arrangements appropriate for a particular Region or District.

2. The main long-term aim of DHSS policy for mental health services, including services concerned with misuse of alcohol, drugs and solvents, is the creation of a comprehensive range of services, provided, where the NHS is concerned, within a District, and in the context of a Regional plan which takes account of District needs and resources and Departmental priorities and policy. Such a service is only possible if, in identifying and meeting needs with District resources, it takes full account of the contribution social, educational, housing, employment and all other voluntary, statutory and independent services can make. It is important to develop, in consultation with other service providers and the consumers, a pattern of service which will enable all those involved to work together and relate to the changing needs of mentally ill people and their families.

3. The elements that go to make up a comprehensive district service are broadly those set out in the *Better Services for the Mentally Ill* White Paper of 1975 complemented by the 1978 Report of a Working Group on the Organisational and Management Problems of Mental Illness Hospitals (the Nodder Report). The urgent tasks for NHS services remain the three set out in para. 5.9 of *Care in Action* (see paras 15–18 below).

District health services — in hospitals

4. Most people with mental illnesses are not in hospital. The hospital, with its specialist staff and facilities, provides a community resource, not simply an in-patient resource. The essential elements are:

(i) A psychiatric department (Health Building Note 35 discusses the function of such a department in a District with the new pattern of services, but is out of date in some respects, and a revised version is in preparation). It needs to provide facilities for in-patient, out-patient and day-patient assessment, treatment and rehabilitation; including support for those discharged after a shorter or longer stay in hospital.

(ii) Accommodation within the District General Hospital will be required for assessment and short-term treatment of elderly people with psychiatric disorders. (Where there is a psychiatric department in the hospital this accommodation usually forms part of it.)

(iii) Local accommodation, perhaps in smaller hospitals or new units, will be needed for continuing care, and relief and intermittent care, for some elderly patients.

(iv) In-patient accommodation is needed still for the 'old long-stay' patients who were admitted before modern methods of treatment and care were available. The task of caring for these patients is concentrated in the 90 or so districts with traditional psychiatric hospitals. Many of these patients regard the hospital as their home, but psychiatrists continue to discharge those for whom suitable arrangements can be made when this seems in the patient's interest. From a combination of discharges and deaths, the number continues to decline quite rapidly [see para 17(iii)].

(v) Continuing in-patient care is also required for a small number of more recently admitted people, the 'new long-stay' patients — people who despite advances in treatment cannot be supported in the community. They should not be expected to live indefinitely in the ordinary busy psychiatric in-patient setting. Plans will be needed for suitable accommodation such as a hospital hostel along the lines discussed in the 1975 White Paper (para 4.4). DHSS has information on current studies in this field.

District health services — in the community

5. Although at present most of the resources of the psychiatric service are concentrated under the hospital roof, a comprehensive service requires resources in the community away from the hospital. Psychiatrists and other health care staff are increasingly involved in the patient's home setting and in working in health centres and with primary health care teams away from their hospital base. The primary care team and associated community support services are crucial to the care of the large number of people with mental health problems — not always diagnosed as such — who have no, or no continuing, contact with specialist services.

6. A Community Psychiatric Nursing service is an important component of health service provision in the community. The nurses work as members of a multi-disciplinary team in a variety of settings, e.g. health centres, GP surgeries, day hospitals, psychiatric departments. Their aim is to provide treatment and nursing care in the community (and so prevent admission to hospital), and to provide after-care services following discharge from hospital. Some districts have also developed specialist CPN services, e.g. in the care of elderly mentally ill people.

7. A day hospital may be attached to an in-patient unit in a hospital or sited separately. In some districts crisis intervention and other services are run by a multidisciplinary team; sometimes mental health centres are set up in the centre of populations to provide ready access. In other districts day hospital staff may join with local authority staff to provide combined day care, linking clinical social and occupational functions to assist with rehabilitation and support. Advice about rehabilitation is provided in *Psychiatric Rehabilitation in the 1980s* (Royal College of Psychiatrists, 1980).

Services provided by local authorities, other statutory authorities, voluntary organisations and private bodies

8. These services need to complement NHS services in the care of people with a mental illness. Sited in the community they serve, they should aim to meet the whole range of accommodation, occupation and support needs of mentally ill people in a given area. Co-operation between all parties and co-ordination of provision are essential if a sensible and comprehensive network of services is to be achieved for all age groups. The range of services can include day centres, residential homes, hostels, sheltered accommodation, supported lodging schemes, ordinary housing, group homes, social clubs, drop-in centres and self-help groups: as well as education, training and employment services.

9. The revised procedures for registering residential care homes, announced in LAC(84)15, have increased local authorities' opportunities to influence standards of care; and changes in Supplementary Benefit Regulations have widened the options for residents' financial support. A code of practice 'Home Life' has been published to provide practical advice and guidance to registering authorities.

10. Private hospitals and mental nursing homes may enable health authorities to find places not otherwise available for particular categories of patient at a cost not disproportionate to the patient's needs.

Joint planning

11. This is essential for the proper use of both existing and any new resources. Collaboration is needed:

— at strategy level to encompass health and local authority services, and the voluntary sector, in an integrated network to meet the full range of needs, to achieve jointly owned policies and to avoid unnecessary duplication of services through parallel developments. To achieve this a mental illness sub-group of the joint care planning team, or some similar joint team, is needed.

— at operational level to create multi-disciplinary teams, to integrate as far as possible professional services such as occupational therapy and community psychiatric nurses/social workers, using the 'key worker' approach when this can improve care to organise joint training where appropriate and to generate ideas for the joint development of services.

12. Joint finance can make an important contribution to developments. It is aimed at encouraging collaboration and should be used to promote joint strategies, rather than isolated schemes outside the agreed pattern of development. 'Care in the Community' offers wider scope for enabling people to move into community care where this will benefit them, in line with the policy aim of switching from hospital to community care. See para. 20 below, HN(82)9 and HC(83)6.

Certain specialised services

13. In addition to general psychiatric services, and services for elderly people with mental illness, which are needed in every district, each region will need a strategy for its adolescent and children's services, for secure units and forensic services, and for alcohol, drug and solvent misuse (1975 White Paper, chapter 5, 7 and 8). Some

of these may require a regional or subregional base, but where possible the aim should be to move towards a District based service, accessible to consumers.

Paragraphs I and II on child and adolescent services are available from the DHSS

(iii) Regions also need to develop a strategy so that the region as a whole can offer a comprehensive range of accommodation for mentally ill (or mentally handicapped) patients who are violent or are offenders, or are for various reasons difficult to place, so that NHS deficiencies in the necessary skills to manage them do not mean that people who ought to be in-patients in NHS hospitals remain in prison, in special hospitals, or in the community. Regional secure units and interim secure units are important elements in this range, but other elements are needed also. For example the Region should know where care can be given to mentally handicapped people who need medium security with a suitable environment; to mentally handicapped people with mental illness; and to mentally ill people who are not expected to improve further with treatment but who need long-term care with medium security (see *Care in Action*, para. 5.10). Under Section 39 of the Mental Health Act, 1983 Regions may now be required to attend Court to give account of facilities which can be made available, either in their own Regions or elsewhere.

(iv) Alcohol Treatment Services should be locally based and although at the present time there are several Regional Alcohol Treatment units it is not expected that more of these will be developed. Most of them have adjusted, or are in the process of adjusting, the service they offer to a smaller catchment area based on single districts or groupings of districts. Future emphasis should be on district services which are multidisciplinary and community based with back-up in-patient provision.

(v) Drug Misuse — Ministers regard the improvement of services for drug misusers as of the highest priority (see Circular HC(84)14/CHC(84)12. In planning services, Regions should take account of the advice in the reports by the Advisory Council on the Misuse of Drugs on Treatment and Rehabilitation (1982) and on Prevention (1984). Services for drug misusers should provide an adequate comprehensive multidisciplinary network which should be firmly rooted in the community. In-patient detoxification facilities should be available at district level, and increasingly the majority of services, including walk-in advice centres, day centres and access to laboratory facilities, should be centred in the District. There is also, however, a need for a regional or sub-regional unit whose main role would be to offer services to the more disturbed drug misuser, and act as a support and advice centre to district services. The need for close co-operation between health services, local authority social services departments and non-statutory agencies providing counselling and longer term residential rehabilitation is essential in developing an effective service.

(vi) Solvent Misuse — services for solvent misusers should be multi-professional and locally based using existing skills, resources and powers to co-operate more effectively to discourage the practice of solvent misuse through education and persuasion. The health service has an important role in detecting the misuse of solvents by individuals and diagnosing and treating any adverse effects on their health. There is a need to identify the minority of children for whom solvent sniffing may have become the inappropriate response to other more severe problems and who will require specialist social work and psychiatric intervention. Doctors including general practitioners and those working in community based health services should work within multidisciplinary networks and help adolescents with associated problems of which solvent inhalation may be a symptom. General practitioner and casualty

departments may use — and through them other helping professionals have access to — the analytical services of the National Poisons Information Service to detect which solvents, if any, have been inhaled.

Staffing

14. *(i)* Medical — the Department has agreed with the Royal College of Psychiatrists on an overall target of one consultant to 40,000 population for district services (although in the light of changing needs and changing consultant roles this is under discussion and may be revised to increase the target number of consultants). How work is distributed among the consultant psychiatrists in each district is a matter for local arrangement following discussion with the GPs being served, usually through the medium of the Local Medical Committee. Where there is geographical sectorisation this should be elastic enough to allow GPs some choice (and two-consultant sectors may have advantages over single-consultant sectors). Specialty and special responsibility appointments will need to cover the psychiatry of old age (and 'Care in Action' asks that each District should have at least one such psychiatrist); alcohol, drug and solvent misuse; forensic psychiatry; rehabilitation; child and adolescent psychiatry; and psychotherapy. The Department has not formulated any targets for the numbers of consultants in the field of child and adolescent psychiatry. The Court Committee's recommendations for child psychiatry have been met in terms of overall numbers, but the regional picture is uneven.

(ii) Nursing: the changing pattern of service will determine how many nurses of each grade a health authority will require. The very nature of matching a service to local needs will inevitably mean that no two services will be alike, particularly in light of the importance of testing different models of care. The White Paper goal of 100 nursing staff per 100,000 population has now been exceeded in most parts of the country, but authorities should continue to bear in mind the need for a satisfactory balance of trained/untrained staff. In meeting the changing educational needs of nurses working in the psychiatric field and ensuring satisfactory standards of nursing care, it is vital that nurse managers and nurse educationalists collaborate to plan basic and post-basic education. Such planning should include preparation of the nurse to work in a variety of settings which, in addition to hospitals, includes other types of residential care as well as the patient's own home. It is important that in developing personnel policies for staff working in this field, and making suitable arrangements for their education and training, that authorities develop strategic manpower plans which not only take into account the continued supply of new recruits but also explore potential for retention of existing staff during a period of change. Authorities should also seek to encourage nurses who may wish to return to the field of mental illness nursing after a period of absence, e.g. the married woman whose children are now grown up. In that context re-orientation and opportunities for further training are essential.

(iii) Social workers with specialist knowledge, as well as general social services, are there to help patients and their families with problems arising from mental illness. They make a contribution to the treatment plan, care and after care, and provide a link to the services and resources the community can offer. It is the responsibility of the Local Authority Social Service Departments to provide social work support to the health service either through hospital based social workers or through the area team, according to local administration arrangements and geography. In all cases there should be social workers, with special knowledge of the needs of mentally ill people and their families, contributing as members of the multidisciplinary teams.

(iv) Others—other key groups of staff include occupational therapists, physiotherapists, other therapists (e.g. art, music, drama), and clinical psychologists. The latter group have an important role in relation to services for the mentally ill. Not only are psychological factors important in the genesis and maintenance of certain problems in the field, they are important in the management of chronic handicaps and the prevention of further deterioration. Psychological techniques are important in assessment, treatment and rehabilitation. Physiotherapists have a key role in assessing patients' physical disorders and in maintaining and improving mobility. They can contribute to the psychological treatment of patients using various physical methods. They also share their skills with other staff to ensure safe and effective methods of lifting and handling. The number of physiotherapists working in hospital and in the community is at present exceedingly small and will need to increase to meet future needs and changes in policy.

(v) Occupational Therapists specialising in mental illness play a significant role in the assessment, treatment and care of patients of all ages, by planning and providing therapeutic programmes. These are aimed at helping patients to improve personal and social performance, recognise and cope with the effects of mental illness, develop or improve skills related to work and leisure and achieve better community integration and an improved quality of life. Improvement of the physical well being is also included. OT's are also involved in a training and advisory role in the NHS and LASS's. The demand for OT continues to grow particularly with the move of services into the community. There is a national shortage of OT's, creating difficulties in filling funded posts as well as limiting developments in the service. Regions should be encouraged to make forward plans to fund students with training. Industrial therapy also has a part to play in the employment of longer stay patients, and in some aspects of helping patients return to work.

Matters of special concern

A: Mental illness in old age

15. Services for the 'psychiatry of old age' currently call for special attention. The need has grown sharply, and will continue to do so for the next ten years, as a result of the increasing numbers in the oldest age groups. In the last five years it has come to be accepted that a specialised service can best meet this need; detailed advice on establishment of such a service is contained in the HAS document *The Rising Tide*. The need is for a comprehensive service which recognises that most old people with mental illness are living at home, and that they and their families need basic community services with access to specialist services; multidisciplinary assessment is always desirable before decisions are taken on where an old person can live. Needs span health and local authority domiciliary care, including specialist community psychiatric nurses; local authority residential care and in-patient care. All districts which do not have local in-patient care should make an early start on providing some suitable accommodation within the district, served by a consultant psychiatrist with a special responsibility for elderly people (see *Care in Action*, para. 5.9(b)).

B: Development of district services

16. In many districts, a psychiatric hospital forms a base for the local services. Present policy is to accept that for the time being such a hospital, if it is suitably situated

in relation to the population of the district in which it is built, may continue to form the base for a comprehensive psychiatric service *for that district*. This implies that the priority tasks in each region will be developments to build up new patterns of comprehensive services in the districts which do not have a suitable psychiatric hospital, and to adjust catchment areas appropriately; while at the same time planning and executing the closure of hospitals which are not being fitted into the new pattern of services in this way (see *Care in Action*, para. 5.9).

17. It is increasingly urgent for regions to decide on a *regional strategy for psychiatric services, including hospital closure* where relevant (Para. 3 of HM(81)4, Annexe A, indicates the region's role in connection with such planning). In the last 25 years the number of in-patients has fallen from 145,000 to about 69,000 of whom about 56,000 are in the 100 or so traditional hospitals. On average, therefore, the number of patients in the latter have fallen by more than half, and will continue to fall over the next 10 years, as a result of not only therapeutic advances but three other factors:

(*i*) Regional programmes to establish psychiatric departments in district general hospitals (there are currently about 80 such departments which have over 50 beds, and a slightly smaller number with fewer beds).

(*ii*) Authorities making better progress than previously with the complementary task of providing local accommodation in each district for elderly patients, often by adaptation (para. 15 above);

(*iii*) The number of 'old long stay' patients remaining in the traditional hospitals reducing by about 2,000 annually, partly by discharge, but mainly by the death of the oldest patients.

18. Money which is saved through the reduction in the number of in-patients should enable progress to be made in establishing good district services. (Para. 2.3.4 of the current 'Land Transactions' handbook requires receipts from sales of land, etc. from hospitals for mentally ill or mentally handicapped people to be used to develop the relevant services.) But reductions in numbers are unlikely to produce matching cost savings unless a hospital is closed. Such closures should be carefully planned, perhaps 5 years ahead, in the context of a regional strategy. The first stage of such a strategy may be to plan the steps by which catchment areas will be aligned with district boundaries, and to plan the successive adjustments to revenue allocations that will be needed to allow development in a district which had previously looked to a neighbouring district for psychiatric care. Movements of both patients and staff need to be worked out so as to minimise the disadvantages to individuals and maximise the advantages. It should be emphasised that the closure of hospitals is a consequence, not a cause, of the reduction of in-patient care. Patients who would be better off outside hospital should have a planned discharge to suitable care even if no closure is foreseen; patients who are better off in in-patient care should receive such care, by a transfer if necessary, even if a closure is planned.

C: Adolescent services

19. There are currently some problems in the provision of services for adolescents with behavioural or developmental disorders. The small numbers involved make planning difficult at district level and it is consequently important that regions should take a close interest in this subject. Particular thought needs to be given to the potential difficulty of providing comprehensive services economically where numbers are small, and the philosophy of care is to retain local links with family and friends; and also to the need to match the service to the actual needs. (Some regions have relied on specialist units which together have enough beds to meet the region's needs, but

find that the admission policies of the various units do not together match the needs which arise for in-patient care, so that the units have empty beds while e.g. the local authorities' children's departments find themselves providing care for young people who need psychiatric care.) The Health Advisory Service is conducting a special exercise during the course of 1985 to look at service provision for this group and aims to produce guidance for authorities by the end of the year.

Policy and management

20. The Psychiatric Services Management Teams described in the Nodder Report need to be re-considered in some respects in the light of changes in management structure below district level (e.g. HC(80)8) and the continuing development of unit management. But the principles discussed in chapter 4 of the report, including the crucial importance of a link with the local authority at this level, and the special problems which arise when care is divided between a psychiatric hospital and a psychiatric department in a DGH, still require attention in all districts.

APPENDIX ON BED AND DAY PLACES REQUIREMENTS

Introduction

1. The paper above brings together the relevant policies from a number of sources. Health authorities may find it useful to have in addition a note setting out the resource implications, as DHSS see them, for the planning of services.

2. This does not attempt to provide a blueprint for a service, because there is considerable variation between districts, not only in the sort of fixed resources that are available, but also in the operational policies which determine how much a particular resource is used. Provision for each district therefore requires individual planning, in consultation with the professional people involved.

3. Provision can conveniently be planned under five headings and these categories can be used to analyse present and future planned provision in any district. It should be noted that this is a categorisation of accommodation etc., not of patients. In the paragraphs 6–20 below each of the headings I–V is followed by discussion of the category and of the organisational factors that will affect the local need.

4. It will also be necessary to take account of any general population factors which affect the level of need; these have been discussed in the psychiatric literature.

5. A necessary preliminary is to determine the catchment area for each district at the relevant future dates. They should normally be adjusted until they correspond with the districts' general catchment areas, and it is important that plans for adjustments should be made early, even if they cannot be executed at once. (Historically, psychiatric catchment areas have been harder to escape from than those for other specialties. It is hoped that as psychiatric resources improve those concerned will be more willing to admit patients from other areas when GPs or patients wish this; meanwhile the catchment area ensures that every patient can gain admission somewhere.)

I. Bed needs: The psychiatric department

6. The 1975 White Paper discussed the 'district general hospital psychiatric unit' which forms the district base in the new pattern of service. (Because HC(80)8 gave

a special meaning to the word 'unit', DHSS now describe this as a 'psychiatric department'.) The White Paper tentatively repeated the guidance in HM(71)97 that such a department if linked, not only to other elements of health care (see below), but also to the complementary social services elements it described, might need about 0.5 beds per 1,000 population (para. 6 of enclosure to HM(71)97, para. 4.8 of White Paper).

7. Because in-patient stays have continued to get shorter, many services with a base in or adjacent to the DGH now use considerably less than 0.5 beds per 1,000. More information about current bed usage in district general hospital departments is expected from a study being undertaken by the Royal College of Psychiatrists in conjunction with the HAS. Meanwhile many mental illness hospitals have built up community elements and community links which enable them to provide a similar type of service in their admission and medium stay wards, so that a fairly similar ratio may be applicable to the relevant beds in these hospitals also. (When planning the building of a new department, it is of course relevant to ascertain how many beds are being used in the service which is to move into the department; though when the move takes place there may be a change in bed use, as a result of changes not only of environment but of staff.)

8. It is likely that in most districts analysis on these lines will suggest planning for between about 0.3 and 0.5 beds per 1,000. The absence of other elements of a community service, for example staffed hostels, will of course tend to raise the level of in-patient care. Operational policies for the interaction between the main base and the other elements of in-patient care are also important. Creation of a separate assessment ward for elderly people (para. 10 below) as recommended in *The Rising Tide* and in para. 4(ii) of main paper will reduce the beds to be planned in the general psychiatric wards commensurately; the same applies if it is also decided to provide separate accommodation for elderly people with functional illness. (If no elderly patients are to use the general wards, it may be sensible to calculate a bed ratio against the 0–65, or 15–65 population).

9. As well as in-patient accommodation the department may be expected to provide for day-patient and out-patient care: these are discussed in paras 17 and 20 below. (In some districts the department will be in effect divided between two locations.)

II. Bed needs: Accommodation for elderly mentally ill people

10. Whilst the majority of elderly people with mental disorder who require in-patient care are likely to be dealt with in the general psychiatric department (and be provided for within the 0.3–0.5/1,000 total population guideline) DHSS also accepts the view of the HAS and RCPsych that services for the elderly should include a ward for assessment and short-term treatment. This may have up to 1 bed per 1,000 population over 65 (again, from the 0.3–0.5 beds per 1,000 total population guideline) depending on how it is to be used. This ward should be in a DGH even where the rest of the psychiatric service may be elsewhere, because of the medical facilities that may be necessary. Where the main psychiatric service is in the DGH the assessment ward may be best placed within it though it should also be near the geriatric department. (The function now seen for the assessment ward is considerably wider than that proposed in HM(70)11, the main function of which was to enable patients to be correctly allocated between the psychiatric and the geriatric services.)

11. Beds for elderly patients requiring continuing in-patient care or admitted to provide for supporters will also be needed. Since it is mainly dementia patients who require this in practice the need to be met is equivalent to the need for 'ESMI beds';

given the increased weight of very old people among the over-65 population the level of care intended in the guideline in HM(72)71 is now equivalent to about 3 beds per 1,000 over 65. (This is in addition to beds provided within the guideline 0.3–0.5 per 1,000 population for general psychiatry.) These beds should be in small units in local hospitals close to the community where the patient has lived and thus easily accessible to family and friends. These units, which do not need to be on the DGH site, will provide beds for continuing in-patient care together with some for short-term relief or respite care. The need for continuing care and respite care beds will vary according to the pattern of care provided and other factors (e.g. the proportion of elderly people isolated from their families; the strength of health and social services community services; the quantity of local authority residential accommodation and its residential policies; the quantity of voluntary and private residential accommodation).

12. It should be emphasised that DHSS has followed professional practice in abandoning the distinction formerly made between 'the elderly severely mentally infirm' i.e. those suffering from forms of dementia and elderly people with other mental ilness. As indicated in *The Rising Tide* the specialised hospital service for the psychiatry of old age would normally cover both functional illnesses and dementia but will not cover 'old long-stay' patients whose illness began when they were younger but who have become old while in in-patient care.

III. Bed needs: Accommodation for 'long-stay patients'

13. As indicated in para. 3 of the Appendix, the categorisation used for planning purposes is essentially a categorisation of accommodation, not patients. 'Long-stay' accommodation is a traditional term for the third major group of in-patient accommodation, which provides continuing care for patients who do not need the facilities of the admission wards (in the old pattern of care), or the psychiatric department (in the new pattern of care). The precise bed needs therefore depend on practice rather than statistics of length of stay: a psychiatrist may think it right to retain one patient in the district general hospital for two years or so to complete his treatment; another patient, particularly if he is known from earlier admissions, may be transferred to 'long-stay' accommodation very quickly.

14. The term 'old long stay' has been used to denote those who became long-stay before modern methods of treatment and care had been developed. Although all the accommodation of such patients is in mental illness hospitals. Although most of the accommodation is today occupied by patients who are over 65, the accommodation is not currently treated as part of the service for the psychiatry of old age (*The Rising Tide*, para. 18).

15. 'New long stay' patients are those who have become long-stay more recently — sometimes a fixed date such as the psychiatric census of 1971 is used. The distinction is not clear-cut because case register studies have shown that (setting aside elderly people in the provision under category II above) most of the long-stay patients who began their latest stay within the last 10 years or so are people who had earlier been 'old long-stay' patients who returned to psychiatric hospital after an absence, perhaps after an unsuccessful experiment in the community, or even sometimes merely after a short stay in another hospital. In districts which are still served by a mental illness hospital there may be little practical value in distinguishing between 'new long-stay' and 'old long-stay'; for planning purposes what is needed is a statistical calculation of probable future bed needs from the rate of decline of both groups (either taken separately or together). Some assistance with such calculations, along with other advice

on calculations of bed needs, is given in the OR publication *The Provision of In-Patient Facilities for the Mentally Ill: A Paper to assist NHS Planners* (G. Robertson), which was circulated to regional statisticians in March 1981. (Rates of decline are not of course immutable: a hospital where the rate has been slow, because of little effort at rehabilitation, may provide scope for many discharges when a consultant with a special interest in rehabilitation is appointed.)

16. The position is different in a district now served by a psychiatric department in a general hospital. Here 'new long-stay' patients may begin to accumulate within the district general hospital. The rate depends on the pattern of care and the use made of community facilities. An accumulation of 'new long-stay' patients in such a district requires the attention of planners because it is undesirable to let patients live in an acute ward, and let the throughput in the DGH progressively decline, and also undesirable to ask the mental illness hospital formerly responsible to take over the care of the DGH's unwanted patients. A possible solution of a hospital hostel (para. 4(v) of main paper) is discussed in para. 4.54 of the 1975 White Paper and in 'A hostel-ward for "new" long-stay patients' (Wykes/Wing: *Psychological Medicine*, Monograph Supplement 2). This also lists some references bearing on rates of accumulation. A paper produced by DHSS Mental Health Division on the provision of Hospital Hostels for New Long Stay Patients is available from Room C424, Alexander Fleming House, Elephant and Castle, London SE1 6BY.

IV. Day care

17. The 1975 White Paper suggested that day patients would need day hospital places at a rate of 0.30 per 1,000 population, and that in-patients would need another 0.35 places; it was envisaged that all or most of the day hospital care would be associated with the in-patient care on the district general hospital site. One advantage of this is that the patient can be under the same staff team as an in-patient and as a day-patient.

18. As indicated above planning now envisages less in-patient care. This does not in itself suggest any need for less day places, since patients who are discharged earlier, or not admitted, may receive day care instead. It may be suggested that 0.65 day places are still needed, though now only say 0.25 will be needed for in-patient and 0.40 for day patients; but some districts have found a lower level of need — see also para. 20(b) below.

19. But change in professional opinion also suggests that in many districts it is better to site at least some of the day hospital places not in the district general hospital, if that is at the edge of the town, but in a central location. The DGH will still need enough day hospital places for its in-patients and for those day patients who can conveniently attend from the community. Travelling day hospitals can be useful.

V. Completing the district service

20. (a) The other NHS elements of the district service do not have major capital implications but it is important that they should be planned in good time jointly by the health and social service staff concerned, so that for example changed patterns of out-patient clinics, or convenient locations where community psychiatric nurses and social workers can meet, can be arranged with all those concerned.

(b) It is particularly important that Health and Social Service Authorities should combine in the planning of day hospitals and day centre care. As indicated in para. 7

of the main paper, it may sometimes be desirable to offer forms of combined day care; and in all areas the pattern of the two types of facilities should make a sensible whole. Day hospitals and day centres for elderly patients need separate consideration. Where transport is required for patients, it is important that arrangements be considered and discussed with the ambulance service, and any other body which may be involved in its provision, at the planning stage.

21. Plans also need to be made for the specialised services discussed in para. 13 of the main paper, often on a regional or sub-regional basis. Here the RHA has a special responsibility in securing plans which amount overall to a comprehensive regional service to meet each need (see HC(82)6, Appendix A, para. 2.2). (The guideline in HM(64)4 for child psychiatric beds is now regarded as too high.)

References

1. DHSS (1973) Health Building Note 35 HMSO. (Published as Hospital Building Note)
2. DHSS (1975) White Paper *Better Services for the Mentally Ill*. Comnd 6233. HMSO.
3. DHSS (1977) *Land Transactions Handbook*.
4. DHSS (1978) *The Nodder Report*.
5. DHSS (1981) *Care in Action*. HMSO.
6. DHSS HN(82)9 and HC(83)6/LAC(83)5; HN(81)4; HC(80)8/LAC(80)3; HM(71)97; HM(72)71; HC(82)6/LAC(82)3; LAC(84)15.
7. DHSS HC(84)14/LAC(84)12. Services for Drug Misusers. (June 1984).
8. DHSS (No(84)5. Report on the Nurse Manpower Project for the NHS Management Enquiry.
9. DHSS Health Trends, Vol. 14 (1982) Dr Dorothy Black *Misuse of Solvents*.
10. Royal College of Psychiatrists (1980) *Psychiatric Rehabilitation in the 1980s*.
11. Royal College of Psychiatrists (1980) *Secure Facilities for Psychiatric Patients: A Comprehensive Policy*.
12. Health Advisory Service (1983) *The Rising Tide*.
13. Advisory Council on the Misuse of Drugs (1982) *Treatment and Rehabilitation*. HMSO.
14. Advisory Council on the Misuse of Drugs (1984) *Prevention*. HMSO.
Note: Unless otherwise indicated, the author is the publisher.
DHSS (MHA) March 1985.

II. Mental Handicap: Policies and Priorities (Draft Revision: February 1985)

Introduction

1. This revised note, prepared by DHSS Mental Health Division, in consultation with professional colleagues, replaces the March 1983 edition which should now be destroyed. In continuing to provide a brief summary of the main policies for services for mentally handicapped people advocated by the Department, this version brings references to policy up to date (e.g. circulars issued since February 1983 in connection with the 'Children's Initiative' and joint planning and finance).

This note does not describe any new policies, or seek to specify the detail of good professional practice, or to prescribe the precise arrangements appropriate for a particular Region or District.

Policy

2. National policies for mentally handicapped people are based on the principles outlined in the 1971 White Paper *Better Services for the Mentally Handicapped*[1] (see Appendix B for references). The overall aims are to develop coordinated health and social services in each locality, and to achieve a major shift from institutional health care for mentally handicapped people to a range of community care according to individual needs, with increasing responsibilities and resources for local authorities. Joint planning and collaboration between the statutory authorities is crucial for the development of mental handicap services. The main aims for field authorities outlined in the White Paper are summarised in Appendix A attached.

3. These broad aims were elaborated in the White Paper into a number of specific guidelines or objectives for field authorities (for example, targets for hospital places or local authority residential care). The 1980 review of mental handicap services (*Mental Handicap: Progress, Problems and Priorities*)[2] endorsed the principles outlined in the White Paper. The review redefined some of the targets for future provision to enable authorities to take account of the age structure of their local population, and modified the target for children's places in health care. National guidelines for provision are intended to help authorities to plan their services, but can provide only a broad guide to what is needed. Health and local authorities together, and in collaboration with the voluntary agencies, must themselves look at local needs and circumstances and formulate specific plans accordingly. Some health and local authorities, either separately or together, have found Case Registers to be a very helpful aid to local long-term planning.

4. The National Development Team for Mentally Handicapped People is available to advise individual health and local authorities and voluntary organisations over the whole range of planning, developmental and operational issues or on specific issues concerning their mental handicap services within the overall resources available to them. It is an independent body consisting of a full-time Director (who is a consultant psychiatrist), two full-time Associate Directors (one with a nursing and the other with a social services background) and a panel of about 80 members including NHS administrators, nurses, psychiatrists, clinical psychologists and social services staff, and relatives of mentally handicapped people.

5. The 1980 review identified a number of questions which, it said, needed further consideration. Two of the questions — the day care needs of profoundly handicapped people and the services required by mentally handicapped people with special needs — were the subject of study by a team of DHSS officials, with the help of Professor Peter Mittler. A report containing information of practical assistance to practitioners and planners was issued in February 1984 (see paragraph 22 below).

6. *Care in Action*,[3] the Government's handbook of policies and priorities for the health and personal social services (February 1981), reiterated the White Paper's principles to authorities and stressed the need for locally based services and for the development of each individual's capabilities for independent living. It also emphasised that care in a health setting should be for people with clear medical or nursing needs, and that joint planning between health and local social services authorities, and close involvement of voluntary bodies and other agencies, such as education and housing authorities, was essential.

Joint planning and finance

7. The importance of joint planning and collaboration between health and local authorities and voluntary organisations in the delivery of services cannot be

overstressed. In general the arrangements remain as in HRC(74)19 and HC(77)17. HN(82)9[4] asked Districts to agree with the corresponding local authorities and neighbouring Districts revised machinery for joint consultation and collaboration following health service restructuring. Regions were asked to inform themselves of these arrangements and consider any problems in the light of the general policy on collaboration.

8. The Government's commitment to the transfer of mentally handicapped people and others who are currently in hospital to community care was stressed in the *Care in the Community* Green Paper.[5] 'Care in the community' includes not only living at home but living in residential units run by the health service, local authorities or voluntary organisations.

9. Three of the proposals made in the Green Paper, which did not require primary legislation, were implemented in March 1983 by the issue of HC(83)6:[6]

— DHAs are able to make continuing annual payments for as long as necessary to local authorities and voluntary organisations for people moving into community care;
— the payment of joint finance for schemes to get people out of hospital may be extended where there are special circumstances and with the agreement of the JCC from 7 to a maximum of 13 years with 100% support for up to 10 years;
— a programme of pilot projects is being promoted and up to £16 million of joint finance funds will be centrally reserved over a period of 5 years to help develop and assess the programme. Thirteen projects, seven involving mentally handicapped people, are being funded for 3 years from April 1984. A further selection of projects is being made for funding from April 1985 for 3 years.

Other proposals required primary legislation, which was introduced with the HASSASSA Act 1983. They were brought into effect from 1 April 1984 (HC(84)9)[7] and were:

(*i*) to enable payments to be made by DHAs for the support of education for handicapped people and of housing, provided by local authorities and other bodies, such as housing associations;
(*ii*) to enable special health authorities to make payments to local authorities and voluntary organisations under Section 28A of the NHS Act 1977;
(*iii*) to enable payments to be made to 'remote' local authorities.

10. The success of these and other developments depends on close collaboration between the statutory authorities and with voluntary organisations, so that the resources available are used as effectively as possible to provide complementary services as part of an agreed pattern of provision. From 1 January 1985, the Joint Consultative Committees should each have 3 members elected from voluntary organisations.

Staffing

11. There are currently no Departmental targets for staff who work with mentally handicapped people.

12. The Royal College of Psychiatrists has suggested a ratio of one consultant in mental handicap for every 200,000 population. The role of the consultant in mental handicap has been changing over the years, and increasingly consultants see their

work as providing a psychiatric service to mentally handicapped people throughout a locality, rather than confining their attention to more generalised medical work in a mental handicap hospital.

13. By far the largest group of NHS staff in direct contact with mentally handicapped people are nurses. *Staffing:* Health authorities should ensure that appropriately qualified nurses (RNMH) with the appropriate grade mix are supplied within the context of their strategies and in the light of the agreed balance of care between health and local authorities. The National Development Team for Mentally Handicapped People, in its Second Report,[8] suggests four nurse to patient ratios based on its classification of mentally handicapped people in long-term care (into four main groups). It discusses the subject further in its Third Report. The NHS Report 1984[9] pointed to an improvement in the nurse to patient ratio between 1976 and 1983, but this increase has been largely among unqualified staff. *Education and Training:* The English National Board issued in 1982 a syllabus of training for mental handicap nurses[10] which is to be fully introduced into schools of nursing by 1987. It highlights the contribution of the mental handicap nurse and the skills and knowledge required, and is based upon a systematic approach to the needs of mentally handicapped people. While professional education for nurses falls within the remit of the English National Board, other training (including in-service) falls to NHSTA, NAHA/health authorities and CCETSW or other bodies such as BIMH. Education and training at basic, post-basic and in-service levels for nurses working in a wide range of NHS residential settings, and as community nurses, is now a major concern for managers at District and Regional Level.

14. Other staff—notably clinical psychologists, speech, occupational and physiotherapists—have a key role to play in mental handicap services. Demand for the services of such staff continues to outstrip supply. This is often due to the slow development of understanding both within and without the particular profession as to the value of their contribution to mental handicap services, resulting in low establishment levels which can be a discouragement to recruitment even at that level. Those concerned with their deployment need to consider how they can contribute most effectively to the services offered to mentally handicapped people. The 1980 review suggested that scarce staff should not confine themselves to providing direct treatment for a limited number of clients, but should devise and communicate programmes that can be carried out by helpers and others—including relatives where appropriate—and participate in in-service staff training. For example, occupational therapy provides its services in this way, and in fact there are many more helpers than qualified staff (171 WTE qualified: 602 WTE helpers in 1982). However, direct contact between occupational therapist and patient is needed in primary and continuing assessments, in specific activities and techniques, and in devising and implementing new programmes and approaches. It is important therefore that the proportion of qualified to helper time is carefully considered in the light of local needs. All staff working with mentally handicapped people may find it helpful to have further in-service training, focussed on specific needs, to broaden their horizons and develop flexibility in the allocations of tasks between disciplines.

15. Health authorities also need to consider with the relevant local authorities, the availability of social services staff to people in health service care. Particularly important will be access to social work help for patients. This should be provided by social workers being based preferably in the community, where they are readily accessible to families, and working into the hospital. For those patients who also have a physical handicap and are living at home or moving into the community, there may be additional difficulties of independent functioning created by the physical

environment. Most social service departments now employ occupational therapists specialising in assessment for and prescription of aids and teaching their use. Along with officers of housing departments and local authority grant officers, they are also involved extensively in the adaptation of properties to meet the needs of handicapped people. In order to enhance the movement of handicapped people into the community, there has to be close liaison between DHA officers and these therapists.

Health service residential provision
for mentally handicapped adults

Number of places, siting and size of units

16. The 1971 White Paper suggested a specific (reduced) target for hospital places for adults, for achievement by 1991, of 74 beds per 100,000 population aged over 16. The Department's 1980 review of services concluded that the White Paper probably over-estimated the number of hospital places for adults which will eventually be required but suggested that the total number of places (provided by the NHS, local authorities and other bodies) should probably be about the same as envisaged by the White Paper. Health and local authorities might therefore use figures on the total residential provision (adding NHS and local authority targets together) envisaged in the White Paper (155 places per 100,000 population aged 16 and over) as a rough guide to the total residential provision needed for adults. Alternatively, Case Registers are increasingly being set up to define local needs more closely.

17. The White Paper recommended 200 beds as the maximum size for new mental handicap hospitals. The 1980 review concluded that few Districts were likely to need more than 150 mental handicap health care places, and that these need not all be on one site. The review did not give any precise guidance on optimum size for hospitals and units but advised authorities to 'think small'.

18. The Jay report[11] proposed a model of care under which those mentally handicapped people who need residential care away from home should receive this in small residential units, preferably in domestic housing and sited in local communities, run either by health or local authorities. The Government accepted this in principle but indicated the need for further consideration of the best way of providing for the special needs of the relatively small numbers of the most severely and multiply handicapped people. Thus health authorities should aim to accommodate eventually in small homely units based in local communities all mentally handicapped people requiring care in a health setting, except possibly for some with special needs (see paragraph 21 below).

19. *Community units on hospital sites:* It will not usually be possible to provide in new or existing buildings on hospital sites units that are truly part of a community unless the hospital is situated alongside an existing population, or a new community is being established there; and the units have their own access to this and are serviced and staffed quite independently from the hospital.

20. The 1980 review suggested that it would be useful to have at least one small health service unit in every District, whose functions could vary depending on local needs and circumstances. How small these units should be will again depend on local circumstances, but they should provide a homely environment. The National Development Team for Mentally Handicapped People suggests that this environment is best achieved in ordinary houses; and in practice it appears to work well. The use of community units (single buildings) as such is no longer recommended by the

Team except in very special circumstances. It would regard a single building with 24 beds as too big by current standards. Where the creation of a community unit is regarded as necessary, the Interim Building Guidance[12] to health authorities (HN(80)21) encourages the provision of individually sited units. Any plan should encourage individual or small group living. The creation of health service units (whether in ordinary houses or other accommodation) should be carried out in consultation with local authorities and in the light of the overall assessment of need for community residential care.

Specialist health services

21. It seems that there may be a need for more specialised health services than will normally be available in the units described above, and which may need to be provided on a supra-district basis. These services might include short and longer term assessment (where assessment cannot be carried out elsewhere) and treatment facilities for people with profound or multiple handicaps or for those with additional mental illness or severe behaviour disorders. There are a number of models on which such services can be provided. None of these requires an establishment such as a large hospital, but some include the maintenance of some 'base' or 'core' units to provide very specialist services and facilities.

22. The arguments about whether such services for some special needs should be provided in specialist units (and what should be their optimum size) are outlined in the Department's report *Helping Mentally Handicapped People With Special Problems*.[13] The information and views collected by the study team on selected groups with particular needs did not point firmly to a single solution. Their report describes the available options and the factors which authorities might bear in mind when planning services. It also includes practical suggestions for staff who are caring for mentally handicapped people with special needs, and managers in the mental handicap service should ensure that the report is available to such staff as well as to the planners.

Health service residential provision
for mentally handicapped children

23. The Government has stated unequivocally that mental handicap hospitals do not provide a favourable environment for children to grow up in, and has stressed that, for mentally handicapped children needing care in a health setting, small homely units in or near to the local community should be provided. To hasten progress and get all long-stay children out of large mental handicap hospitals and into more appropriate accommodation, HC(81)13[14] (November 1981) asked health authorities to make sure that all mentally handicapped children in their care were identified and their needs reviewed jointly with the relevant local authority in order to decide the best way of making more suitable provision for those unsuitably located, taking account of their long-term needs and consulting their families and care staff.

24. HC(83)21[15] (issued September 1983) followed up this earlier circular by asking Regional Health Authorities to monitor the progress made by their Districts and to be prepared to report progress in the run up to the annual review meetings with Ministers. In particular this report was to indicate: (a) when the process of joint review is likely to be completed, and (b) when authorities expect all children to be appropriately located.

Additional central funding

25. HC(83)21 described the scheme providing additional funding to assist health authorities with special problems, details of which had been sent to administrators in January 1983 (DA(83)2).[16] Under the scheme £9 million has been made available over a period of 4 years from 1983/4 to meet the capital and initial revenue costs of new projects designed to get children with health care needs out of hospital into more appropriate accommodation in the local community. To date 32 projects (out of a total of over 80 applications) have been approved, and these will bring some 250 children out of long-stay hospitals. When considering the applications submitted, priority was given to schemes which would establish a local residential service in a District which previously had no health service provision outside mental handicap hospitals or which would provide for a return to their home communities of children who had been admitted to mental handicap hospitals at a distance from their home District.

£ for £ scheme

26. The £ for £ scheme (guidelines in HC(81)13) has made a total of £1 million available over four years from November 1981 to match on a £ for £ basis funds raised by voluntary bodies for *capital* expenditure on local projects which will get children under 16 out of hospital and into more suitable accommodation. All projects submitted to the Department for consideration must have the backing of the relevant local and health authorities. To date seven grants totalling some £600,000 have been made from this scheme.

Assessment

27. The 1971 White Paper recommended a comprehensive multidisciplinary assessment for all children where mental handicap is detected or suspected. The aim of the assessment should be to formulate a continuous plan or programme of management designed to meet a child's specific health education and social needs, and to reach a decision about the support and advice which should be provided to the child's family. It is important that this assessment should involve a wide spectrum of professional mental handicap experience, and, wherever possible, the child's family.

Respite care

28. Most families with a mentally handicapped child will be able to care for that child for a longer period at home if the child can, from time to time, be admitted to short-term care, which can be provided by health or local authorities or by private or voluntary organisations. This form of care is important not only for the relief it offers parents but because it allows the child to be seen by staff over longer periods when emerging problems can be identified. The question of whether and when a child should be admitted to short-term care should be discussed in detail with the family.

Day services

29. The 1971 White Paper suggested that 35 places per 100,000 population for in-patients and 10 places per 100,000 population for day patients were needed for

occupation and training in mental handicap hospitals. The 1980 review did not alter these targets, but pointed out that hospitals are often too isolated to provide day services for people in their catchment area, and that there might be a need for separate NHS day provision if it is felt that some people require services which cannot be provided in an ATC. For people in hospital the aim should be to ensure that they have suitable training and leisure activities, whenever possible away from the ward on which they live. Wherever possible this should take advantage of community resources and facilities to encourage integration and provide a realistic environment to help patients transfer their skills from a hospital environment to a community one as part of the progression towards community living.

30. Day services for the most severely handicapped people are often regarded as a hospital responsibility, but the National Development Group for the Mentally Handicapped[17] recommended that all ATCs should have a special care section, and many local authorities have been successfully developing special care units. These units need to have, or at least have available to them, staff with particular expertise in the care and management of these severely handicapped people, many of whom will have associated physical handicaps. Physiotherapists, occupational and speech therapists and nurses can greatly help the work of these units. Both the NHS and local authorities at present have a valuable contribution to make to special care provision and decisions as to how to provide day services, and the form that these should take should be discussed thoroughly at local level — health and local authorities should jointly ensure that provision is available to meet the current and foreseeable needs of mentally handicapped people.

Community services

31. One of the most important developments in recent years has been the movement of health services out of hospitals and into a variety of community settings. A number of authorities provide (or are planning to provide) specialist advice and help to families or others caring for mentally handicapped people in a day or residential setting, through the operation of multidisciplinary District Handicap Teams and Community Mental Handicap Teams, consisting of health and social services staff. The National Development Team has commented on the increasing number of — now some 500 — community mental handicap nurses in post (although not all of them work in teams), and has suggested that for Districts with no or very little in the way of mental handicap services the appointment of community mental handicap nurses to form, with a social worker, the core of a team is a good starting point. (The Team suggests that one community mental handicap team can serve a population of 60–80,000, depending on local factors.) These core team members should have, as a named resource, other members from various disciplines upon whom they can call — notably clinical psychologists, physiotherapists and occupational and speech therapists.

APPENDIX A

Aims for field authorities outlined in the 1971 White Paper

(*i*) Ensuring that the family with a handicapped member has the same access to general social services as other families and to special additional help as required.

(ii) Preventing unnecessary segregation of mentally handicapped children or adults from other people of similar age and from the general life of the local community.

(iii) Preventing mental handicap if possible and reducing the severity of its effects.

(iv) Providing a comprehensive initial assessment and periodic reassessment of the needs of each handicapped person and his family.

(v) Providing stimulation, social training and education, and purposeful occupation or employment for each mentally handicapped person.

(vi) Enabling each mentally handicapped person to live with his own family if this does not impose an undue burden on them or him.

(vii) Enabling the mentally handicapped person who has to leave home temporarily or permanently to maintain links with his own family.

(viii) Providing a home-like substitute home for those mentally handicapped people who need one, with sympathetic and constant human relationships.

(ix) Providing an adequate range of residential services for mentally handicapped people in every area.

(x) Fostering proper co-ordination of relevant services and in the application of relevant professional skills to individual mentally handicapped people and their families, regardless of administrative frontiers.

(xi) Developing LA personal social services for mentally handicapped people as an integral part of services provided under the LA Social Services Act, 1970 (and other legislation).

(xii) Fostering close collaboration between LA personal social services for mentally handicapped people and services provided by other LA departments and with GPs, hospitals and other services for people who are disabled.

(xiii) Fostering partnership in the planning and operation of hospital and LA services.

(xiv) Encouraging voluntary help for mentally handicapped people and their families.

(xv) Encouraging understanding and help from the immediate and wider community for the mentally handicapped person and his family.

APPENDIX B

References

1. *Better Services for the Mentally Handicapped* — Cmnd 4683, 1971.
2. *Mental Handicap: Progress, Problems and Priorities.* A review of mental handicap services in England since the 1971 White Paper — DHSS (1980).
3. *Care in Action: A handbook of Policies and Priorities for the Health and Personal Social Services in England* — DHSS (1981).
4. National Health Service Restructuring: Collaboration between the NHS and Local Government — HN(82)9 (February 1982).
5. *Care in the Community: A Consultative Document on Moving Resources for Care in England* — DHSS (July 1981).
6. *Care in the Community and Joint Finance* — HC(83)6 (March 1983).
7. Collaboration between the NHS, Local Government and Voluntary Organisations — HC(84)9 (March 1984).
8. National Development Team for Mentally Handicapped People — First, Second and Third Reports — HMSO (1978, 1980, and 1982) [Fourth Report due 1985].
9. *The Health Service in England: Annual Report* — DHSS (1984).

10. Syllabus of Training: Professional Register — Part 5 (Registered Nurse for the Mentally Handicapped) — English National Board for Nursing Midwifery and Health Visiting (1982).
11. *Report of the Committee of Enquiry into Mental Handicap Nursing and Care* — HMSO (1979).
12. Interim Building Guidance, Health Services Residential Accommodation for the Mentally Handicapped — Annex III of HN(80)21 (September 1980).
13. *Helping Mentally Handicapped People with Special Problems* — Report of a DHSS Study Team (1984).
14. *Helping to get Mentally Handicapped Children out of Hospital, £1 Million for £1 Million Scheme* — HC(81)13 (November 1981).
15. *Helping to get Mentally Handicapped Children out of Mental Handicap Hospitals* — HC(83)21 (September 1983).
16. *Helping to get Mentally Handicapped Children out of Hospital* — DA(83)2 (January 1983).
17. *Day Services for Mentally Handicapped Adults, National Development Group for the Mentally Handicapped* — Pamphlet Number 5 (July 1977).

III. Mental Illness and Mental Handicap — Key Figures

Mental illness

Numbers of *mental illness units* in general hospitals increased from 120 in 1974 to 145 in 1982.

Numbers of *in-patients* in MI hospitals and units fell from 104,600 in 1971 to 69,030 in 1983.

Day hospital places have more than doubled from 6,000 in 1970 to 16,361 in 1983. *Day centre places* increased from 5,083 in 1975 to 8,932 in 1984.

Numbers of places in *residential accommodation* increased from 4,145 in 1975 to 5,564 in 1984 (provisional figures).

Consultant psychiatrists in adult mental illness increased from 796 (WTE) in 1973 to 1,067 (WTE) in 1983. *Nurses* in MI hospitals and units increased from c37,000 (WTE) in 1970 to 57,770 (WTE) in 1983. *Community psychiatric nurses* increased from 663 (WTE) in 1976 to 1,911 (WTE) in 1983 [figures for CPNs based in mental illness hospitals and units only and likely to be incomplete; the results of a CPNA survey in November 1981 suggested over 2,000 CPNs in practice]. *Clinical psychologists* increased from 550 (WTE) in 1973 to 1,310 (WTE) in 1983.

Mental handicap

About *120,000* (2.5 in 1,000) severely m.h. people in England and Wales. There is no agreed estimate of the number of mildly m.h. people, some of whom may require services.

Numbers of *m.h. people in NHS hospitals and units* fell from *56,000* in *1969* to about *40,000* in *1983*. Some *15,000* hospital residents could move into community care immediately if resources were available.

Numbers of *m.h. children in NHS hospitals and units* fell from *7,100* in *1969* to about *1,250* in *1983*. Since the Children's Initiative was launched in December 1980, number of children in NHS hospitals and units has fallen by nearly half.

Between 1978 and 1983 in England, number of consultants rose from 135 to 145 (7.4%); other medical staff from 156 to 210 (35%); nursing staff from 25,400 to 31,300 (23%). Were also increases in the number of clinical psychologists, physiotherapists and occupational therapists.

Ratio of *nurses* to hospital residents up from *1:3.9* in *1969* to *1:1.3* in *1983*.

Day services for m.h. people have also increased, with Adult Training Centre places doubling from *23,000* in *1969* to *47,419* in *1984*. Day hospitals, which offered *141* places in *1972*, provided more than *1,100* in *1983*.

Places in *local authority homes and hostels* more than trebled from *4,300* in *1969* to *14,346* in *1984*.

Local authority revenue spending on m.h.: At 1982/83 prices, gross expenditure on personal social service grew by 51% in real terms between 1976/77 and 1982/83 (to £193.1m).

Hospital and Community Health Service revenue spending on m.h.: At 1982/83 prices, gross expenditure on hospital services grew by 10% in real terms between 1976/77 and 1982/83 (to £422.8m).

IV. Note on Joint Finance and the Care in the Community Initiative

Joint finance

1. Joint finance was introduced in 1976 to encourage joint planning and collaboration between health and local authorities and to promote a shift from hospital to community care.

2. The current legal basis is Section 28A of the NHS Act 1977 (inserted by Section 1 of the HASSASSA Act 1983) and brought into force on 1 April 1984.

3. This provision gives DHAs and SHAs for the London Postgraduate Teaching Hospitals the power to make grants to LAs to assist with their functions in the provision of personal social services, education and housing for disabled people (including mentally disordered people) and to voluntary organisations (VOs) providing such services. Housing associations and statutory housing bodies may also receive payment for housing provision.

Conditions for grant

4. As follows:

(i) projects must be recommended by the Joint Consultative Committee;

(ii) in the opinion of the DHA the expenditure may be expected to make a better contribution in terms of total care than would the deployment of equivalent resources directly on health services;

(iii) up to 100% of cost of capital projects may be met;

(iv) revenue support may be given for up to 7 years (longer with the Secretary of State's approval) at reducing amounts as the LA/VO takes over the funding; 100% of costs may be met for up to 3 years;

(v) the LA/VO accepts a firm commitment to continue revenue support when joint finance comes to an end.

Uses, allocation and distribution

5. Health authorities are free to use any of their funds for joint finance.

6. Each year certain sums are allocated specifically to joint finance. These can

only be used to support personal social services, housing or education projects or for expenditure on primary health care closely linked to a PSS project receiving support.

7. The designated funds are distributed to RHAs on the basis of managed populations weighted to take account of the population over 75, the mentally ill and the mentally handicapped; an adjustment is also made for inner city areas and for the provision of hostels for alcoholics.

8. About 40% of joint finance has been spent on services for the elderly and about 33% on services for the mentally handicapped. The remainder has mainly been spent on services for the mentally ill or for the younger physically handicapped. Virtually all the money is spent on one or other of the priority groups.

9. Each year the proportion of allocated funds spent has risen. Any unspent money is added to the following year's total. In April 1983 this amounted to about £17.4 million for all authorities out of a total allocation of £326 million.

Increases in joint finance allocations

10. Since 1978/79 joint finance allocations have been increased by 51% in real terms. Counting the 1984/85 allocation of about £100 million the total allocation since the scheme started amounts to some £520 million.

Care in the community

11. The Care in the Community initiative followed consultation in 1981 on possible ways to remove obstacles to the shift of NHS resources to Social Services to get people out of hospital and into community care.

12. The main details are:

(*i*) The normal joint finance rules are modified in the case of projects to get people out of hospital. If the Joint Consultative Committee is satisfied either at the outset or subsequently that there are circumstances which justify an extension of the total period over which payments may be made, then revenue support can be given by the health authority for 13 years with the first 10 of these years being 100% health funding.

(*ii*) Health authorities can now meet the full or part of the revenue cost of a project to get people out of hospital from their *main* allocation *without time limit*.

(*iii*) Health authorities can now make payments towards education and housing for mentally or physically handicapped people from joint finance and other resources.

13. A programme of centrally funded pilot projects is under way to demonstrate and evaluate what can be achieved. 13 projects were selected from over 120 applications for the first tranche — these will cost about £8 million of the £15.6 million reserved centrally for the pilot programme. The second tranche will start in 1985/86 (the closing date for applications was October 1984).

Local authority expenditure implications

14. There is a concession in the Rate Support Grant arrangements whereby year-on-year increases in expenditure by local authorities on each jointly-financed scheme are disregarded in calculating any grant hold-back. This concession started in 1984–5 and applies to projects to which the health authority is still contributing. A scheme

ceases to be regarded as jointly financed when the local authority meets 100% of the costs. The increase alone is disregarded because to do more could involve double counting — previous year's spending is taken into account for many authorities in setting the authority's expenditure target.

15. Local government expenditure financed from *NHS* funds under joint finance arrangements is outside the controls on local government spending and always has been. This applies equally to NHS funding of Care in the Community projects.

DHSS guidance

16. Circular HC(83)6 on the Care in the Community programme issued in March 1983, also contained consolidated guidance on joint finance and strengthened the monitoring and accountability arrangements.

17. Circular HC(84)9 issued in March 1984 gave further guidance including the extension of joint finance to housing and to education for disabled people.

Index

44